GREAT AMERICAN
WORLD WAR II STORIES

GREAT AMERICAN
WORLD WAR II STORIES

EDITED BY TOM McCARTHY

LYONS
PRESS

Essex, Connecticut

An imprint of Globe Pequot, the trade division of
The Rowman & Littlefield Publishing Group, Inc.
4501 Forbes Blvd., Ste. 200
Lanham, MD 20706
www.rowman.com
Distributed by NATIONAL BOOK NETWORK

British Library Cataloguing in Publication Information available

Library of Congress Cataloging-in-Publication Data
Names: McCarthy, Tom, 1952- editor.
Title: Great American World War II stories / edited by Tom McCarthy.
Other titles: Great American World War Two stories
Description: Essex, Connecticut: Lyons Press, [2024] | Series: Lyons Press classics
Identifiers: LCCN 2023059534 (print) | LCCN 2023059535 (ebook)
 | ISBN 9781493081462 (trade paperback) | ISBN 9781493084296 (epub)
Subjects: LCSH: World War, 1939–1945—Personal narratives, American. | World War,
 1939–1945—United States. | United States—Armed
Forces—Biography.
Classification: LCC D769.A2 G74 2024 (print) | LCC D769.A2 (ebook)
 | DDC 940.54/8173—dc23/eng/20240108
LC record available at https://lccn.loc.gov/2023059534
LC ebook record available at https://lccn.loc.gov/2023059535

∞™ The paper used in this publication meets the minimum requirements of American
National Standard for Information Sciences—Permanence of Paper for Printed Library
Materials, ANSI/NISO Z39.48-1992.

Contents

CONTENTS

Introduction

GREAT AMERICAN WORLD WAR II STORIES BREAKS THE MOLD
Painstakingly chosen from the most moving and graphic stories available, and through inspiring, cautionary detail, this book will bring readers into the largest war ever fought.

For the Americans who fought, most of whom were volunteer soldiers, sailors, and Marines, courage and duty were watchwords. Freedom and principle mattered more than their own lives.

Here are accounts that are told with startling clarity, showing how young Americans almost casually put their lives on the line routinely in battles on land, sea, and in the air.

This is the courage that led Admiral Chester W. Nimitz to describe the actions of American Marines on Iwo Jima as a performance where "uncommon valor was a common virtue."

Before the war, before the United States poured everything it had into the fight for democracy, it is unlikely any of the soldiers whose wrenching, uplifting, and heroic stories are told in this collection would have thought their actions would be celebrated more than eighty years later.

But here it is.

Most were kids, still in high school, worried about things adolescents concern themselves with—grades or jobs or football scores or getting a date for the senior prom. Most were barely old enough to shave, let alone storm the beaches at Normandy or assault Iwo Jima or battle for weeks on Okinawa. Most had not been exposed to death, let alone have had any experience in watching a friend they had trained with die under a raking stream of machine-gun fire.

Before that war, most had never been away from home, yet they would find themselves hunkered down on a desolate beach on a godforsaken island in the South Pacific or hiding from German patrols on a lonely Mediterranean outpost.

Many had not yet driven a car, but some would learn to fly and take part in aerial battles that required finely honed instincts, reflexes, and the nerve to send an enemy plane to Kingdom Come and bring their damaged aircraft back to the safety of their base.

The soldiers, sailors, Marines, and pilots whose actions are recounted in these stories grew up fast. Some would return home, many would not. Many never got the chance to reach adulthood, their dreams and hopes dying with them thousands of miles from home.

Still they served.

There was much at stake. The very foundation of the United States was in peril, and they would have none of that. These young men were willing, even enthusiastic, about defending the elements of the American Constitution that made the United States unique—the guarantee of civil rights and individual liberty, freedom of the press and of religion, and the right to vote and choose our leaders without interference or challenge.

Those young men would die for those rights.

The stories in this collection, on the one hand, are a stark reminder of the price of freedom and the cost many paid to allow future generations to live and prosper in a free and open society.

On the other hand, the stories here are a breathtaking and admirable homage to courage and selflessness. Every soldier, sailor, or Marine whose heroism is recounted in these stories was honorable, courageous, and brave.

Here are the Marines on Iwo Jima and Okinawa, the soldiers and the general who led them onto the beaches of Normandy.

Here also is the story of the USS *Nautilus*, which engaged the enemy in fourteen different patrols from the Battle of Midway to the liberation of the Philippines. You will also find an oral history of the pilots who helped control the skies and a highly personal account of a pilot downed and alone in the jungles of Burma and the travails and ultimate rescue of the crew of a sunken submarine.

Here also is a little known and ill-fated attempt by American commandoes in the Mediterranean, and an indefatigable crew of a "crash boat" crew whose mission was to rescue downed pilots, often under fire.

Great American World War II Stories is, above all else, a tribute to American duty, honor, and victory.

ONE.

Omaha Beach

Following General Cota

Noel F. Mehlo Jr.

On the morning of June 6, 1944, the transport USS *Charles Carroll* delivered landing craft to the western approaches of Omaha Beach. Under the command of Cdr. Harold Woodall Biesemeier from August 13, 1942, to June 13, 1944, this ship and her crew conducted assault landings in North Africa and in Italy, including at Sicily and Salerno, while under fire.

At 5 a.m., she stood eleven miles off the Normandy coast, rolling slightly in a wind-flecked channel swell, and at 5:20 a.m., her skipper gave the command, "Away all boats!" This was the signal to disembark for all personnel headed ashore. The ship cleared its twenty landing craft over its davit falls as twenty- to thirty-foot waves threatened to smash some of them against their mother ship. Through the skill of the trained crew, all were launched without damage.

After setting the landing craft into the channel, the crew of the USS *Charles Carroll* swung large cargo nets over her sides, with four each to starboard and port. The soldiers aboard, who were slated as second-wave assault troops, gathered along the ship railings to climb down the nets to the waiting craft.

General Norman Cota and the Detachment 29th Division headquarters and Headquarter Company, part of the 116th RCT, gathered amidships at Debarkation Station 11 and boarded Landing Craft 71. This designation was the official reference to General Cota's landing party. His group is also referred to as the provisional brigade headquarters for the 29th Infantry Division, the Advance Division Headquarters of the 29th Infantry Division, or, commonly, "Cota's Bastard Brigade."

1st Lieutenant Jack Shea, General Cota's aide-de-camp, chronicled the entire D-Day chain of events involving General Cota in a November 1, 1944, combat narrative for Headquarters, Second Information and Historical Service, to which he was assigned as of that point in the war. Much of Cota's D-Day story derives from his report.

> Landing craft 71, crewed by an unknown ensign and Coxswain Ricardo Feliciano, carried the first echelon of command troops ashore for the 29th Division.
> Landing craft 71 cleared the USS *Charles Carroll* at 6:10 a.m. (H–20) for an inshore trip of eighty-five minutes. They continued forward in conditions with three miles of good visibility.
> They then reached a point four to six hundred yards offshore, where the beach landings were directed by eight stationary British Armored Motor Launches (AMLs). The AMLs' job was to efficiently direct all landing craft into the proper mine-swept lanes by use of loud-hailers. Lieutenant Shea noted that the incoming tide was about two-thirds full, having reached the band of angled-timber groin beach obstacles.

The 146th Special Underwater Demolition Battalion had yet to complete the task of blowing up these obstacles, having mislanded some two thousand yards to the east. Approximately one-third of these obstacles had Tellermines wired to the seaward face of the timbers. The US Navy's 5th Engineer Special Brigade

(ESB) landed in the first wave with the mission of clearing beach defenses. These men were all heroes. As General Cota approached the beach, they were furiously attempting to accomplish their own assignments under murderous fire. Their *After Action Report* recorded the critical beach conditions as Cota landed.

> Army and Navy doctors and Aid men worked as they could to give emergency treatment to the wounded. A surgeon of the 16th Regimental Combat Team noticed a high proportion of casualties caused by rifle bullet wounds in the head. Wounded men, lying on the exposed sand, were frequently hit a second or third time. Officer casualties were high. Companies A, C and D of the 116th Regimental Combat Team lost all but one officer each, and the 2nd Battalion of the same regiment lost two Company Commanders on the beach.
>
> The confusion of the first hour of the Invasion mounted during the period from 0730 to 0830 hours. Landings continued, but men and vehicles could not move off the beach. A majority of the units piled up behind the shingle bank, where they lay in rows sometimes three deep. In many cases these units were leaderless, their officers having been killed or wounded.

The solitary craft entered its landing lane at the right western edge of Dog White Beach, located approximately seven hundred meters northeast of Vierville, when it was noticed by the coxswain that the beach was under heavy enemy fire. They altered course slightly to avoid floating mines. This craft approached the shore alone and made landfall amid the breakwaters at the Dog White and Dog Red boundary. While nearing shore, Coxswain Ricardo Feliciano lost seaway and cut the throttle before beaching as they began navigating the maze of beach obstacles not previously destroyed. The craft sideslipped and was swept against an angled-timber groin by the three-knot easterly crosscurrent traversing along the face of the beach. The waves were four to six feet high and thrust Landing Craft 71 into the timber obstacle multiple times.

These collisions dislodged an attached Teller mine, which failed to explode. The coxswain gunned the motor and maneuvered the boat free, advancing closer to shore, and then Landing Craft 71 grounded on a sandbar approximately seventy-five yards from the high-water mark at 7:26 a.m. (H+56). The boat skipper dropped the ramp under heavy machine-gun, mortar, and light-cannon fire and called to the men, "Disembark!"

Between the sandbar where the ramp went down and the high-water mark at the seawall was a runnel with a varying depth of three to six feet, requiring some soldiers to swim or wade ashore. Several men found themselves immersed to their armpits. As the men emerged from the runnel, many made their way to the shelter of the tanks of the 743d Tank Battalion.

Lieutenant Shea's report continued,

"Moderate small arms fire was directed at the craft as the ramp was lowered. This consisted of rifle, and judging from the sound, machine gun fire. It continued to cover the group as they made their way inland. Having landed in about two or three feet of water, it was necessary to cross a runnel (about five feet deep and thirty feet wide) which ran parallel to the high-water mark. During this phase of the landing, which necessitated wading through about 40 yards of water, Major John Sours, Regimental S-4, was killed. He was hit in the chest and upper body by automatic fire, fell face down in the water. His body was later recovered as it floated in the shallows."

Two other soldiers were likewise killed in these moments. General Cota continued the advance through all of this, under the first of what would be many documented instances of threat to his life over the next thirty hours.

According to official records, all officers and men interviewed about the D-Day landings reported that there was positively no evidence of friendly aerial bombardment and little evidence of naval bombardment of the beaches. There were no craters to use for cover, and the enemy beach installations remained intact.

General Cota's party sought cover behind the nearest tank as the group moved across the beach under the cover of the tank that had engaged German antitank weapons to its near right front. The Duplex Drive amphibious tanks of Company C, 743d Tank Battalion, were the first real cover available. The tanks landed at H–6, and there were an estimated eighteen tanks standing just above and advancing along with the rising tide. They all faced the bluffs and were spaced at intervals of approximately seventy to one hundred yards. This placed them about twenty-five feet from the seawall, from which position each of them fired at enemy positions immediately in front of each tank. Two tanks were burning to the west near the Vierville exit. One, identified as Tank "C-5," was noticeably damaged from several rounds of direct 88-mm fire from the German WN 72 casemate. 1st Lieutenant Alfred H. Williams Jr., Company C, 743d Tank Battalion, and his crew managed to escape that destruction.

General Cota and his men screened themselves behind a tank that was firing to its right front instead of its previously assigned target to the west: the enemy artillery positions at Pointe et Raz de la Percée. These German strongpoints were armed with two 75-mm artillery pieces situated high on the bluffs and were able to fire down the beach well beyond Dog Red.

At some point during these moments, something in General Cota must have triggered his fortitude for what followed. From this moment on, he was no longer only one of many soldiers landing under fire on the beach; he rose to the occasion and led his men to a victory snatched from the jaws of imminent defeat.

An official account by Headquarters, 29th Infantry Division, recounted, "Realizing that immediate steps had to be taken to move the men from the dangerous area of the beach, General

Cota, exposing himself to enemy fire, went over the seawall giving encouragement, directions and orders to those about him."

After observing the tanks in action, General Cota noticed that these tanks were not firing per operational plans, and the enemy gun positions were able to profitably employ their fire. Brigadier General Cota observed at this point that the enemy guns fired one flat trajectory shell at each landing craft just before it touched down. The Germans held fire until the point that a landing craft touched down. If they missed, they determined distance by line of sight, splash, and water ricochets. The German observers then adjusted fire within a three-second interval and fired a second shot that found its mark. Direct hits were achieved by no later than the third round.

Cota's group suffered another casualty behind the tank from machine-gun fire, and the group advanced to the seawall approximately nine hundred yards from the Vierville exit to seek better cover. This seawall was four to five feet high and had twenty- to thirty-foot-long timber-rail breakwaters seaward at about fifty-yard intervals.

By the end of D-Day, only twenty-one of fifty-one of the 743d Tank Battalion's medium tanks would survive to continue the fight. The 743d Tank Battalion's commander, Lieutenant Colonel John S. Upham, was wounded by machine-gun fire later in the morning.

At this point (H+60), nearly one hundred disorganized men from the Beach Brigade, 1st Battalion of the 116th RCT, Naval Aid Group men, naval fire control parties, naval beach maintenance men, 2d Rangers, and others took shelter from enemy rifle and machine-gun fire from the bluffs above. The troops were hopelessly jumbled, unled, and firmly pinned down. No Americans had advanced past the seawall at the inland border of the beach.

As the soldiers lay pinned down by machine-gun fire, clustered in the bays formed by the seawall and breakwaters, the enemy was beginning to bring effective mortar fire to bear on those hidden behind the wall.

Sergeant Francis E. Huesser, light machine-gun squad leader, Company C, 116th Infantry, and Captain Robert J. Bedell, Company C, 116th Infantry, leader of 1st Assault Section, landed at 6:53 a.m. They described a "tremendous blossom of orange flame and black, oily smoke." Captain Bedell saw General Cota only a minute or so later.

> They ran forward to the little wooden seawall banked with shingle. Huddled there beneath the low timber wall. It was there that they saw General Cota for the first time. All of them remembered seeing Cota, just after touching down on the beach. "He was waving a .45 around, and I figured if he could get up there so could I." [Captain Bedell] remarked that Cota came up to him, and prompted that "Well, we gotta get 'em off the beach. We've gotta get going."

Sergeant Huesser discussed how General Cota influenced his group's actions as they blew a gap with a Bangalore torpedo. Cota "came up to us, waving that pistol around and said we had to get off the beach. That we had to get through the wire. I guess all of us figured that if he could go wandering around like that, we could, too." They snaked the pipes of the torpedo under the fencing and pulled the friction igniter. Nothing. Lieutenant Schwartz scurried over, did something to it, and took cover, and then it blew.

One critically important detail become all too apparent in the flow of events at about 7:30 a.m.: an estimated three-fourths of all radios, particularly the SCR 300s, were either destroyed by enemy fire or ruined by the salt water.

The 29th Infantry Division later reported that they believed the Germans specifically targeted radiomen either purposefully or because they mistook the backpack radios for flamethrowers.

Company H arrived in the vicinity of the breakwaters at approximately 7:30 a.m. Private First Class Arden Earll remembered seeing the first of the group of tanks working in this sector. The tank would go in reverse to the water's edge and gather up soldiers in need of cover. The tank would advance to the seawall and then fire a few rounds, allowing the wet soldiers to take cover at the seawall and then reverse to do the dance all over. This allowed the tanks not to become stationary targets and easy picking for the Germans.

Private First Class Arden Earll, mortarman, MOS 504, Company H, 2d Battalion, 116th Infantry, 29th Infantry Division

I got there by that tank, and I had to go around it because the tide had come in by that time, and I got right behind the tank. One enemy artillery round hit out in the water. I thought to myself: "Arden, get out of here, they are after this tank." I couldn't move, I was loaded so heavy, I couldn't move very fast. The next round came in right close to the tank. It didn't hurt the tank. But I got my first Purple Heart right there. I still got part of that artillery shell in my right wrist and hand. I wasn't hurt too bad. I had seen an American panic, before, on the way in. And I started, I began to feel, and I thought, "For God's sakes Arden, you're not hurt bad. Keep Going." So I did. Our Aid-man was a hero that day. That's all we had. We didn't have any first aid, uh, hospital, or anything like that. Now, I think there was hospital ships out there, but they couldn't get in to get us off the beach, and so, a lot of the guys just laid there. I was bleeding a little bit, but I could still walk, I could still go, I carried my load. I kept going. . . . We moved to the west down the beach to the sector General Cota landed in and was working. By the time I saw General Cota, a lot of us were hunkered down. We were waiting to see what was; we knew something was wrong, but we waited for somebody to tell us what to do next, and that's when I saw General Cota. I do know that he walked up and down along the beach, quite a lot, and exposed himself to enemy fire at all times.

Herb Epstein, Intelligence NCO, 5th Ranger Infantry Battalion, HQ Company

As A and B were preceding us into the beach, Colonel [Max] Schneider decided to land at the Vierville Draw because the men that preceded us in the 29th division were under murderous fire on the beach and having a hard time getting out of the boats. The fire was so intense and Colonel Schneider was observing this fire, we were in the lead boat at the time. As we got close to the shore, Schneider commanded the boat flotilla captain to swing the whole group left, parallel to the beach. So instead of landing at Dog Green according to the battle plan, we landed further to the east. As we were going parallel to the beach Schneider saw an area that wasn't too hot and ordered the flotilla commander "to get us in and get us in fast." We turned again another 90 degrees and they got us to water that wasn't very deep, at least it was reasonably dry where they landed my boat. There was a lot of artillery and mortar fire coming in and a lot of men lying on the beach.

The 5th Ranger Infantry Battalion (RIB), under the command of Lieutenant Colonel Max Schneider, had the primary mission of landing at Pointe du Hoc as a follow-up force to Lieutenant Colonel James Earl Rudder and his three companies of 2d Ranger Infantry Battalion engaged there. After not receiving communications to land there, Schneider made his way to their secondary landing objective at Dog Green. As the battalion approached, the men witnessed the carnage that befell Companies A and B and the remnants of the 29th Infantry. Remaining calm and drawing on his experience as a former Darby's Ranger who fought in the Mediterranean, Schneider swung his flotilla of two waves of landing crafts to the east and headed in at the breakwaters where Cota and his men were.

Private First Class Randall Ching was a member of 2d Platoon, Company B, 5th Ranger Infantry Battalion, and was in one of the westernmost bays formed by the breakwaters. He was the only Chinese American Ranger during World War II. He was born in the States, but during the Great Depression, his family emigrated back to China. As a result, he was conscripted into the Chinese army and fought the Japanese in the late 1930s before returning to the States at the outset of US involvement in the war, and he volunteered as a Ranger.

Private First Class Randall Ching, Company B, 5th Ranger Infantry Battalion

> I landed on Dog White Beach with our whole 5th Ranger Battalion. It took the Rangers five minutes to get from the beach to the seawall. I watched artillery coming up to the seawall, to the left, to the right, when I was at the seawall. It walked, it come up, because the Germans got the seawall all zeroed in. And they opened up, with three shells, Boom, Boom, Boom, all over the seawall. And I thought, oh hell, this is gonna' come up pretty close to me pretty soon. It just so happened, that two landing craft landed and both ramps dropped. Both had two ramps down. So the artillery turned their attention to those landing craft. They hit both of them. The first one was hit, was the nearest on to me, so I saw that. They hit it with three shells. People started to jump overboard because of the fire. That is the worst part of the memory in my mind. One of the persons on the landing craft was carrying a flamethrower, and the flamethrower exploded.

A vivid account of the morning of June 6, 1944, was sent in a letter to Mr. Cornelius Ryan on June 16, 1958, in response to Ryan's plea for stories associated with D-Day so that he could incorporate them into his epic *The Longest Day*. This moving account brought forth the horrors experienced and witnessed by all on that beach.

Private First Class Max D. Coleman, Company C, 5th Ranger Infantry Battalion

> In your interviews with various participants of the "D" Day Operations, try to get a picture of the sky in the early dawn. I have witnessed many sunrises in my thirty-four years, but this one stayed in my mind. Apparently it was unusual not only to me, for I have asked many others about it. I am not capable of an accurate description. There was a storm of high winds, as you well know; but it was a storm with few clouds. The first rays of the sun turned the few clouds to crimson. It would have captured the imagination of any artist or poet. You may want to know about the two landing craft that had run aground because of the storm. The sounds of the men in pain and terror as shell after shell fell on the decks could be heard above the din of other combat. Men would jump screaming into the sea only to rise as floating corpses. One man with a flame thrower on his back disintegrated into a flaming inferno.

Lieutenant Colonel Harold A. Cassell, XO, 116th Infantry, was aboard Landing Craft 91 along with the alternate headquarters for the regiment. As they were on the beach in positions bracketing the vessel, Cota's men witnessed the landing as it beached and was subsequently devastated. Cassell and some fifteen men had disembarked before the blast, and the remaining survivors leapt overboard, many of them in flames. Cota's men reported that a lot of the men who did make it to shore were badly burned.

Cota worked to the west down the beach and by some accounts made it as far as half the distance to the D-1 exit near the manor, Hamel au Prêtre.

All accounts place him calmly and tactically walking in that direction, exhorting men to action. This amounted to a distance of between one-half and three-quarters of a mile. When he turned to head back to the breakwaters, he calmly walked away from these German positions. The thought of turning one's back to this amount of active firepower is astounding.

While in the vicinity of elements of Company C, 116th Infantry, General Cota happened upon a section of seawall with a low mound of earth approximately five yards beyond it. He crawled forward to reconnoiter the firing position and then personally directed the placement of a Browning Automatic Rifle there. He told the gunner to lay down suppressive fire and shoot at any enemy movement along the bluffs.

This fire was intended to cover the soldiers as they breached the wire and made their way toward the foot of the bluffs. After this, General Cota personally supervised the placement of a Bangalore torpedo in the double-apron barbed wire fence. The barbed wire in this area was standard agricultural-style barbed wire, not the heavier, squarish military concertina wire expected by the men. The wire was along the inner border of the promenade, the ten-foot-wide, asphalt-surfaced road that ran parallel with the seawall along Dog Beach.

This started elements of Companies C and D, up the bluffs. During this action, Cota interacted with Lieutenant Colonel Robert Ploger, CO, 121st Engineer Combat Battalion, to secure the needed Bangalore torpedoes. The general acted above and beyond the call of duty in this instance alone at the risk of his life as he was under observation by the Germans.

Lieutenant Colonel Robert Ploger, commander, 121st Engineer Combat Battalion, 29th Division:

> While I was walking west along the beach looking for some of my engineers, I ran into General Cota. He said, "Ploger, bring me some Bangalore torpedoes so we can blow this wire." I went off to look for some. A little while later I ran into Gen. Cota again, and this time he asked me for some minefield marking tape which came in long rolls of white cloth. He wanted it to

mark lanes through minefields beyond the wire and up the bluff. I immediately went off on another search.

The second wave of the 5th Ranger Infantry Battalion landed at 7:50 a.m. on the eastern edge of Dog White Beach, extending east into Dog Red Beach over a 250-yard front. Major General Raaen provided testimony regarding the Ranger landing on the beach in relation to General Cota.

Major General John C. Raaen Jr., USA (Ret.), June 6, 2018, Witness Statement to Congress for Cota Medal of Honor Upgrade

My LCA touched down on the east edge of Omaha Dog White Beach on June 6, 1944, at 0750 British Double Daylight Time. The rest of my battalion's, the 5th Ranger Infantry Battalion, 12 boats landed to my left on Dog Red Beach. The beach was chaos. Machine gun and rifle fire poured down the beach from the enemy positions to my right. Artillery fire was concentrated on the landing craft at the water's edge. Smoke, fire, the cracking of bullets overhead, the detonation of artillery striking Landing Craft added to the chaos. The beach was littered with burning debris from materiel destroyed by enemy fire. The dead, the dying, the wounded lay everywhere.

The situation on Dog Red Beach was desperate. The tide had reached a point about 50 to 60 yards from the wooden seawall. No troops had left the beach. Those who survived crossing the beach were piled on top of one another at the base of the four-foot seawall. Tides and wind from the storm had scattered the landing craft and many had landed as far as two miles from planned landing locations. Most troops were leaderless, no idea where they were, where they were supposed to go.

I had been on the beach no more than ten minutes, checking the men for firearms, ammunition and other equipment while awaiting orders from battalion. Several of my men called my attention to a man about 100 yards to my right moving along the edge of the beach. He was chewing on a cigar, yelling and waving at the men in the dunes and at the seawall. He was taking no action to conceal himself from the enemy who continued to pour small arms fire.

We thought him crazy or heroic. Everyone else was seeking cover, while this man was exposing himself not only to the enemy, but to the troops he was rallying. As he approached the bay (formed by breakwaters and the seawall) I was in, I rose to meet him. As he rounded the end of the breakwater, I saw his insignia of rank. Brigadier General!

I reported to him with a hand salute. "Sir, Captain Raaen, 5th Ranger Battalion."

He responded, "Raaen, Raaen. You must be Jack Raaen's son."

"Yes, sir."

What's the situation here?"

"Sir, the 5th Ranger Battalion has landed intact, here and over a 250-yard front. The battalion commander has just ordered the companies to proceed by platoon infiltration to our rallying points."

"Where is your battalion commander?"

"I'll take you to him, sir," pointing out the location of Lt. Col. Schneider.

"No! You remain here with your men."

As General Cota started away, he stopped and looked around saying, "You men are Rangers. I know you won't let me down."

And with that, he was off to see Schneider. During this whole conversation, General Cota never took cover nor flinched as the bullets cracked by us and artillery detonated some 50 yards away at the waterline.

Captain Raaen was not alone in his witness of General Cota's actions over the next ten to twenty minutes. Several other 29er's and Rangers provided testimony in one form or another over the years. In many cases, the men providing the testimonials had no interaction with each other as they told their stories. The facts of their stories are in alignment in terms of General Cota's gallantry above and beyond the call of duty on the beach.

Major Richard P. Sullivan, executive officer, 5th Ranger Infantry Battalion

I watched the approach on an LCI to the beach, with troops all lined up to run down the gangway to the beach, when an artillery shell containing liquid fire (napalm?) exploded on the deck covering all with flame, causing most of the men to jump into the sea. This happened only a few yards from shore and was probably the man seen by other Rangers. He was carrying a flamethrower and took a direct hit from an artillery shell and was vaporized along with his equipment. The activities of Brigadier General Cota seemed to be stupid at the time, but it was actually nothing but the sheer heroism and dedication of a professional soldier and fine officer that prompted him to walk up and down the landing beach urging the men forward. I remember his aide-de-camp being a nervous wreck trying to get the General to stop his activities.

T/4 Lee Brown, HQ Company, 5th Ranger Infantry Battalion

We were told to keep our heads down, but I did peek up and the "zip, zip, zip" of machine-gun fire had us ducking back down quickly. Lieutenant Colonel Schneider, and I think Captain [Hugo W.] Heffelfinger, were in my LCA—the British LCA driver did a great job getting us into the beach, I did not even step into any water—I was up onto dry beach. When the ramp went down on our LCA, the lead officer hesitated and because of that hesitation it saved many lives. The reason was because in the time of the hesitation a machine gun strafed right in front of the LCA ramp and would have cut down many of us coming right off—I was 5th, 6th or 7th off and likely would have been cut down. The officer who hesitated and didn't charge right off, like they had been told to do was Schneider.

He had paused to take off his Mae West and toss it down on the beach. The delay likely saved my life. I ran all the way to the sea wall as fast as I could with my M1 rifle, there really wasn't anything to hide behind until you got there. Many men fell around me on the run in to the wall. Getting to the sea wall I looked back and saw an LCT get hit and blow up.

There were bodies flying in the air—I turned to the radio man next to me and I said, "This is war!" I remember General Cota approaching us and him specifically talking to Captain John Raaen first and asking if he was Jack Raaen's son. He was then speaking with Schneider and I remember him exhorting them to lead the way on the beach. I was in awe of Cota's bravery in standing upright over them all hunkered down behind the wall and being impervious to fire.

Staff Sergeant Richard N. Hathaway Jr., Company A, 5th Ranger Infantry Battalion

Back on Omaha, I was lying on the shingle, attempting to gather my men in order to breach the concertina barbed wire on top of the beach wall when a voice behind me asked, "What outfit is this?" At the very same moment, that German machine gun, which had given us so much trouble on the way in, opened up.

I answered the voice and said, "We're the Rangers."

I got a response of, "Well, let's get off this beach!"

In a rather excited voice, I said, "We will, as soon as I blow this f-ing wire." I then turned and noticed where the voice came from. It was from a short stocky man with the stub of a cigar in his mouth, wearing a field jacket with a silver star on his shoulder, the rank of a brigadier general.

It was Brigadier General Norman Cota, the Assistant Division Commander of the Twenty-ninth Infantry Division. I couldn't help but wonder what in hell was he doing on this beach. I turned back, still looking for that German machine gun when I heard my Bangalore man yell, "Fire in the hole!"

The Bangalore exploded, and with Lieutenant Charles Parker leading, we took off through the gap in the wire. I was sixth in line as we started up the bluff.

As a result of this interaction, the Rangers' official motto was born from General Cota's lips, under fire, at a time when their spirit and fighting tenacity were critically needed: "Rangers, Lead the Way!"

Lieutenant Colonel Max Schneider, CO, 5th Ranger Infantry Battalion, issued orders, the Rangers blew four gaps into the wire along their entire front, and the men began to pour through. General Cota himself moved to the Rangers of Company C at 8:07 a.m. and exhorted their advance. They moved at the double and cleared any communications trenches along the foot of the bluffs and then began the ascent in columns. The bluffs were on fire from naval shelling, and this slowed the advance but at the same time offered a smoke screen to their movements from German eyes. The Rangers were off the beach by 8:10 a.m. LCI(L) 92 came ashore at 8:10 a.m., approximately two hundred yards to the left of the Rangers' gaps in the wire and suffered the same fate as LCI(L) 91.

With the Ranger battalion on the move, General Cota turned his attention to soldiers remaining on the beach. With a gap blown in the wire in his vicinity, the first man through the wire was hit by a heavy burst of machine-gun fire and died in just minutes. Joe Balkoski tentatively identified this Stonewaller as either Private Ralph Hubbard or Private George Losey. ("Stonewaller" refers to those members of the forerunning units of the 29th Infantry Division who served under General Stonewall Jackson during the American Civil War.)

As the soldier lay dying, the others could hear his pleas: "Medic, medic, I'm hit. Help me."

He moaned and cried for a few minutes as life slipped away from him. Soldiers nearby heard the man call for his "mama" several times, and then it was over. This death demoralized these troops, and they stalled any advance to be made.

General Cota, with a desire to urge them on, stood up and charged through the gap next. Men rallied behind him, and they crossed the road unharmed and dropped into a field of marsh grass beyond. The 29er's followed a system of shallow communications trenches until they reached taller grass beyond, near the base of the bluffs. No antipersonnel mines or booby traps were discovered in the trenches as the men moved. Cota's men began the ascent on a diagonal to the right, up the bluffs, through the smoke. They reached the top of the bluffs about one hundred yards to the west of a small concrete foundation positioned twenty-five yards below the bluff. This feature of the landscape remains.

Cota remained at the foot of the bluffs and then met up again at 8:30 a.m. with Colonel Canham, who had set his first CP on the bluffs near the bottom. The radiomen tried using their SC300 radios to establish contact with the 1st Infantry Division off to the east. Their attempts were unsuccessful, as the radios were damaged. As the CP began to try to function, the Germans zeroed in on it as a target and fired five or six rounds of ranged-in two-inch mortars at the group.

The fragments killed two enlisted men within three feet of the general. His radio operator, T/3 C. A. Wilson, was seriously wounded and thrown twenty to thirty feet up the bluff, while Lieutenant Shea, the general's aide, was thrown seventy-five feet down the bluff.

As a result, Colonel Canham hurriedly moved the CP up the bluff. The attack on the western portion of Omaha Beach was arrested and disorganized such that at 8:30 a.m., the commander of the 7th Naval Beach Battalion ordered a temporary halt of landings on Omaha in the face of the deteriorating situation.

Arden Earll's testimony about General Cota paints a profound picture of the courage and leadership he exhibited on the beach. The importance of this testimony is that it defines what it means to go from a near-catastrophic defeat to a heroic victory, as is often said of the US forces that assaulted Omaha Beach west on D-Day. You can see in his words the change from hopelessness to victory in action for the American infantryman—a change that was brought on by "Dutch."

Private First Class Arden Earll, mortarman, MOS 504, Company H, 2d Battalion, 116th Infantry, 29th Infantry Division

So there the first waves were, we landed, and everybody had been told that it was going to be like a cake-walk. Just walk in, and I remember myself, when we got off of the LCVP, Sgt. Washburn was right ahead of me, and I looked around and that beach was just as flat as this tabletop, no shell craters, no nothing. We had been told we didn't need to worry about digging a fox hole, there would be so many shell craters; you could just drop into one. But there was nothing. So, why did the 29ers hunker down? Maybe I shouldn't say this, but I will. They had not been told the truth.

Maybe it wasn't General Eisenhower or General Montgomery's fault, but all the preparations for before our landing had not come to pass. So the foot troops got on there; "Hey, this isn't the way it's supposed to be!" And what did they do? Right away it affected the soldiers in their heads. They hunkered down. What do we do next? And that's the reason.

General Cota directly and positively affected this battlefield condition and caused us to overcome our fear.

We were all hunkered down behind the seawall, or whatever protection we could get, and Cota went along, prodding us on, to keep going. He said, "You're gonna' die out here. It's better if you go inland to die." He did not seem to be scared of anything. He stood upright and just walked along. "Come on, keep going, keep going."

General Cota had no fear for his own safety.

General Cota was exposed to enemy sniper fire, small arms fire, and everything they could throw at him, and it didn't seem to worry him at all. He just walked along, and "Come on, you've got to go!" He didn't seem to be scared of anything. He could have been shot by a sniper. He could have got hit by artillery, he could have got hit by anything. He was the only high-ranking officer I witnessed do that. Everybody else was as low as they possibly could be. So he was the only one, the only physical human target that the Germans had to shoot at. Here he was, a General, and he was the target.

He said, "If you stay here, you're gonna get killed. If you go inland, you may get killed. But let's go inland and get killed. Not stay on this damn beach. The tide was coming in. Don't stop. Get the hell out of here, and get 'em."

I think that inspired a lot of people, a lot of the guys, to keep moving. They had a General tell them these things.

If it hadn't have been for a few people like him, D-Day could have very well been turned into what the British went through at Dieppe. It could have very well turned into that. It very well might have been. But General Cota thought, even if he didn't do anything, or say anything, if they just saw him, walking up and down the beach, "By God, if he could do it, we could do it!" So, that is what I think. Other men also thought, "If a General can do that, we can do it." He did these actions for his entire time on the beach.

It took courage for him to stand there in the wide open amongst all that chaos, in the midst of a lot of scared kids. General Cota probably looked like and was the age of many of their dads. His leadership became infectious. Because when they saw the General, walking up and down and in plain sight, it inspired them to move. The General was armed only with his pistol.

Seeing General Cota gave me a lot of courage. All I could think of was, "Arden, you gotta keep going. You gotta keep going. If you're ever going to get home, there's only one way to get home, and that's to keep going." I didn't know when my time might be up. I think all of us felt that way. Our time could be up anytime, but we have to keep going.

In his first hour ashore, General Cota took what was nearly a total disaster and began an arduous journey to exert command and control over the battlespace. He reinvigorated the demoralized men. His actions during that second hour saved the remaining thousand or so men on the beach who had not already fallen as honored dead or as casualties.

The fact that so many men from so many different units and locations directly witnessed his actions on the beach is clear evidence of his movement up and down the beach during Cota's first hour in combat. Communications were nonexistent, and contact was yet to be established with the 1st Infantry Division or with General Charles Gerhardt afloat aboard the USS *Ancon*. General Bradley considered diverting the remaining follow-up forces to Utah Beach. But on the beach, now at the toe of the bluff, General Cota saw what had to be done. He had just missed his own death by mere feet after the mortar fire struck the Advance CP. He would lead the men to Vierville and beyond.

In Cota's postwar words to his grandson, "There's nothing like being shot at."

Two.

Taking Mount Suribachi

Colonel Joseph H. Alexander

D-DAY

Weather conditions around Iwo Jima on D-day morning, February 19, 1945, were almost ideal. At 0645 Admiral Turner signaled: "Land the landing force!"

Shore bombardment ships did not hesitate to engage the enemy island at near-point-blank range. Battleships and cruisers steamed as close as two thousand yards to level their guns against island targets. Many of the "Old Battleships" had performed this dangerous mission in all theaters of the war. Marines came to recognize and appreciate their contributions. It seemed fitting that the old *Nevada*, raised from the muck and ruin of Pearl Harbor, should lead the bombardment force close ashore. Marines also admired the battleship *Arkansas*, built in 1912, and recently returned from the Atlantic where she had battered German positions at Pointe du Hoc at Normandy during the epic Allied landing on June 6, 1944.

Lieutenant colonels Donald M. Weller and William W. "Bucky" Buchanan, both artillery officers, had devised a modified form of the "rolling barrage" for use by the bombarding gunships against beachfront targets just before H-hour. This concentration of naval gunfire would advance progressively as the troops landed, always remaining four hundred yards to their front. Air spotters would help regulate the pace. Such an innovation appealed to the three division commanders, each having served in France during World War I. In those days, a good rolling barrage was often the only way to break a stalemate.

The shelling was terrific. Admiral Hill would later boast that "there were no proper targets for shore bombardment remaining on Dog-Day morning." This proved to be an overstatement, yet no one could deny the unprecedented intensity of firepower Hill delivered against the areas surrounding the landing beaches. As General Kuribayashi would ruefully admit in an assessment report to Imperial General Headquarters, "we need to reconsider the power of bombardment from ships; the violence of the enemy's bombardments is far beyond description."

The amphibious task force appeared from over the horizon, the rails of the troopships crowded with combat-equipped marines watching the spectacular fireworks. The Guadalcanal veterans among them realized a grim satisfaction watching American battleships leisurely pounding the island from just offshore. The war had come full cycle from the dark days of October 1942 when the 1st Marine Division and the Cactus Air Force endured similar shelling from Japanese battleships.

The marines and sailors were anxious to get their first glimpse of the objective. Correspondent John P. Marquand, the Pulitzer Prize-winning writer, recorded his own first impressions of Iwo: "Its silhouette was like a sea monster, with the little dead volcano for the head, and the beach area for the neck, and all the rest of it, with its scrubby brown cliffs for the body." Lieutenant David N. Susskind, USNR, wrote down his initial thoughts from the bridge of the troopship *Mellette*: "Iwo Jima was a rude, ugly sight. . . . Only a geologist could look at it and not be repelled." As described in a subsequent letter home by US Navy lieutenant Michael F. Keleher, a surgeon in the 25th Marines:

The naval bombardment had already begun, and I could see the orange-yellow flashes as the battleships, cruisers, and destroyers blasted away at the island broadside. Yes, there was Iwo—surprisingly close, just like the pictures and models we had been studying for six weeks. The volcano was to our left, then the long, flat black beaches where we were going to land, and the rough rocky plateau to our right.

The commanders of the 4th and 5th Marine Divisions, Major Generals Clifton B. Cates and Keller E. Rockey, respectively, studied the island through binoculars from their respective ships. Each division would land two reinforced regiments abreast. From left to right, the beaches were designated Green, Red, Yellow, and Blue. The 5th Division would land the 28th Marines on the left flank, over Green Beach, the 27th Marines over Red. The 4th Division would land the 23rd Marines over Yellow Beach and the 25th Marines over Blue Beach on the right flank. General Schmidt reviewed the latest intelligence reports with growing uneasiness and requested a reassignment of reserve forces with General Smith. The 3rd Marine Division's 21st Marines would replace the 26th Marines as corps reserve; thus, releasing the latter regiment to the 5th Division. Schmidt's landing plan envisioned the 28th Marines cutting the island in half then returning to capture Suribachi, while the 25th Marines would scale the Rock Quarry and then serve as the hinge for the entire corps to swing around to the north. The 23rd Marines and 27th Marines would capture the first airfield and pivot north within their assigned zones.

General Cates was already concerned about the right flank. Blue Beach Two lay directly under the observation and fire of suspected Japanese positions in the Rock Quarry whose steep cliffs overshadowed the right flank like Suribachi dominated the left. The 4th Marine Division figured that the 25th Marines would have the hardest objective to take on D-day. Said Cates, "If I knew the name of the man on the extreme right of the right-hand squad, I'd recommend him for a medal before we go in."

The choreography of the landing continued to develop. Iwo Jima would represent the pinnacle of forcible amphibious assault against a heavily fortified shore, a complex art mastered painstakingly by the Fifth Fleet over many campaigns. Seventh Air Force Martin B-24 Liberator bombers flew in from the Marianas to strike the smoking island. Rocket ships moved in to saturate near-shore targets.

Then it was time for the fighter and attack squadrons from Mitscher's Task Force 58 to contribute. The navy pilots showed their skills at bombing and strafing, but the troops naturally cheered the most at the appearance of F4U Corsairs flown by Marine Fighter Squadrons 124 and 213, led by Lt. Col. William A. Millington from the fleet carrier *Essex*. Col. Vernon E. Megee, in his shipboard capacity as air officer for General Smith's Expeditionary Troops staff, had urged Millington to put on a special show for the troops in the assault waves.

"Drag your bellies on the beach," he told Millington.

The marine fighters made an impressive approach parallel to the island, then virtually did Megee's bidding, streaking low over the beaches, strafing furiously. The geography of the Pacific War since Bougainville had kept many of the ground marines separated from their own air support, which had been operating in areas other than where they had been fighting, most notably the Central Pacific. "It was the first time a lot of them had ever seen a marine fighter plane," said Megee. The troops were not disappointed.

The planes had barely disappeared when naval gunfire resumed, carpeting the beach areas with a building crescendo of high-explosive shells. The ship-to-shore movement was well under way, an easy thirty-minute run for the tracked landing vehicles (LVTs). This time there were enough LVTs to do the job: 68 LVT(A)4 armored amtracs mounting snub-nosed 75mm cannon leading the way, followed by 380 troop-laden LVT 4s and LVT 2s.

The waves crossed the line of departure on time and chugged confidently toward the smoking beaches, all the while under the climactic bombardment from the ships. Here, there was no coral reef, no killer neap tides to be concerned with. The navy and marine frogmen had reported the approaches free of mines or tetrahedrons. There was no premature cessation of fire. The "rolling barrage" plan took effect. Hardly a vehicle was lost to the desultory enemy fire.

The massive assault waves hit the beach within two minutes of H-hour. A Japanese observer watching the drama unfold from a cave on the slopes of Suribachi reported, "At nine o'clock in the morning several hundred landing craft with amphibious tanks in the lead rushed ashore like an enormous tidal wave." Lt. Col. Robert H. Williams, executive officer of the 28th Marines, recalled that "the landing was a magnificent sight to see—two divisions landing abreast; you could see the whole show from the deck of a ship." Up to this point, so far, so good.

The first obstacle came not from the Japanese but from the beach and the parallel terraces. Iwo Jima was an emerging volcano; its steep beaches dropped off sharply, producing a narrow but violent surf zone. The soft black sand immobilized all wheeled vehicles and caused some of the tracked amphibians to belly down. The boat waves that closely followed the LVTs had more trouble. Ramps would drop; a truck or jeep would attempt to drive out, only to get stuck. In short order, a succession of plunging waves hit the stalled craft before they could completely unload, filling their sterns with water and sand, and broaching them broadside. The beach quickly resembled a salvage yard.

The infantry, heavily laden, found its own "foot-mobility" severely restricted. In the words of Corp. Edward Hartman, a rifleman with the 4th Marine Division: "The sand was so soft it was like trying to run in loose coffee grounds." From the 28th

Marines came this early, laconic report: "Resistance moderate, terrain awful."

The rolling barrage and carefully executed landing produced the desired effect, suppressing direct enemy fire, providing enough shock and distraction to enable the first assault waves to clear the beach and begin advancing inward. Within minutes, six thousand Marines were ashore. Many became thwarted by increasing fire over the terraces or down from the highlands, but hundreds leapt forward to maintain assault momentum.

The 28th Marines on the left flank had rehearsed on similar volcanic terrain on the island of Hawaii. Now, despite increasing casualties among their company commanders and the usual disorganization of landing, elements of the regiment used their initiative to strike across the narrow neck of the peninsula. The going became progressively costly as more and more Japanese strongpoints along the base of Suribachi seemed to spring to life.

Within ninety minutes of the landing, however, elements of the 1st Battalion, 28th Marines, had reached the western shore, seven hundred yards across from Green Beach. Iwo Jima had been severed—"like cutting off a snake's head," in the words of one marine. It would represent the deepest penetration of what was becoming a very long and costly day.

The other three regiments experienced difficulty leaving the black sand terraces and wheeling across toward the first airfield. The terrain was an open bowl, a shooting gallery in full view from Suribachi on the left and the rising tableland to the right. Any thoughts of a "cakewalk" quickly vanished as well-directed machine-gun fire whistled across the open ground and mortar rounds began dropping along the terraces. Despite these difficulties, the 27th Marines made good initial gains, reaching the southern and western edges of the first airfield before noon.

The 23rd Marines landed over Yellow Beach and sustained the brunt of the first round of Japanese combined arms fire. These troops crossed the second terrace only to be confronted by two huge concrete pillboxes, still lethal despite all the pounding. Overcoming these positions proved costly in casualties and time.

More fortified positions appeared in the broken ground beyond. Col. Walter W. Wensinger's call for tank support could not be immediately honored because of congestion problems on the beach. The regiment clawed its way several hundred yards toward the eastern edge of the airstrip.

No assault units found it easy going to move inland, but the 25th Marines almost immediately ran into a buzz saw trying to move across Blue Beach. General Cates had been right in his appraisal. "That right flank was a bitch if there ever was one," he would later say. Lt. Col. Hollis W. Mustain's 1st Battalion, 25th Marines, managed to scratch forward three hundred yards under heavy fire in the first half-hour, but Lieutenant Colonel Chambers's 3rd Battalion, 25th Marines, took the heaviest beating of the day on the extreme right, trying to scale the cliffs leading to the Rock Quarry.

Chambers landed fifteen minutes after H-hour. "Crossing that second terrace," he recalled, "the fire from automatic weapons was coming from all over. You could've held up a cigarette and lit it on the stuff going by. I knew immediately we were in for one hell of a time."

This was simply the beginning.

While the assault forces tried to overcome the infantry weapons of the local defenders, they were naturally blind to an almost imperceptible stirring taking place among the rocks and crevices of the interior highlands. With grim anticipation, General Kuribayashi's gunners began unmasking the big guns—the heavy artillery, giant mortars, rockets, and antitank weapons held under tightest discipline for this precise moment. Kuribayashi had patiently waited until the beaches were clogged with troops and material. Gun crews knew the range and deflection to each landing beach by heart; all weapons had been preregistered on these targets long ago. At Kuribayashi's signal, these hundreds of weapons began to open fire. It was shortly after 10:00 a.m.

The ensuing bombardment was as deadly and terrifying as any the marines had ever experienced. There was hardly any cover. Japanese artillery and mortar rounds blanketed every corner of the 3,000-yard-wide beach. Large-caliber coast defense guns and dual-purpose antiaircraft guns firing horizontally added a deadly scissors of direct fire from the high ground on both flanks. Marines stumbling over the terraces to escape the rain of projectiles encountered the same disciplined machine-gun fire and minefields which had slowed the initial advance. Casualties mounted appallingly.

Two marine combat veterans observing this expressed a grudging admiration for the Japanese gunners. "It was one of the worst blood-lettings of the war," said Major Karch of the 14th Marines. "They rolled those artillery barrages up and down the beach—I just didn't see how anybody could live through such heavy fire barrages."

Said Lt. Col. Joseph L. Stewart, "The Japanese were superb artillerymen. . . . Somebody was getting hit every time they fired." At sea, Lieutenant Colonel Weller tried desperately to deliver naval gunfire against the Japanese gun positions shooting down at 3rd Battalion, 25th Marines, from the Rock Quarry. It would take longer to coordinate this fire: The first Japanese barrages had wiped out the 3rd Battalion, 25th Marines' entire shore fire control party.

As the Japanese firing reached a general crescendo, the four assault regiments issued dire reports to the flagship. Within a ten-minute period, these messages crackled over the command net:

1036: (From 25th Marines) "Catching all hell from the quarry. Heavy mortar and machine-gun fire!"

1039: (From 23d Marines) "Taking heavy casualties and can't move for the moment. Mortars killing us."

1042: (From 27th Marines) "All units pinned down by artillery and mortars. Casualties heavy. Need tank support fast to move anywhere."

1046: (From 28th Marines) "Taking heavy fire and forward movement stopped. Machine-gun and artillery fire heaviest ever seen."

The landing force suffered and bled but did not panic. The profusion of combat veterans throughout the rank and file of each regiment helped the rookies focus on the objective. Communications remained effective. Keen-eyed aerial observers spotted some of the now-exposed gun positions and directed naval gunfire effectively. Carrier planes screeched in low to drop napalm canisters. The heavy Japanese fire would continue to take an awful toll throughout the first day and night, but it would never again be as murderous as that first unholy hour.

Marine Sherman tanks played hell getting into action on D-day. Later in the battle these combat vehicles would be the most valuable weapons on the battlefield for the marines; this day was a nightmare. The assault divisions embarked many of their tanks on board medium landing ships (LSMs), sturdy little craft that could deliver five Shermans at a time. But it was tough disembarking them on Iwo's steep beaches. The stern anchors could not hold in the loose sand; bow cables run forward to "deadmen" LVTs parted under the strain. On one occasion the lead tank stalled at the top of the ramp, blocking the other vehicles and leaving the LSM at the mercy of the rising surf. Other tanks bogged down or threw tracks in the loose sand.

Many of those that made it over the terraces were destroyed by huge horned mines or disabled by deadly accurate 47mm anti-tank fire from Suribachi. Other tankers kept coming. Their relative mobility, armored protection, and 75mm gunfire were most welcome to the infantry scattered among Iwo's lunar-looking, shell-pocked landscape.

Both division commanders committed their reserves early. General Rockey called in the 26th Marines shortly after noon. General Cates ordered two battalions of the 24th Marines to land at 14:00; the 3rd Battalion, 24th Marines, followed several hours later. Many of the reserve battalions suffered heavier casualties crossing the beach than the assault units, a result of Kuribayashi's punishing bombardment from all points on the island.

Mindful of the likely Japanese counterattack in the night to come—and despite the fire and confusion along the beaches—both divisions also ordered their artillery regiments ashore. This process, frustrating and costly, took much of the afternoon. The wind and surf began to pick up as the day wore on, causing more than one low-riding DUKW to swamp with its precious 105mm howitzer cargo. Getting the guns ashore was one thing; getting them up off the sand was quite another. The 75mm pack howitzers fared better than the heavier 105s. Enough marines could readily hustle them up over the terraces, albeit at great risk. The 105s seemed to have a mind of their own in the black sand. The effort to get each single weapon off the beach was a saga in its own right.

Somehow, despite the fire and unforgiving terrain, both Col. Louis G. DeHaven, commanding the 14th Marines, and Col. James D. Waller, commanding the 13th Marines, managed to get batteries in place, registered, and rendering close fire support well before dark, a singular accomplishment.

Japanese fire and the plunging surf continued to make a shambles out of the beachhead. Late in the afternoon, Lt. Michael F. Keleher, USNR, the battalion surgeon, was ordered ashore to take over the 3rd Battalion, 25th Marines, aid station from its gravely wounded surgeon. Keleher, a veteran of three previous assault landings, was appalled by the carnage on Blue Beach as he approached: "Such a sight on that beach! Wrecked boats, bogged-down jeeps, tractors and tanks; burning vehicles; casualties scattered all over."

On the left center of the action, leading his machine-gun platoon in the 1st Battalion, 27th Marines' attack against the southern portion of the airfield, the legendary "Manila John" Basilone fell mortally wounded by a Japanese mortar shell, a loss keenly felt by all marines on the island. Farther east, Lt. Col. Robert Galer, the other Guadalcanal Medal of Honor marine (and one of the Pacific War's earliest fighter aces), survived the afternoon's fusillade along the beaches and began reassembling his scattered radar unit in a deep shell hole near the base of Suribachi.

Late in the afternoon, Lt. Col. Donn J. Robertson led his 3rd Battalion, 27th Marines, ashore over Blue Beach, disturbed at the intensity of fire still being directed on the reserve forces this late on D-day. "They were really ready for us," he recalled. He watched with pride and wonderment as his marines landed under fire, took casualties, and stumbled forward to clear the beach. "What impels a young guy landing on a beach in the face of fire?" he asked himself. Then it was Robertson's turn. His boat hit the beach too hard; the ramp wouldn't drop. Robertson and his command group had to roll over the gunwales into the churning surf and crawl ashore, an inauspicious start.

The bitter battle to capture the Rock Quarry cliffs on the right flank raged all day. The beachhead remained completely vulnerable to enemy direct-fire weapons from these heights; the marines had to storm them before many more troops or supplies could be landed. In the end, it was the strength of character of Capt. James Headley and Lt. Col. "Jumping Joe" Chambers who led the survivors of the 3rd Battalion, 25th Marines, onto the top of the cliffs. The battalion paid an exorbitant price for this achievement, losing twenty-two officers and five hundred troops by nightfall.

Two.

The two assistant division commanders, Brigadier Generals Franklin A. Hart and Leo D. Hermle, of the 4th and 5th Marine Divisions, respectively, spent much of D-day on board the control vessels, marking both ends of the Line of Departure, four thousand yards offshore. This reflected yet another lesson in amphibious techniques learned from Tarawa: Having senior officers that close to the ship-to-shore movement provided landing force decision-making from the most forward vantage point.

By dusk, Gen. Leo D. Hermle opted to come ashore. At Tarawa he had spent the night of D-day essentially out of contact at the fire-swept pier-head. This time he intended to be on the ground. Hermle had the larger operational picture in mind, knowing the corps commander's desire to force the reserves and artillery units onshore despite the carnage in order to build credible combat power. Hermle knew that whatever the night might bring, the Americans now had more troops on the island than Kuribayashi could ever muster. His presence helped his division to forget about the day's disasters and focus on preparations for the expected counterattacks.

Japanese artillery and mortar fire continued to rake the beachhead. The enormous spigot mortar shells (called "flying ashcans" by the troops) and rocket-boosted aerial bombs were particularly scary—loud, whistling projectiles, tumbling end over end. Many sailed completely over the island; those that hit along the beaches or the south runways invariably caused dozens of casualties with each impact. Few marines could dig a proper foxhole in the granular sand ("like trying to dig a hole in a barrel of wheat"). Among urgent calls to the control ship for plasma, stretchers, and mortar shells came repeated cries for sandbags.

Veteran marine combat correspondent Lt. Cyril P. Zurlinden, soon to become a casualty himself, described that first night ashore:

At Tarawa, Saipan, and Tinian, I saw Marines killed and wounded in a shocking manner, but I saw nothing like the ghastliness that hung over the Iwo beachhead. Nothing any of us had ever known could compare with the utter anguish, frustration, and constant inner battle to maintain some semblance of sanity.

Personnel accounting was a nightmare under those conditions, but the assault divisions eventually reported the combined loss of 2,420 men to General Schmidt (501 killed, 1,755 wounded, 47 dead of wounds, 18 missing, and 99 combat fatigue). These were sobering statistics, but Schmidt now had 30,000 marines ashore. The casualty rate of 8 percent left the landing force in relatively better condition than at the first days at Tarawa or Saipan. The miracle was that the casualties had not been twice as high. General Kuribayashi had possibly waited a little too long to open up with his big guns.

The first night on Iwo was ghostly. Sulfuric mists spiraled out of the earth. The marines, used to the tropics, shivered in the cold, waiting for Kuribayashi's warriors to come screaming down from the hills. They would learn that this Japanese commander was different. There would be no wasteful, vainglorious *banzai* attacks, this night or any other. Instead, small teams of infiltrators, which Kuribayashi termed "Prowling Wolves," probed the lines, gathering intelligence. A barge full of Japanese special landing forces tried a small counterlanding on the western beaches and died to the man under the alert guns of the 28th Marines and its supporting LVT crews.

Otherwise, the night was one of continuing waves of indirect fire from the highlands. One high velocity round landed directly in the hole occupied by the 1st Battalion, 23rd Marines' commander, Lt. Col. Ralph Haas, killing him instantly. The marines took casualties throughout the night. But with the first streaks of dawn, the veteran landing force stirred. Five infantry regiments looked north; a sixth turned to the business at hand in the south: Mount Suribachi.

SURIBACHI

The Japanese called the dormant volcano Suribachi-yama; the marines dubbed it "Hot rocks." From the start the marines knew their drive north would never succeed without first seizing that hulking rock dominating the southern plain. "Suribachi seemed to take on a life of its own, to be watching these men, looming over them," recalled one observer, adding, "The mountain represented to these Marines a thing more evil than the Japanese."

Col. Kanehiko Atsuchi commanded the two thousand soldiers and sailors of the Suribachi garrison. The Japanese had honeycombed the mountain with gun positions, machine-gun nests, observation sites, and tunnels, but Atsuchi had lost many of his large-caliber guns in the direct naval bombardment of the preceding three days. General Kuribayashi considered Atsuchi's command to be semiautonomous, realizing the invaders would soon cut communications across the island's narrow southern tip. Kuribayashi nevertheless hoped Suribachi could hold out for ten days, maybe two weeks.

Some of Suribachi's stoutest defenses existed down low, around the rubble-strewn base. Here, nearly seventy camouflaged concrete blockhouses protected the approaches to the mountain; another fifty bulged from the slopes within the first hundred feet of elevation. Then came the caves, the first of hundreds the marines would face on Iwo Jima.

The 28th Marines had suffered nearly four hundred casualties in cutting across the neck of the island on D-day. On D+1, in a cold rain, they prepared to assault the mountain. Lt. Col. Chandler Johnson, commanding the 2nd Battalion, 28th Marines, set the tone for the morning as he deployed his tired troops forward: "It's going to be a hell of a day in a hell of a place to fight the damned war!" Some of the 105mm batteries of the 13th Marines opened up in support, firing directly overhead. Gun crews fired from positions hastily dug in the black sand directly next to the 28th Marines command post. Regimental executive officer, Lt. Col. Robert H. Williams, watched the cannoneers fire at Suribachi "eight hundred yards away over open sights."

As the marines would learn during their drive north, even 105mm howitzers would hardly shiver the concrete pillboxes of the enemy. As the prep fire lifted, the infantry leapt forward, only to run immediately into very heavy machine-gun and mortar fire. Col. Harry B. "Harry the Horse" Liversedge bellowed for his tanks. But the 5th Tank Battalion was already having a frustrating morning. The tankers sought a defilade spot in which to rearm and refuel for the day's assault. Such a location did not exist on Iwo Jima those first days. Every time the tanks congregated to service their vehicles they were hit hard by Japanese mortar and artillery fire from virtually the entire island. Getting sufficient vehicles serviced to join the assault took most of the morning. Hereafter, the tankers would maintain and reequip their vehicles at night.

This day's slow start led to more setbacks for the tankers; Japanese antitank gunners hiding in the jumbled boulders knocked out the first approaching Shermans. Assault momentum slowed further. The 28th Marines overran forty strongpoints and gained roughly two hundred yards all day. They lost a marine for every yard gained. The tankers unknowingly redeemed themselves when one of their final 75mm rounds caught Colonel Atsuchi as he peered out of a cave entrance, killing him instantly.

Elsewhere, the morning light on D+1 revealed the discouraging sights of the chaos created along the beaches by the combination of Iwo Jima's wicked surf and Kuribayashi's unrelenting barrages. In the words of one dismayed observer:

> The wreckage was indescribable. For two miles the debris was so thick that there were only a few places where landing craft could still get in. The wrecked hulls of scores of landing boats

testified to one price we had to pay to put our troops ashore. Tanks and half-tracks lay crippled where they had bogged down in the coarse sand. Amphibian tractors, victims of mines and well-aimed shells, lay flopped on their backs. Cranes, brought ashore to unload cargo, tilted at insane angles, and bulldozers were smashed in their own roadways.

Bad weather set in, further compounding the problems of general unloading. Strong winds whipped sea swells into a nasty chop; the surf turned uglier. These were the conditions faced by Lt. Col. Carl A. Youngdale in trying to land the 105mm-howitzer batteries of his 4th Battalion, 14th Marines. All twelve of these guns were preloaded in DUKWs, one to a vehicle. Added to the amphibious trucks' problems of marginal seaworthiness with that payload was contaminated fuel. As Youngdale watched in horror, eight DUKWs suffered engine failures, swamped, and sank, with great loss of life. Two more DUKWs broached in the surf zone, spilling their invaluable guns into deep water. At length, Young-dale managed to get his remaining two guns ashore and into firing position.

General Schmidt also committed one battery of 155mm howitzers of the corps artillery to the narrow beachhead on D+1. Somehow these weapons managed to reach the beach intact, but it then took hours to get tractors to drag the heavy guns up over the terraces. These, too, commenced firing before dark, their deep bark a welcome sound to the infantry.

Concern with the heavy casualties in the first twenty-four hours led Schmidt to commit the 21st Marines from corps reserve. The seas proved to be too rough. The troops had harrow-ing experiences trying to debark down cargo nets into the small boats bobbing violently alongside the transports; several fell into the water. The boating process took hours. Once afloat, the troops circled endlessly in their small Higgins boats, waiting for the call to land. Wiser heads prevailed. After six hours of awful seasickness, the 21st Marines returned to its ships for the night.

Even the larger landing craft, the LCTs and LSMs, had great difficulty beaching. Sea anchors needed to maintain the craft perpendicular to the breakers that rarely held fast in the steep, soft bottom. "Dropping those stern anchors was like dropping a spoon in a bowl of mush," said Admiral Hill.

Hill contributed significantly to the development of amphibious expertise in the Pacific War. For Iwo Jima, he and his staff developed armored bulldozers to land in the assault waves. They also experimented with hinged Marston matting, used for expeditionary airfields, as a temporary roadway to get wheeled vehicles over soft sand. On the beach at Iwo, the bulldozers proved to be worth their weight in gold. The Marston matting was only partially successful—LVTs kept chewing it up in passage—but all hands could see its potential.

Admiral Hill also worked with the Naval Construction Battalion (NCB) personnel—Seabees, as they were called—in an attempt to bring supply-laden causeways and pontoon barges ashore. Again, the surf prevailed, broaching the craft, spilling the cargo. In desperation, Hill's beach masters turned to round-the-clock use of DUKWs and LVTs to keep combat cargo flowing.

Once the DUKWs got free of the crippling load of 105mm howitzers, they did fine. LVTs were probably better, because they could cross the soft beach without assistance and conduct resupply or medevac missions directly along the front lines. Both vehicles suffered from inexperienced LST crews in the transport area who too often would not lower their bow ramps to accommodate LVTs or DUKWs approaching after dark. In too many cases, vehicles loaded with wounded marines thus rejected became lost in the darkness, ran out of gas, and sank. The amphibian tractor battalions lost 148 LVTs at Iwo Jima. Unlike Tarawa, Japanese gunfire and mines accounted for less than 20 percent of this total.

Thirty-four LVTs fell victim to Iwo's crushing surf; eighty-eight sank in deep water, mostly at night.

Once ashore and clear of the loose sand along the beaches, the tanks, half-tracks, and armored bulldozers of the landing force ran into the strongest minefield defenses yet encountered in the Pacific War. Under General Kuribayashi's direction, Japanese engineers had planted irregular rows of antitank mines and the now-familiar horned antiboat mines along all possible exits from both beaches. The Japanese supplemented these weapons by rigging enormous makeshift explosives from five-hundred-pound aerial bombs, depth charges, and torpedo heads, each triggered by an accompanying pressure mine. Worse, Iwo's loose soil retained enough metallic characteristics to render the standard mine detectors unreliable. The marines were reduced to using their own engineers on their hands and knees out in front of the tanks, probing for mines with bayonets and wooden sticks.

While the 28th Marines fought to encircle Suribachi and the beach masters and shore party attempted to clear the wreckage from the beaches, the remaining assault units of the VAC resumed their collective assault against Airfield No. 1. In the 5th Marine Division's zone, the relatively fresh troops of the 1st Battalion, 26th Marines, and the 3rd Battalion, 27th Marines, quickly became bloodied in forcing their way across the western runways, taking heavy casualties from time-fuzed air bursts fired by Japanese dual-purpose antiaircraft guns zeroed along the exposed ground. In the adjacent 4th Division zone, the 23rd Marines completed the capture of the airstrip, advancing eight hundred yards, but sustaining high losses.

Some of the bitterest fighting in the initial phase of the landing continued to occur along the high ground above the Rock Quarry on the right flank. Here, the 25th Marines, reinforced by the 1st Battalion, 24th Marines, engaged in literally the fight of its life. The marines found the landscape, and the Japanese embedded in it, unreal.

The second day of the battle had proven unsatisfactory on virtually every front. To cap off the frustration, when the 1st Battalion, 24th Marines, finally managed a breakthrough along the cliffs late in the day, their only reward was two back-to-back cases of "friendly fire." An American air strike inflicted eleven casualties; misguided salvos from an unidentified gunfire support ship took down ninety more. Nothing seemed to be going right.

The morning of the third day, D+2, seemed to promise more of the same frustrations. Marines shivered in the cold wind and rain; Admiral Hill twice had to close the beach due to high surf and dangerous undertows. But during one of the grace periods, the 3rd Division's 21st Marines managed to come ashore, all of it extremely glad to be free of the heaving small boats. General Schmidt assigned it to the 4th Marine Division at first.

The 28th Marines resumed its assault on the base of Suribachi—more slow, bloody fighting, seemingly boulder by boulder. On the west coast, the 1st Battalion, 28th Marines, made the most of field artillery and naval gunfire support to reach the shoulder of the mountain. Elsewhere, murderous Japanese fire restricted any progress to a matter of yards. Enemy mortar fire from all over the volcano rained down on the 2nd Battalion, 28th Marines, trying to advance along the eastern shore. Recalled rifleman Richard Wheeler of the experience, "It was terrible, the worst I can remember us taking."

That night the amphibious task force experienced the only significant air attack of the battle. Fifty kamikaze pilots from the 22nd Mitate special attack unit left Katori Airbase near Yokosuka and flung themselves against the ships on the outer perimeter of Iwo Jima. In desperate action that would serve as a prelude to Okinawa's fiery engagements, the kamikazes sank the escort carrier *Bismarck Sea* with heavy loss of life and damaged several other ships, including the veteran *Saratoga*, finally knocked out of the war. All fifty Japanese planes were expended.

Two.

It rained even harder on the fourth morning, D+3. Marines scampering forward under fire would hit the deck, roll, and attempt to return fire—only to discover that the loose volcanic grit had combined with the rain to jam their weapons. The 21st Marines, as the vanguard of the 3rd Marine Division, hoped for good fortune in its initial commitment after relieving the 23rd Marines. The regiment instead ran headlong into an intricate series of Japanese emplacements, which marked the southeastern end of the main Japanese defenses. The newcomers fought hard all day to scratch and claw an advance of two hundred net yards. Casualties were disproportionate.

On the right flank, Lieutenant Colonel Chambers continued to rally the 3rd Battalion, 25th Marines, through the rough pinnacles above the Rock Quarry. As he strode about directing the advance of his decimated companies that afternoon, a Japanese gunner shot him through the chest. Chambers went down hard, thinking it was all over: "I started fading in and out. I don't remember too much about it except the frothy blood gushing out of my mouth. . . . Then somebody started kicking the hell out of my feet. It was [Captain James] Headley, saying, "Get up; you were hurt worse on Tulagi!"

Captain Headley knew Chambers's sucking chest wound portended a grave injury. He sought to reduce his commander's shock until they could get him out of the line of fire. This took doing. Lt. Michael F. Keleher, USNR, now the battalion surgeon, crawled forward with one of his corpsmen. Willing hands lifted Chambers on a stretcher. Keleher and several others, bent double against the fire, carried him down the cliffs to the aid station, and eventually on board a DUKW, making the evening's last run out to the hospital ships.

All three battalion commanders in the 25th Marines had now become casualties. Chambers would survive to receive the Medal of Honor; Captain Headley would command the shot-up

3rd Battalion, 25th Marines, for the duration of the battle. By contrast, the 28th Marines on D+3 made commendable progress against Suribachi, reaching the shoulder at all points. Late in the day, combat patrols from the 1st Battalion, 28th Marines, and the 2nd Battalion, 28th Marines, linked up at Tobiishi Point at the southern tip of the island. Recon patrols returned to tell Lieutenant Colonel Johnson that they found few signs of live Japanese along the mountain's upper slopes on the north side.

At sundown, Admiral Spruance authorized Task Force 58 to strike Honshu and Okinawa, and then retire to Ulithi to prepare for the Ryukyuan campaign. All eight Marine Corps fighter squadrons thus left the Iwo Jima area for good. Navy pilots flying off the ten remaining escort carriers would pick up the slack. Without slighting the skill and valor of these pilots, the quality of close air support to the troops fighting ashore dropped off after this date. The escort carriers, for one thing, had too many competing missions, namely combat air patrols, antisubmarine sweeps, searches for downed aviators, and harassing strikes against neighboring Chichi Jima. Marines on Iwo Jima complained of slow response time to air-support requests, light payloads (rarely greater than one-hundred-pound bombs), and high delivery altitudes (rarely below 1,500 feet). The navy pilots did deliver a number of napalm bombs. Many of these failed to detonate, although this was not the fault of the aviators; the early napalm "bombs" were simply old wing-tanks filled with the mixture, activated by unreliable detonators. The marines also grew concerned about these notoriously inaccurate area weapons being dropped from high altitudes.

By Friday, February 23 (D+4), the 28th Marines stood poised to complete the capture of Mount Suribachi. The honor went to the 3rd Platoon (reinforced), Company E, 2nd Battalion, 28th Marines, under the command of 1st Lt. Harold G. Schrier, the company executive officer. Lieutenant Colonel Johnson ordered Schrier to scale the summit, secure the crater, and raise a fifty-four-by-twenty-eight-inch American flag for all to see. Schrier led his forty-man patrol forward at 08:00.

The regiment had done its job, blasting the dozens of pillboxes with flame and demolitions, rooting out snipers, knocking out the masked batteries. The combined-arms pounding by planes, field pieces, and naval guns the past week had likewise taken its toll on the defenders. Those who remained popped out of holes and caves to resist Schrier's advance, only to be cut down. The marines worked warily up the steep northern slope, sometimes resorting to crawling on hands and knees.

Part of the enduring drama of the Suribachi flag-raising was the fact that it was observed by so many people. Marines all over the island could track the progress of the tiny column of troops during its ascent ("Those guys oughta be getting flight pay," said one wag). Likewise, hundreds of binoculars from the ships off-shore watched Schrier's marines climbing ever upward. Finally, they reached the top and momentarily disappeared from view. Those closest to the volcano could hear distant gunfire. Then, at 10:20, there was movement on the summit; suddenly the Stars and Stripes fluttered bravely.

Lusty cheers rang out from all over the southern end of the island. The ships sounded their sirens and whistles. Wounded men propped themselves up on their litters to glimpse the sight. Strong men wept unashamedly. Navy Secretary Forrestal, thrilled by the sight, turned to Holland Smith and said, "The raising of that flag means a Marine Corps for another five hundred years."

Three hours later an even larger flag went up to more cheers. Few would know that Associated Press photographer, Joe Rosenthal, had just captured the embodiment of the American warfighting spirit on film. *Leatherneck* magazine photographer Sgt. Lou Lowery had taken a picture of the first flag-raising and almost immediately got in a firefight with a couple of enraged Japanese. His photograph would become a valued collector's item. But Rosenthal's would enthrall the free world.

Capt. Thomas M. Fields, commanding officer of Company D, 2nd Battalion, 26th Marines, heard his men yell "Look up there!" and turned in time to see the first flag go. His first thought dealt with the battle still at hand: "Thank God the Japs won't be shooting us down from behind anymore."

The 28th Marines took Suribachi in three days at the cost of more than five hundred troops (added to its D-day losses of four hundred men). Colonel Liversedge began to reorient his regiment for operations in the opposite direction, northward. Unknown to all, the battle still had another month to run its bloody course.

THREE.

Doolittle Hits Tokyo

Colonel Robert Barr Smith (Ret.) and Laurence J. Yadon

THE SPRING OF 1942 WAS NOT A HAPPY TIME FOR THE UNITED States and her allies. America had lost the Philippines; Britain had lost Malaya and was falling back in Burma; Holland had lost her possessions in the Dutch East Indies. Naval losses for all three nations had been heavy, and many people were deeply concerned with the vital short-term need to salvage whatever could be saved from the ruin. And all of these nations had Hitler's rampant Germany to contend with, plus her arrogant ally, Italy, in addition to Japan.

But some of those same people already had their thoughts and dreams focused on something else, something far more satisfying: revenge. Admiral Yamamoto, the able architect of Japan's aggression in the Pacific, had put it perfectly in responding to congratulations on Japan's successful attack on the Hawaiian Islands.

"I fear," he said, "that all we have done is awaken a sleeping giant."

He was, as most Americans would say, right on the money.

President Roosevelt was one of those intent on striking back, and the sooner the better. And so, just two weeks after the sneak attack on Pearl Harbor, in a meeting with the Joint Chiefs of Staff at the White House, he voiced his notion that the United States should bomb Japan as soon as possible, in order to boost American morale. Planning began immediately.

Since there was no base close enough to Japan from which to fly off bombers against the home islands of Imperial Japan, it became obvious that the raiders would have to come by sea. Taking off from one of the Navy's carriers might just be possible, with some modifications of the bombers and a lot of luck. The raiders would have to be multi-engined bombers, and those belonged to the Army Air Corps. The Navy's aircraft carriers would have to sail deep into the Pacific, dangerously close to Japan's home waters, if the Army's bombers were to carry a decent bomb load and have any chance of flying from their targets on to some place of reasonable safety where the crews might survive.

For the bombers could not return to the carrier from which they had been launched, even if they could manage a carrier landing, a problematical possibility itself. The carriers would have to clear out at high speed once they had launched the strike. Waters that were close to Japan were far too dangerous, and America's small carrier force was far too precious to risk by loitering for most of a day so near Japan. In order to reach Japan from any distance with a decent load of bombs—a half ton per plane was the goal—the multi-engine Army aircraft had to be capable of taking off from a carrier flight deck.

No four-engine bomber would even fit on a carrier flight deck, let alone take off from one. So it would have to be a medium bomber, and the planners carefully looked over the available aircraft. Two types were rejected because their wingspan was too broad for the carrier; in the end the planners settled on the B-25 Mitchell. It was twice tested, and both times took off successfully from the USS *Hornet*.

Work began immediately on major modifications. The interior changes to the plane were mostly to accommodate extra gas tanks to almost double the bomber's regular fuel capacity, but there were more. The treasured Norden bombsight was replaced by a crude device dreamed up by one of the pilots, called the "Mark Twain" and costing a whole twenty cents. The belly turret and one radio were removed to save weight, and a pair of dummy guns were added to the stern of each B-25.

Starting on the 1st of March, the crews began rehearsals in Florida, flying at night and over water, practicing low-altitude bombing and takeoffs from a section of runway painted in the shape and size of a carrier deck. And on the 1st of April, 1942, sixteen modified bombers were loaded on the *Hornet* at Alameda Naval Air Station on San Francisco Bay. Each aircraft had a crew of five, and a two-hundred-man maintenance and support detachment went to sea with them.

Next day the task force sailed, out into the broad Pacific: *Hornet*, its sister-ship *Enterprise*—providing fighter cover for the little task force—and three heavy and one light cruisers, eight destroyers, and two fleet oilers. On April 17, the oilers refueled everybody, and then they and the destroyers turned for home. The carriers and cruisers pushed on at high speed for their launching point in the dangerous seas east of Japan.

They were unobserved most of the way, but on the morning of April 18, the little fleet ran into a Japanese picket boat, *Nitto Maru*. Light cruiser *Nashville* promptly sent *Nitto Maru* to the bottom, but she had gotten off a radio signal before she sank. On the correct assumption that the presence of American ships was now known by the Japanese naval command, Captain (later Admiral) Mark Mitscher of *Hornet* made a hard but wise decision. He would launch the strike immediately, although the task force was still some 170 nautical miles short of the planned launch point, and ten hours ahead of schedule.

All sixteen B-25s got into the air in everybody's first real carrier takeoff. Each bomber carried three 250-pound bombs and a bundle of incendiaries, rigged to break apart and scatter over a broad area once it was dropped. Several bombs had medals attached to them, Japanese "friendship medals" given to Americans in a less hostile time. Now they would be returned . . . with interest.

Flying in at "zero feet," Doolittle's men arrived over Japan and split up, their coming apparently a complete surprise to the Japanese defenders in spite of the little picket boat's radio warning. There was some light antiaircraft fire and attacks by a few fighters, as the bombers struck at ten targets in Tokyo, two more in Yokohoma, and one each in Nagoya, Kobe, Yokosuka, and Osaka. Only one B-25 was damaged, and gunners on *Hara Karier* got two Japanese fighters; *Whirling Dervish* shot down another one. The bombers' nose gunners sprayed everything in sight, and the force was gone into the west, as suddenly as it had come.

The raid's planners had laid out a course southwest across the East China Sea that would bring the aircraft over China in about twelve hours. There were bases there that could receive them, primarily at a place called Zhuzhou, for which fifteen of the bombers headed. The sixteenth aircraft was gobbling gasoline at a frightening rate, and its commander wisely elected to turn for the closer Soviet Union, landing near Vladivostok. The Russians had a problem: At the time they had a non-aggression pact with Japan, so they decided they could not honor a request from the United States to release the crew. The American crew was therefore interned; well-treated, but still not free. That is, until they were moved to a town near the Iranian border.

There the plane commander managed to bribe a man he thought was a smuggler, who got the Americans across the border into sanctuary at a British consulate. It much later developed that the providential "smuggling" was in fact the work of the Soviets' NKVD law enforcement agency, achieving clandestinely what their government could not legally do in the cold light of day.

The other crews either bailed out or crash-landed in China. They got much unselfish help from the Chinese, soldiers and civilians alike, and also from an American missionary. Sixty-nine men escaped the Japanese; three were killed in action when their B-25 crashed and a fourth died when he fell from a cliff after bailing out. Two crews were missing and unaccounted for, until, in August, the Swiss consul in Shanghai advised that two crew members had drowned after their aircraft landed at sea, and the other eight were prisoners of the Japanese.

In August, the Japanese announced that all eight had been "tried" and sentenced to death, although several sentences had been commuted, they said, to life in prison. In fact, three Americans were shot by firing squad. The rest were imprisoned on starvation rations. One man died; the remaining emaciated aircrew were freed by American troops in August 1945. Remarkably, one of those four, Corp. Jacob DeShazer, later returned to Japan as a missionary and served there for more than thirty years. Greater love hath no man.

The raid was a tremendous psychological blow to Japan, although as predicted, the material damage was relatively light. Until now the holy home islands were thought to be safe from the inferior westerners. By contrast, the delight in America overflowed; a bright ray of sunshine for a country deeply angry at the nation that smiled and talked peace even while its carriers were steaming into position to strike at Pearl Harbor. One of the authors still remembers his father's comment when the news of the raid on Japan broke: "Take that, you bastards!"

Not only in Japan, but all across America, people asked, "Where did the American bombers come from?"

Why, from Shangri-La, said President Roosevelt, using the name of the hidden mountain paradise created in James Hilton's classic novel *Lost Horizon*. The Japanese navy tried hard to find the American ships from which they knew the raid was launched, but they only managed to add to their embarrassment. Even though they used five carriers and a multitude of other ships, they still failed to find the American task force, let alone attack it, adding to the great shame of allowing the enemy to penetrate so deeply into the holy waters of Imperial Japan in the first place.

The dark side of the raid was the predictable Japanese reaction in China, especially in the eastern coastal provinces that could harbor American airmen as they did the Doolittle raiders. Operation *Deigo* did its evil best to ensure that no Chinese who helped the American raiders would ever do so again. The generally accepted civilian death toll from Japanese reprisals was ten thousand. Other estimates run as high as a quarter of a million.

There was an unexpected consequence, too. There is a suggestion that the strike on Japan may have reinforced Admiral Isoroku Yamamoto's decision to strike at Midway Island, or at least forced his hand on timing, setting the stage for the US Navy's decisive whipping of the Japanese in June of 1942. Midway was a startling, massive American victory, gutting Japan's carrier force and, maybe more importantly, destroying much of her cadre of experienced carrier pilots.

America rejoiced at the daring raid on the Japanese homeland. Jimmie Doolittle, who thought he might be court-martialed for losing his entire command, instead received the Congressional Medal of Honor and was promoted two grades to brigadier general.

The bombs didn't do much damage; nobody expected them to. But while Japan was deeply ashamed and could never feel secure again, America smiled. And one small step had been taken toward the far-off day of complete retribution. Japan had sowed the wind at Pearl Harbor. Four years later a big, sleek bomber named *Enola Gay* would bring the very fires of hell to the islands of Japan.

Four.

Treacherous Passage

Douglas A. Campbell

THE SEA WAS IN A FURIOUS MOOD. PILED ON ITS SURFACE WERE great, gray waves, living monsters who could humble even the greatest warships. Yet, the USS *Flier* was but a submarine, at about 300 feet, one of the smaller vessels in the navy. Even when submerged, it pitched and rolled like a slender twig. But inside *Flier* were no ordinary sailors. They were submariners: men—most of them quite young—selected from the ranks for their virtues of fearlessness and its companion trait, optimism. Their mood was bright. Despite the beastly roar and hiss of the sea above them, none believed that on this day his death was at hand.

The Reaper might come later, when their boat reached the actual battle lines in this, the third year of World War II. And probably not then, either, they thought. The momentum of the conflict had turned in their favor. There was a sense, pervasive on board, that destiny was with the Allies. Everyone expected to be around for the final victory. These were young men—many of them green—led by a handful of sailors creased by the experience of having survived at sea. Death was for someone else, the enemy, even on January 16, 1944, even on the Pacific Ocean, the greatest naval battleground in history, a place where tens of thousands of Americans had already died.

But the men aboard the *Flier* could not ignore the thrashing as she bucked and twisted. For the one young cowboy in the crew, it had to make him think rodeo bull. He and his mates joked uneasily about the sobriety of the welders who had built the submarine back in Groton, Connecticut.

In these angry seas they approached the atoll known as Midway, one of the Navy's refueling depots. Once beyond Midway, their first wartime patrol aboard *Flier* would begin, and their record—distinguished or dreadful—would be tallied in tons of enemy shipping sunk. With young hearts and a sense of invincibility, they knew that the slamming of their submarine by the sea was only a tune-up for the coming combat. And they had no fear.

On August 12, the now-battle-tested *Flier* approached Sibutu Passage like a slugger stepping into the batter's box. On the far side of this strait was the Sulu Sea, nearly 90,000 square miles of unbroken blue water shaped roughly like a baseball diamond. Sibutu Passage was home plate. The opposing team—the Japanese soldiers and sailors—had taken all the land around that diamond two years earlier. They were scattered along the first-base line, a string of islands called the Sulu Archipelago that ended in Mindanao, more than 200 miles to the northeast. More Japanese troops were strung along the islands from first base to second—Mindoro, at the top of the diamond, 500 miles due north. The enemy also held third base—the small island of Balabac to the northwest. And the huge island nation of Borneo, due west of Sibutu Passage, was thick with supporting troops, like the bench-dwellers in the dugout. Throughout the more than 7,000 Philippine Islands and their Indonesian and Malaysian neighbors, the Japanese navy and army were arrayed in what until now had been an almost impenetrable defense. Americans entered the Sulu Sea only by submarine, and when they did, they knew it was kill or be killed in this deadly World Series.

Flier's general orders, drafted back in Fremantle, became specific on the evening of August 13 as the submarine approached Balabac Strait. The word came around dinnertime, the normal hour for submarine headquarters in Australia to broadcast the war news along with any special instructions for the submarines on patrol. On this, the third consecutive day, there was a message for the submarine *Robalo*, which was scheduled to return from its most recent patrol. The message asked for the boat's location and estimated time of arrival in Fremantle. There was no urgency in the transmission. A returning submarine could easily be a few days late.

There was a message for *Flier*, as well. When the radioman's message was typed into the machine, the officer informed the captain, Commander John Crowley, of the new orders. The submarine *Puffer*, which had been patrolling in the northern Philippines, had encountered a Japanese convoy heading south. *Puffer* had sent torpedoes into several of the ships in the convoy and was now trailing "cripples," the message said. The rest of the convoy, thwarted by *Puffer* from entering Mindoro Strait on the northern end of Palawan, was now traveling southwest, along the western shore of Palawan in the South China Sea. Until now, *Flier*'s assignment had been to patrol the South China Sea, looking particularly for four Japanese submarines making supply runs from Vietnam. The new orders directed *Flier* to go after *Puffer*'s convoy. There was no need for Crowley to change course. *Flier* was already headed for Balabac Strait, and that would take the submarine right into the path of the approaching convoy.

Crowley was energized. The patrol had just begun and already there were targets. The word was passed along by intercom, and the crew knew they were back in the war.

On this evening, Baumgart had lookout duty after dinner, so he donned a pair of red glasses after seven o'clock and wore them for a half hour before he went to the control room. At eight o'clock, he climbed the ladders up through the conning tower. The glasses, filtering the harsh incandescent submarine lighting, prepared his eyes for scanning the darkened ocean. He was wearing his navy denims and boots. The warmth of a night in the tropics required nothing else. And despite his continuing anger over the way he had been assigned this duty, he was beginning to enjoy the hours he spent standing on the A-frame above the deck, cooled by the breeze as *Flier* made eighteen knots across the surface.

The conning tower was crowded with its usual complement of officers and crew. Jim Liddell, the executive and navigation officer, stood at the foot of the ladder leading to the bridge so that he could talk with Crowley, whose stool was on deck beside the hatch. Jim Russo stood beside Liddell, helping him with the charts. Arthur Gibson Howell was at the rear of the compartment, operating the radar. Beside him, Charles Pope, the hero who nearly drowned on the trip between Midway and Hawaii, ran the sonar.

Howell's radar presented him with an image of the nearest shoreline, many miles away. They had traveled on the surface throughout the day and had seen neither Japanese ships nor aircraft, and the radar screen still showed no enemy threats. The night was going as easily as had the day.

Admiral Ralph W. Christie's orders directing *Flier* through Balabac Strait remained unchanged by the message the radioman had transcribed earlier. Crowley was to take the deepest water route through the strait that he could. In deep water, it was assumed, mines could not be anchored. Specifically, the orders directed Crowley to use the Nasubata Channel, one of eight channels between the Sulu and South China seas allowing east and westbound ships to pass through the reef-strewn Balabac Strait. Nasubata Channel was the deepest—more than 500 feet deep in spots—and the broadest, with about five miles' leeway between Roughton Island's reefs to the north and Comiran Island to the south.

As he approached the channel, Crowley had several concerns, as would any skipper. While the ability to navigate safely around natural obstructions such as reefs was always a consideration, in wartime a captain had two more problems to solve. He had to give himself enough room to maneuver if an enemy ship attacked, and he also had to be wary of shallow water where mines could be anchored. Roughton Island's extensive reefs to the north took away maneuvering room and presented a navigation problem. Crowley, talking the matter over with Liddell through the conning-tower hatch, decided he would try a more southerly route through the channel. If he stayed in fifty fathoms—300 feet or more of water—Crowley believed *Flier* would pass through the channel untroubled.

Mines were the only military threat Crowley felt he faced that night. He trusted his radar and its operator, Chief Howell, and felt the device could find a target the size of a surfaced submarine—with the possible exception of a midget submarine—at a range of more than three miles. Unless the Japanese had developed a superior night periscope, he believed that on a night as dark as this one, a submarine could not make a submerged attack. And as Howell reported from below what he was seeing on the radar, Crowley was convinced the only things out there in the dark were islands and mountains, a few of which he knew harbored enemy soldiers. *Flier* could make it through.

Chief Howell relayed a constant stream of radar readings to Liddell, who passed them along to the skipper. And Chief Pope, watching the sonar, gave depth readings. With the radar showing the nearest land about 5,000 yards away, *Flier* was traveling in sixty-five to ninety fathoms of ocean when Pope reported a reading of forty-one fathoms. *Flier* wasn't about to scrape bottom, but the depth was shallow enough to raise Crowley's concern about mines. He asked Liddell, a veteran of a Philippine tour before the war, what he thought.

Crowley was standing in the forward end of the bridge, leaning over the open hatch in the bridge floor to talk with Liddell about taking a new course, when the explosion came. The blast caused the entire submarine to whip to one side and then snap back like an angry stallion trying to throw its rider. Crowley felt the violent motion, but the concussion was without sound, like the thunder from the electrical storms that played their lightning fingers across those distant mountains.

Jim Russo's job had been simply to help handle the conning-tower charts. He was at Liddell's side when the explosion rocked the boat as if it had rammed a wall. Instinctively, he looked down at the hatch to the control room. Something slammed into his cheek below his eye, ripping his flesh like a bullet. A shaft of air was venting straight up from below, blasting out through the hatch to the bridge. Blood was draining down his cheek when Russo felt himself lifted by the column of air, along with Liddell, the 200-pound ex-football-player, straight up to the bridge. Once above deck, Russo—by instinct and without hesitation—followed Liddell, whose shirt had been ripped off by the blast, to the rear of the bridge where, at the railing, they dove into the ocean. When Russo turned around in the water, *Flier* was gone.

Wesley Miller, standing on the A-frame above the bridge, was nearly thrown from his watch but managed to hook his legs over a railing to avoid falling. He was confused. Somehow, he had lost his binoculars, and he was concerned about the discipline that would result. Then there was screaming coming from below and air was blasting out of the hatch in the bridge floor under him. He stood frozen on the A-frame for an instant, although it seemed longer, until he heard someone yell, "Abandon ship!" and saw the bow of the submarine go under. Then the ocean was swelling around him, dragging him down into its darkness. The radio antenna had snagged him. Miller struggled to free himself and then swam and swam, reaching for the surface. Then he was alone in the water, and the submarine was gone.

Al Jacobson, lost in his reverie, watching the lightning and the mountains silhouetted in the darkness, felt the blast of air and, curiously, found Lieutenant Reynolds standing on the deck beside him, complaining that his side hurt. Jacobson told Reynolds to lie down, and then he crouched over the lieutenant, hoping to help him. He assumed that an air bank, used to store compressed air for use in diving and surfacing, had blown, and he told Reynolds to lie still. But as he talked with Reynolds, he saw Ensign Mayer and Ed Casey diving over *Flier*'s side. Just then, water rose around Jacobson and Reynolds, and the submarine sank below them, sucking them down with it. The image in Jacobson's mind was of the two huge propellers at the rear of the boat, still spinning as they passed him, slicing him to bits. He struggled to swim up and away from his death. It took a few seconds before he surfaced in a slick of diesel fuel that floated on warm, calm seas. Baseball-size chunks of cork from inside *Flier* floated around him. He could feel them. But there was no light to see what, or who, else was there.

Crowley, who had been standing to port at the front of the bridge, saw a geyser shoot toward the sky from the forward starboard side of the submarine. The next thing he knew, he was standing against the aft railing of the bridge, near Jacobson. He ran forward to trigger the collision alarm that was mounted on the bulwark just above the conning-tower hatch. When he got there, he smelled diesel fuel. He looked down into the conning tower but it was dark. There was no time!

"Abandon ship!"

The skipper's yell carried across the deck and perhaps a short way down into the submarine, where many in the crew already were being thrown about by the air blast and the flooding that made Crowley's command superfluous. On the bridge, the skipper felt the shaft of air rising from within the submarine, carrying with it the sounds of rushing water and the screams of seventy-one men trapped inside. Some men were climbing the ladder from the conning tower, just in time because the deck was heading under, *Flier*'s engines still driving it like a train entering a tunnel. Crowley found himself in a raging stream of water as the sea poured around the bulwark and into the bridge, and then he was washed out the rear of the bridge, into the sea. In a matter of just twenty seconds after the blast, *Flier* was gone, and after its passing, the ocean was calm. The dead sailors of the Japanese minelayer *Tsugaru* had once again struck from their graves.

A mine had touched the side of *Flier*—just a glancing blow, but enough to trigger its explosives. The geyser had appeared near the rear of the forward torpedo room. The explosion, quiet as it was on the surface, would have been enough to punch a hole through the submarine's superstructure and one or more of its watertight welded-steel compartments.

On this night, Crowley had ordered battle stations for the conning tower, but the rest of the crew was not on alert. If the watertight doors were not dogged in place with their big handles, the blast from the mine—having opened a huge hole in *Flier*'s side—flooded the forward torpedo room and the officers' quarters immediately. At the same time, a rupturing of the tanks full of compressed air sent a shockwave through the submarine's ductwork ahead of the flooding water. The seawater raced to the rear, in seconds reaching the control room where Ensign Behr would have been among the first in its path, followed by the bow and stern planesmen and the other sailors handling the various controls.

The flooding would stop the engines as *Flier* sank deeper, and the darkness that Crowley had seen when he looked down the hatch from the bridge would spread throughout the submarine. For the men in the rear, there was but one hope to temper their panic—an escape hatch in the aft torpedo room. If they could get the hatch open, then for the first time since their submarine training in Connecticut, they would strap on their air tanks and take their chances floating to the surface.

But what then?

The darkness was nearly absolute. Al Jacobson could see nothing, but he could taste diesel fuel on his lips. His body felt the warm, wet embrace of the sea as his uniform clung to his arms and legs. All was quiet except for the lapping of small waves. And then there were shouts, the sounds of a human voice, the first indication to the ensign that he was not alone. He began swimming toward the voice, floating easily in the salt water but slowed by the weight of his shirt, trousers, and boots. The strap of his binoculars was still around his neck, and the glasses floated harmlessly by his chest as he did the sidestroke. *Flier's* sinking had disoriented him, snatching him from the tranquility of a warm ocean night, plunging him into a struggle for survival.

Several of the men had responded to the same yell that had drawn Jacobson. Once they were all together, they shared what they knew and tried to decide what had happened to *Flier*. It could have been an explosion in the batteries, but Crowley discarded that notion. The diesel engines had been running and the batteries were idle, not a situation in which they were likely to explode. The other topic concerned who else from the crew had escaped the boat. With almost no light, they could not expect to see other survivors, so their only choice was to call for them. Soon they had gathered more men into their group. A headcount was taken.

A total of fifteen men responded to the roll call. All fifteen men were already getting a lift. Not only had they escaped the terrifying death of their seventy-one trapped shipmates, but they had also surfaced on a sea that was unusually docile for this time of year. Summer is monsoon season, and storms can whip the Sulu Sea into a froth. Swimming in those waves would have been exhausting, and the chances of all these men finding and communicating with each other would have been slim. With lightning flashing on distant islands, there remained the possibility that a storm could still come, funneling winds between the mountains.

But for now, here on the open ocean, the wind was light and the waves were gentle. As long as each man could stay afloat, he could remain with the group. For the next two hours, as they assessed their situation and developed a plan, that is what the men did.

There was a sense shared by most of the men that they were still part of a military unit. Perhaps this was because of their training, to always follow the lead of Crowley and Liddell. It took time for them to realize that there was no longer a formal chain of command, and that neither Crowley nor Liddell was in charge. They needed a plan.

The first thing to consider was their location. The skipper and his executive officer knew where they were. Liddell began explaining the options, most of which everyone already understood. There was land on three sides, Liddell said. To the west was Balabac, the largest chunk of land in the vicinity, roughly ten miles away. Each man was aware that the Japanese occupied that mountainous island. They could swim in that direction and with some certainty, due to the island's long shoreline, land on Balabac's beaches. To the south was Comiran Island, less than two miles away. Every survivor could probably swim that far, despite injuries. But there was a problem with this option: Comiran was tiny—only a few hundred feet across. If, swimming in this opaque darkness, they missed Comiran, they would have another forty miles of ocean before they reached land on one of northern Borneo's islands.

The lightning occasionally lit a mountainside to the north-west, but judging from what they could see, that land was about thirty miles away.

And if they headed toward any eastern quadrant, the Sulu Sea threatened them, with hundreds of miles of ocean, uninterrupted by land of any kind.

These were the options Liddell presented, each one unpromising. And none was worth even attempting right now. There were no stars to guide the men, and no moon, only clouds overhead. And the occasional lightning flash on the horizon, while it gave them something of a beacon, left their eyes blinded for several minutes.

But even the strongest among the survivors could not expect to stay afloat forever, and so they adopted two rules. First, they would turn so that the waves were lapping their left cheeks, and then they would swim in the direction they were facing. The course was randomly chosen, as far as young Jacobson knew. Perhaps Crowley and Liddell had a reason. But the skipper and his second in command did not share their thinking.

The second rule was Crowley's idea—a death sentence for several of the men, and everyone knew it: It would be each man for himself. The cruel reality was that wherever they were going, it was a long way off. Some of the injured men could not swim the distance without help, and if the whole group waited for the injured, the chances were overwhelming that no one would survive.

Crowley was uninjured, but he was the oldest, at thirty-five, and his physique after several years of sedentary submarine service was not particularly athletic. Crowley could be among the first victims of his edict. But like their skipper, all of the men agreed to the pact, and all fifteen began swimming across the waves, which lifted them a few inches and then gently lowered them in a mesmerizing rhythm.

Chief Pope called out in the night for Jim Liddell, asking the distance that lay ahead of them before they reached shore. After two hours in the water, the men still felt little wind. Liddell, pondering Pope's question, knew the entire swim could be fifteen miles or more, but he wanted to be encouraging.

"About nine miles, Chief," Liddell replied.

"Oh, fuck it!" Pope said in disgust. With that, the chief stopped swimming and said no more, his faint image dissolving forever behind the swimmers in the night.

It was not much later that Jacobson, keeping pace with Ed Casey, saw him veer. Instead of calling him back to the course as he had done before, the ensign swam over to his mentor.

"Ed, rest a minute, and then just float on your back and put your feet on my shoulders and I'll push you back," Jacobson offered.

"Remember, we agreed every man for himself?" Casey said, refusing his young friend's gesture. But the two of them swam back toward the group, talking as they went. They were joking about a blowout party they had planned to throw in Perth when the patrol was over, and as they talked, they reached the wake of the others.

Ten minutes later, Casey disappeared in the darkness. When Jacobson and the others called to him, there was no response. The lieutenant had chosen not to burden his shipmates any longer.

Paul Knapp had been struggling like Casey, but was keeping in line with the others. Jacobson saw him swim off to the side without a word. The ensign thought little of it until Knapp did not return. Then he realized the courage it had taken for Knapp to separate himself.

As the night wore on, one after another of the men, when they felt they could swim no more, silently turned to the side and disappeared, each man choosing for himself when his time had come.

If anyone among the survivors were thinking about the beasts that swam below them, none gave voice to the image. But the reefs of the Sulu Sea were habitat for a vast assortment of large animals. Sharks of every description shared the water with barracudas and rays. Some were harmless, like the white and blacktip sharks, and the guitar sharks. But others were legendary, like the hammerheads and bull sharks, predators that would eat another shark as quickly as they would consume a human being.

If the swimmers were ignoring the carnivores beneath them, it may have been because their minds were filled with the death they had just dodged, and, not that far below the sea, their shipmates already dead inside *Flier*. The thing that now would keep these men alive was their determination to keep swimming.

The overcast sky that had kept the stars hidden was overcome at about three o'clock that morning by the moon, rising grudgingly in the east to give the swimmers a navigational beacon. By now, only nine of the original fifteen survivors remained in the group. Wesley Miller straggled far behind the main pack but could hear their voices in the dark, and shouted to them to maintain contact.

At about five o'clock, when the first hint of daybreak was tingeing the sky from black to gray, helmsman Gerald Madeo began to panic. He fell below the surface, and after seven hours in the water, no one had the strength to help him. They simply continued swimming, led away from Madeo by the moon toward an unknown destination.

The trio of Howell, Baumgart, and Jacobson kept pace with each other throughout the morning, cooled under the blazing tropical sun by the same glass-clear sea that had warmed them during the night. Slowly, they drew toward their island, probably helped by a change in the tide or the currents.

It was one o'clock in the afternoon when Jacobson checked his wristwatch. The approaching drone of an airplane came from a distance, and when the men stopped swimming to look, they saw a low-flying Japanese craft, coming directly toward them. A half-dozen heads on the surface of the Sulu Sea were too tiny for the pilot to notice, however, and the plane kept going. The swimmers resumed their strokes, their luck apparently intact.

CHOOSING FREEDOM

The jungle island floated in the distance like a thin, green wafer. Little about its shore could be determined, but it was closer than anything else, and distance was important for the men, who by now had been in the water for nearly seventeen hours. Jacobson, Howell, and Baumgart had managed to stay close to each other since they had first spotted land. If there was anyone else afloat, they were no longer in sight. There were only the three and the island.

And then ahead, almost on a line toward the island, the men noticed something else in the water. It was long, and above it rose some perpendicular objects. Perhaps it was a native fishing boat, they thought, and the objects were the fishermen. They waved, but there was no response, so they decided to avoid the unfriendly thing. Swimming the straight route toward the island, they nevertheless drew closer to it and discovered it was a bamboo tree, its buoyant trunk riding lightly on the surface, its limbs rising toward the afternoon sun. Eager for some rest, they swam to the tree and Jacobson climbed up to have a look at the surrounding area. Howell and Baumgart struggled up beside where he balanced as the ensign scanned the sea. A short way off he saw more swimmers. He began shouting, joined by his mates, their voices carrying across the now-choppy water, their arms waving in excited arcs.

At daylight, when the island was first spotted, Crowley had given the order to anyone within shouting distance: Swim toward land at your own pace. He soon fell behind the rest, alternately swimming and resting when exhaustion overcame him. That he continued to swim is indisputable. What kept him moving is less certain.

Early in the afternoon, Crowley had seen Liddell ahead of him, clinging to another floating tree. The skipper and his executive officer stayed together then until they heard the shouts from Jacobson's group. It took a few minutes for Crowley and Liddell to reach the larger tree and cling to it. For the skipper, the plant had become a lifesaver. Exhausted, he had felt—even with the island in sight—that he could no longer swim. But the shouts from Jacobson and the others gave him new energy.

Breaking branches from the tree for paddles, the five men now straddled its trunk, urging the tree toward the shore. Off to one side, they saw Don Tremaine, swimming alone. He waved back when they shouted and gestured, but he avoided them. Tremaine had seen them but he could not hear them, and had assumed they were natives. If they were too unfriendly to pick him up, he reasoned, he would not chance swimming toward them.

The water changed from dark blue to a pale aqua a few hundred yards from the shore where the coral reef began, and then it was shallow enough for the men to walk. Their feet were wrinkled and white from seventeen hours in the water, and the entire seabed on which they stepped was coral. It was like walking on crushed glass rather than gravel, and the sharp coral edges sliced into the soft soles of their feet. Abandoning their bamboo tree, they stumbled, trying to keep their balance as the hot afternoon sun dried the salt water from their backs. The pain in their feet was numbed by their eagerness to feel dry land. And up on the beach stood Jim Russo, urging them on.

Staggering ashore, the men could, for the first time since *Flier* sank, see each other from head to toe. The sight was shocking. In the ten hours since daylight, the unrelenting rays of the sun had bombarded their water-softened white flesh. Now, where their skin was exposed, they were scalded red. Baumgart alone had long trousers on, saving his legs from the scorching. But like the others, he waded from the ocean with his face and arms as red as if the seawater had been boiling, and his blood drained into the sand from the coral slashes in his feet.

Byan Island, roughly triangular in shape, is just east of Mantangule Island. In 1944, the island was uninhabited by humans. A few hours after the men reached Byan Island, the sun settled beyond sprawling Mantangule and the air grew cool. Crowley and Liddell believed they were on Mantangule Island and that the big land to the west was Balabac, which they knew was occupied by the Japanese. To build a fire, if they could manage it, might attract attention, so they faced a night of cold. Even before sunset had cooled the air, they were swept alternately by fever chills and sweats. In the dusk, they huddled together for warmth, lying directly on the sand and, having successfully outlasted death for a day, sought the peace of sleep.

Neither sleep nor peace was to be theirs, however. Roused by their fevers, they would seek a more comfortable position, only to have the grains of the beach rasp across their sunburned flesh like sandpaper. At times, they were awakened by rats nibbling on their feet. Young Jacobson lie awake, his body shaking, the watch on his wrist slowly ticking off the seconds and minutes. He wanted nothing more than for the hours to pass and the day to come, bringing with it warmth.

They had learned in their first stumbling hours ashore before nightfall that the area near the beach offered neither food nor water. So when the sun rose on August 15, 1944, the *Flier* survivors knew they had to begin a search. Crowley directed Tremaine, Russo, and Howell, who had injured his knee when he had jumped off the submarine, to stay on the beach and improve the lean-to shelter. Jacobson and Baumgart were to head east and scout out the island, while Crowley and Liddell would head the other way.

Howell, Russo, and Tremaine started gathering scraps of wood and palm leaves in the hope of creating some real shelter for the coming night. At the same time, Ensign Jacobson and Baumgart hobbled along the shore, Baumgart in trousers and an undershirt, the ensign in his underwear with binoculars dangling from his neck. There were coconuts everywhere along the water's edge. They picked up the ones that looked whole and opened them with their bare hands by smashing them on coral. But each one that broke open left them disappointed, its meat rotten, its milk spoiled.

They trudged for hours without success. And then they rounded a point and ahead they saw a string of islands. Still ankle-deep in the sea and standing on coral beds, they splashed forward until they found a sandy beach where driftwood had gathered. Then they decided it was time to head back. Realizing that if they crossed the island, it should take less time than circling the beach, they tried to climb ashore up the coral cliffs. But the thorns and vines repelled them, and they waded once more into the shallows across the coral, retracing their painful steps toward their shipmates.

They had another reason for leaving together: They wanted to talk about the prospects for the group's ultimate survival. Crowley was familiar with the territory only from having studied nautical charts. Liddell had served on a submarine in the Philippines before the war and had a deeper understanding of the locale. What they had found so far was that they could not stay on this island. It was little more than a coral reef with no food or shelter. The jungle that began at the shore was a tangle of thorns and vines.

Rounding the western tip of the island, they saw their two options: to the northeast, beyond two more small islands, lay a large island, which Liddell identified it as Bugsuk Island. And behind them, to the southwest, beyond long, flat Mantangule Island, was the mountainous mass they knew had to be Balabac. Intelligence reports that they had reviewed back in Australia said that the Japanese were on Balabac. But from what they remembered, there was less chance of finding the enemy on Bugsuk, which was about five or six miles away. The trip could be made manageable by hopping only to the next island, Gabung, and resting before going on. There were tremendous currents that funneled between islands like these, Crowley and Liddell knew, and in their weakened state, the survivors could easily be swept out to sea if they tried to swim across. They needed another plan, and more information. So Liddell decided to leave Crowley behind and explore a bit further on the northern side of the island. The lieutenant had walked some distance when, coming around a curve in the shore, he saw a man ahead on the beach—a white man, clothed only in underwear.

At daybreak, the day before, Wesley Miller had lost contact with the other swimmers. But he saw several islands on the horizon, and, since it was in the direction he had been swimming, he kept going for the closest one. As the afternoon wore on, however, he found that the current was sweeping him to his left, past the nearest island. He would never be able to reach it, he knew, so he began to swim for the next island. But when he was perhaps two miles from his target, the current increased, carrying him fast along the beach. Still he swam toward the shore, cutting the distance in half when, to his left, he saw the end of the island approaching. After that, there was nothing, and Miller believed that his long trek from the Oregon ranch to the middle of the Pacific Ocean was at an end.

It was startling when, letting his feet fall below him, Miller felt his toes touch the bottom. He began walking now, and soon the water was only waist-deep, and to his left the coral actually rose above the surface. Then the sun set over Balabac and Mantangule and the water grew deeper. He no longer could wade. Although he must swim again to survive, his arms and legs were unwilling to move. So he willed himself toward the beach, and when he could touch bottom again, he was too tired to stand. Sand and coral rose beneath him as he leaned forward in the water so that his knees, not his feet, propelled him ashore while his body and arms floated listlessly. Crawling as an infant might, he worked his way out of the sea and partway up the sand, where his thoughts and his will ceased and he fell asleep. Awakened in the middle of the night by rising water, he dragged himself to higher ground, up against the coral cliff, and slept once more.

In the morning, Miller began to walk along the shore, looking for a way to scale the cliffs. As he stumbled on, he searched for clams in the sand. In a mile of hiking, he had found only solid rock cliffs along the bank, with jungle growth snarling out of their cracks.

Then Liddell found Miller and led him back to Crowley. The skipper, perhaps noticing the sailor for the first time, realized that this crewman was little more than a boy, a child who was pathetically grateful to find that he was not a sole survivor.

Later that afternoon, everyone assembled at the beach and reported on their work. Jacobson and Baumgart had found neither food nor water, but they told of locating a pile of driftwood on the northern beach. Howell, Russo, and Tremaine, when they were not working on the lean-to, had set out seashells to collect water, should it rain. And they had found water seeping out of the coral cliffs. They had set some shells below the cliffs and collected some water, one drip at a time—three shells full, in all. Everyone shared it, each person drinking a couple of teaspoons. It was merely seawater that had splashed onto the coral at high tide, but their thirst convinced the men they were getting fresh water.

If they continued to wet their lips with this water for long, they were going to be doomed. The human body, in order to rid itself of excess salt, passes the salt through the kidneys where it is washed away in urine. That means that the body is losing water as well as salt. The more salt in the system, the more water must be expelled. In a short time, the consumption of salt water will actually dehydrate the body, increasing the level of salt in the bloodstream and damaging bodily tissues. Soon, the drinker will die. But first, normal body functions will be damaged. Saliva will dry up, leaving the mouth and tongue without lubrication, exposing them to infection. Drying of the tongue may cause it to swell and split. Death might be preferable.

With the other reports submitted, Crowley told the men of their options. They could head west, eventually reaching Balabac where there was food and shelter—and Japanese soldiers. They would probably be captured and become prisoners of war. (Earlier in the afternoon, another Japanese patrol plane had flown low over the island, the red rising sun insignia on its wings easily seen by the survivors.) Or, they could use the driftwood that Jacobson and Baumgart had found, build a raft, try to reach Bugsuk, and, accepting the uncertainty of finding food and water there, remain free men.

To a man, they chose freedom. They would begin work in the morning.

Sunrise brought all the men back onto their feet. The agony of standing on those festering cuts was not enough to keep them on the beach, and soon the eight were hobbling in the shallow water, where vegetation coated some of the coral, making it less sharp. Splashing up Byan Island's eastern shore, they could see Gabung Island in the distance. When they reached the place where the two islands were closest together—just under a mile separated the lands—they began building their raft. Liddell and Russo, both strong men, reached into the jungle from the edge of the beach and tore out vines. As some of the men used the vines to lash the bamboo driftwood logs together, Chief Howell sat on the beach, improvising two paddles by splitting slender bamboo poles partway, inserting small pieces in the split crossway and then tying them in place with thin vines. Occasionally, he would lick moisture that he found on the leaves.

Crowley saw how his men slowed in their work as the day wore on, their movements becoming uncoordinated, their attention wandering. Thirst was on everyone's mind. But even though they scoured the coast looking for edible coconuts, they found none all day.

It was about two thirty that afternoon, just before slack tide, when the eight men surrounded their little raft and pushed it out toward Gabung. Ahead of them was a crossing of slightly less than one mile. The water was the pale blue of reef water (out for several hundred yards off the beach), and the reef resumed on the far side of the channel where dark blue water indicated a depth that no one would be able to wade. They had brought two long poles with them, and for the first quarter of the voyage, the younger men took turns poling the raft, on which Crowley was the only permanent passenger. The rest of the men leaned on the raft for support as they walked in the shallows across another long bed of razor-sharp coral. Crowley paddled.

Before they had made it halfway across the channel, they saw the daily patrol plane coming in low. Crowley and the man poling slipped into the water, and everyone tried to hide under the raft. The plane kept going, and the men, clinging to the sides, kicked in the deeper water, slowly moving the raft across the channel.

Now on the open water, they found themselves directly in the path of an oncoming squall. Abruptly, they were pelted with large, pure droplets, delicious on their lips, and everyone tipped his head back and opened his mouth. But while the raindrops splattered off their foreheads and cheeks, none of it seemed to find their tongues before the squall passed on into the ocean, leaving the scorching sun in its wake.

They had not yet reached the reef on the far side of the channel when the tide seemed to shift and a new current swept between the islands. With only a quarter of a mile to go, they suddenly seemed unable to make any progress, and the raft appeared to be drifting away from Gabung Island. The men on the sides kicked with all their feeble power. Crowley, feeling like a very elderly thirty-five, paddled, and the raft circled the end of the island and settled in its lee; the current having deposited the men close enough to shore that they could swim the final leg.

It was seven o'clock, more than four hours since they had left Byan Island a mile to the south, and the sun had already set. They found a sandy beach and were content to collapse where they could find room. The little slivers of coconut they had eaten earlier had done little to curb their appetite, and their thirst was only growing. But no one had the energy to forage. More than food and water, right now they wanted sleep.

Sunrise the following morning—August 17—brought with it relief from the tremors of the night and hope that this would be the day the men would eat. Before launching their raft, they gathered to discuss their next steps. It would be another nine or ten hours until the tides allowed them to leave this island for the next one in the chain. Crowley and Liddell took suggestions, and the group decided that their time could be best used by traveling around the island the long way. There would be more chance of finding food if they were covering a longer shoreline. It meant more walking, but now empty stomachs and parched mouths were overpowering the screaming pains from their feet and the swollen and blistered burns on their backs and arms. They pushed the raft into the shallow water and began circling the island to the west. Once more, the coral in the shallow water was softened by plants that grew on it, so wading was less painful than it might have been. But there was a trade-off, because when they were not swimming, their burns were always exposed to the sun, as it rose high above the island.

On the eastern side of Byan the day before, the men had walked along the beach with an open ocean to their right. Now, walking along Gabung's western coast, they felt surrounded by islands. Mantangule's long, low bulk stretched out to the southwest, and Bugsuk's broad sweep consumed the view to the northeast, only three or so miles across the reef-strewn water. To the north, another large island—Pandanan—was indistinguishable from Bugsuk. And to the northwest, more, smaller islands rose above the reefs to hide the horizon. With their goal of Bugsuk in sight, the men could think of food and water and let those images draw them ahead. But there were distractions. Swarms of stinging insects flew around them, and their thoughts drifted uncontrollably, clouded by the lack of food and water.

Apo Island was on the far side of a strait nearly two miles across, with the dark blue of deep water again in the middle, between the two shores. The men had about two hours to wait for slack tide and the passing of the next enemy patrol plane, and they gathered more coconuts from the beach, but as so often before, none was edible. Surrounded by a sea full of fish and water, they were dying of thirst and starvation.

The airplane arrived on schedule and continued south over the island. Certain the danger had passed, the men pushed their raft back to sea. The water was shallow enough for them to wade and to keep the weight off their feet as they leaned on the raft. Pushing and splashing, they moved their craft into the dark blue of the deeper water.

They were midway between the two islands, with no retreat possible, when someone noticed the fins. Two sharks cruised just beneath the surface, looking for food. The men kept paddling, splashing and kicking, and the sharks, perhaps sensing the hunger that drove these eight beings, stayed clear.

Aided by the shallow water, the raft crossed between Gabung and Apo islands in only three hours, and the men found a sandy beach just before dark. By now, they knew what to expect. They posted their rat guards and waited in troubled dreams and fitful sleep for the morning.

Sunrise was again their alarm clock, but they lingered until about eight o'clock before gathering around their sole possession, the raft, and heading to the west. Apo is a small, round island, but in all other ways it seemed no different from Byan and Gabung. Again, the men had chosen to take the long way, and each grudging step along the curved shoreline revealed some new aspect of the land ahead. Before noon, they had found the first indication of humans—a dugout canoe abandoned on the beach. The boat was riddled with holes and useless, so they left it and went on. Then they saw a trail leading up over the coral cliff, and Jacobson and Baumgart decided to explore. A trail like this meant human activity. But after a few hundred yards of walking on the coral pavement of the path, the men turned back, leaving the place to the monkeys that chattered and scampered in the trees around them. Joining the other men, they continued north along the shore.

Ancient trees, their trunks varicose and black, their roots writhing like serpents, the weave of their arched branches creating darkened tunnels, grew out from the coral cliffs along the north-western shore of Apo Island. The men walked under the trees, hidden from observation, until, in the distance, they saw the green shoreline of their destination, Bugsuk Island.

They stood transfixed, for there, under coconut trees that swayed like tall, slender dancers lining the edge of a broad, sandy beach, were houses. There were no Japanese launches on the shore and no sign of activity around the buildings. That did not mean there were no risks. So they would wait and watch.

But not for long.

SPIRITS OF THE LAND

There were eyes behind the towering coconut trees that swayed in the sea breeze along Bugsuk Island's sparkling beach in a gentle hula. The eyes were watching the *Flier* survivors.

All that Crowley and his men saw when they looked toward the island were the apparently tranquil settlement of houses and, in their imaginations, food and water. But they were cautious. With their raft in tow, they worked their way around the north-ern edge of Apo Island to a point on the beach where they could no longer see the houses. Their plan was to arrive on Bugsuk just before sunset and to use the half-light of dusk to sneak toward the settlement. By now, their starvation and thirst had robbed the men of whatever athletic ability they had once possessed, so when they swam across the narrow channel between the islands, they would lack the strength to swim against the flow. But if they judged the current correctly, they would land about a mile and a half from the houses. Then they would have enough cover to sneak closer, undetected. There was no more than a half-mile between Apo and the far shore, and all of it was the pale blue of reef water. They expected no problems.

Late that afternoon, they pushed the raft off the sandy beach. Most of the men waded at its side, and when they reached the far shore, they climbed out of the water on to another long stretch of white-sand beach under their tender feet. Stowing the raft, they walked west toward the setting sun. They were on a narrow peninsula on the far side, of which was the tidal mouth of a salt-water stream. Crossing the peninsula with a wary eye toward the far shore, they waded into the stream. When they climbed the far bank, they were on the same beach that, to the west, passed in front of the Bugsuk houses. Here a grove of baring trees, a species that, like mangroves, sinks its roots in salt water, blocked their view of the settlement. The men worked their way through the shallow water under the trees, with the low rays of the sun slanting between the tree trunks and then moved ashore, peering through the grove at what appeared to be a once-thriving but now-abandoned village. The houses that they had seen from Apo Island were surrounded by a coconut grove, and between the survivors and those houses were the remnants of bamboo and palm-leaf native huts.

Jacobson and Baumgart were the last to arrive, their arms filled with coconuts. For the first time in five days, the *Flier* survivors would have unspoiled food to eat, and apparently a place to sleep. The main building in this settlement—well built of bamboo and lumber, with a thatched roof—looked like the home of a person of wealth. But the home had been ransacked, the furniture carted out of its now-barren rooms, and any remnant of the former owners' presence stripped from the now-naked walls.

The house had a good wooden floor for sleeping, probably free from rats and certainly protected from sand crabs. But weary as they were, the men were also excited by their discoveries and were not yet ready for rest. They wanted to explore. Standing in front of the main house and looking south, they could imagine that they were in an exotic resort. A lawn fifty yards deep or more and shaded by the high canopy of coconut trees led to the beach of pure, white, soft sand, framed in this view by drooping coconut palm fronds. Beyond the beach was an island paradise. Stretching out to the left was the chain of islands the men had spent the last four days hopping, and between the last—Byan—and Mantangule, on the right, rose the distant blue mountains of Balabac. A good-size wooden boat—Al Jacobson guessed it was thirty-eight feet long—was beached in front of the house and looked like it had been intentionally destroyed. Nearby was another launch of about the same size that appeared to have been under construction. On either side of the house and inland from it were several clearings, which suggested that the owners had raised vegetables. And farther inland, some of the men reported, there was a stream. In its clear water swam schools of fish, meals for days to come.

Exploring by himself, Earl Baumgart found a curious concrete structure just behind the main house. It stood about five feet high and was another six feet long, and when he climbed atop it, he was elated. Someone had built a cistern to collect rainwater, probably from the roof of the house. There was all the water the men would ever need, and more! He called out his discovery to the others, who came running.

Once more, the skipper lived up to his reputation for cautiousness outside of the realm of battle. He told his gathered crew that they should drink sparingly from the cistern. They wanted to guzzle to their thirst's content, he knew. But having gone without water for five days, and with almost no food in the same period, their bodies could not handle much. When he had explained this, each man took a small sip from Baumgart's pool and then went away. Only Chief Howell ignored Crowley's caution. He drank until his belly was full, and then he drank some more.

Now Jacobson and some others set about opening the good coconuts. They found a sharp rock in the ground and smashed each nut against it until they had removed the soft green outer shell. Then they punched out the eye of the inner, hard brown shell, drained the milk, and crushed the nut into pieces that could be chewed.

With these small pleasures, the men began to settle in for the night. Jacobson found a bamboo door that he laid on the floor as his mattress, and he stretched out on it, content. Images filled his head as the palm leaves rustled above him. There were fish and coconuts to eat, a roof over his head, water to drink, and, it appeared, no enemies within miles. There was no more need to walk, so his feet could heal. There was shade from the sun, so his blisters would dry and disappear. This was a place where a man could wait out the war, if he had to.

Not long after Chief Howell drank his fill from the cistern, he began to feel ill. His condition worsened during the night, but there was no help for him. If some of the others showed little sympathy, it may have been because they knew his sickness, self-inflicted as it was, was not lethal. In time, his body would acclimate. The little bit of coconut in their stomachs had satisfied their appetites, and they knew there would be more meals to come. With a home around them to keep away the chilling breezes, they succumbed to their exhaustion, dreaming untroubled dreams.

Once more, they arose with the sun and began planning their day. There was work to be done, and Crowley and Liddell started organizing teams. One group would catch some fish while another would build a fire for cooking. They had no matches, but Jacobson still had his binoculars, and their lenses would make perfect magnifying glasses for focusing the sun's rays in an incendiary beam on dry tinder. Someone needed to scout the area, and the group would need more coconuts.

Jacobson was the first one up, and he was standing looking out a window toward the rear of the house and the jungle beyond when he saw two small boys—they might have been thirteen or fourteen—emerge from the trees. Jacobson told his shipmates what he saw, and they all were quickly on their feet. It was obvious to them that the boys knew the sailors were there, so they filed out of the house and approached the visitors. The boys were wearing ragged shorts and tattered shirts, and their feet were bare, like the sailors.' Crowley stepped forward.

"Americans or Japanese?" he asked.

"Americanos!" one of the boys, Oros Bogata, said, smiling. "Japanese!" he said, drawing a finger across his throat as if slitting it.

The men felt a collective wave of relief. Then the boy pointed to the cistern by the house.

"Don't drink water," he said.

Perhaps they misunderstood his puzzling words, they thought. But with their *Que sera, sera* attitude, they disregarded that comment and asked whether the boys had any food. Oros patted his small stomach.

"Rice," he said, and he motioned for the men to follow him and his silent friend back into the jungle. Stepping in line behind the boys, they found themselves on a narrow path. The boys, seeing that they were being followed, scampered ahead to a spot where they had left poles with small packs tied at the ends. Each balanced his pole on his shoulder, and then Oros led the file of hobbling, nearly naked men while his friend followed, sweeping the trail behind them to camouflage evidence of the group's passing.

In a short distance, they reached an abandoned sugarcane field. Oros motioned for the men to sit down, and he and his companion cut sections of cane a yard long and offered each man his own piece. The heart of the cane was a sweet and juicy bundle of fibers, and for the next half-hour, Crowley and his men chewed in bliss, until they simply had no more strength left in their jaws.

Back on the path, the boys led the men a short way to a clearing about the size of a football field. In one corner of the field was a raised wooden platform with a thatched roof supported on bamboo poles, but with no walls. Again the boys motioned for the men to sit and rest. Then they dropped their poles and opened their packs. One took a stick, sharpened at one end, and placed the tip in a notched piece of wood that he drew from his pack. He spun the stick between his palms, and in less time than it would have taken to remove a match from a box and strike it, he had some tinder smoldering. Jacobson, the Eagle Scout who had been taught to start fires with a bow and a stick, was impressed.

Then the boys produced a small pot, and one left and got water from a nearby stream. They poured rice from their pack into the pot, and while the fire brought the water to a boil, they cut leaves from a banana tree and made plates for their guests. Now the same boy who had cautioned them against drinking from the cistern gave them a cup of muddy water and, by sign language, told them they should drink it. The men hesitated, so the boy drank some himself. *Que sera, sera!* The men drank, as well.

When the rice was cooked, the boys spread it on the banana leaves. Then they produced three dried fish from the bounty of their packs and divided them among the men. There was enough for everyone.

Four days earlier, Crowley and his men had chosen survival with freedom over survival with food when they had elected to head away from Balabac. Theirs was a decision that prolonged the pain of hunger and thirst, which might easily have been cut short had they allowed themselves instead to come under Japanese control. Now, without hesitation, they had turned themselves over to the authority of two small boys whose friendship they accepted as a stray dog does that of a man with a scrap of food. Led by their stomachs, the sailors had followed the boys into the jungle with only the promise of rice, and now, with the smell of steaming hot rice and fish rising to their nostrils, they attacked their meal.

Their focus changed abruptly when, looking up from his food, one of them saw nine men, bristling with weapons—rifles, blow-guns, and bolos—stepping into the clearing from every point of the compass.

They were surrounded!

FOUR.

The *Flier* survivors had traded their safety for scraps of sustenance. The price of their meal now stared across the clearing at them.

Wesley Miller was ready to bolt like a startled fawn, but these fierce-looking warriors were everywhere. No one budged. The shredded soles of their feet precluded it.

"Hello!" one of the armed men called. His voice was cheerful and a smile lit his face. He dashed across the grass to the platform where the sailors still sat. Crowley struggled to his feet, as did his men at the approach of this stranger. When the man reached them, he grasped the hands of the *Flier* crew, shaking them vigorously.

"Welcome to Bugsuk Island," the man said. "I am Pedro Sarmiento."

Sarmiento said he was the leader of the local bolo battalion, indicating the men who were with him. Sarmiento had instructions from the guerrilla headquarters that if he found any Allied survivors, he was to ship them to a guerrilla outpost on Palawan's southern tip.

Crowley and Liddell were becoming comfortable with Sarmiento, and they were prepared to follow his instructions. At this point someone recalled the earlier direction from the two boys, to not drink the water in the cistern, and asked Sarmiento to explain.

"Oh," he replied, "earlier in the war, when the Japanese had driven the owner of the home from his property, Sarmiento had poisoned the water with arsenic in hopes that Japanese soldiers would drink it!"

Everyone looked at Chief Howell. The man had a cast-iron gut!

A Japanese patrol would reach Bugsuk later in the morning, Sarmiento told the sailors, and so they could not remain at the schoolhouse. The Japanese soldiers would inspect the area and then would spend the night in the house where Crowley and his men had slept so peacefully the night before. So the sailors would have to hike at least a mile inland to be safe. The Japanese were afraid to penetrate the center of the island, Sarmiento said.

Sarmiento reported that his instructions from the guerrilla leader, Captain Mayor, were to take any survivors all the way north across the center of Bugsuk and then to bring them by boat to the guerrilla outpost at Cape Buliluyan, the southernmost tip of Palawan. He told Crowley and Liddell that it was important to begin the hike soon. When they said they were ready, he told them to finish their breakfast. Then he sent the two boys back to the beach to make sure the Americans had not left any evidence behind.

A few minutes later, the boys returned with the lens that the sailors had removed from Jacobson's binoculars, with which they had planned to start their fires. Someone offered the lens to Sarmiento, who produced a pipe and tobacco that he lit with the lens. He smiled with gratitude. Then, seeing that they had finished their rice and fish, he invited the men from *Flier* to begin their cross-island trek.

FIVE.

Sugar Loaf

George Feifer

OKINAWA'S SOUTH. MAY 1945.
The Okinawan campaign was already longer than those for Saipan and Iwo Jima, and although its casualties were still about a quarter less than Iwo Jima's, the brass knew the greatest bloodletting lay ahead. It was time to shorten it by breaking the back of the defense. The ventures of Paul Dunfrey's platoon across the muddy Asakawa on May 9 and 10 were feelers for a general offensive the following day, General Buckner's response to demands that he get moving again.

The full-scale attack on May 11 was intended to penetrate the second and best line, which guarded Shuri. It would take place across the full width of the island where the 10th Army was stalled, about twenty miles south of the landing beaches. The 7th Army Division was enjoying a brief rest after a brutal month taking the Pinnacle and another defensive system at a group of hills near Kochi (where it unknowingly engaged Captain Kojo's battalion). Each of the other four divisions faced extremely formidable barriers at their places in the line. A large hill mass called Conical Hill confronted the 96th Army Division on the Pacific coast. The heights of Shuri itself awaited the 77th Army Division.

On those heights' other flank, the 1st Marine Division faced Wana Ridge and Wana Draw, a giant moat that might have been created for the slaughter of anyone mad enough to enter it. The obstacles in the path of General Shepherd's (and Paul Dunfrey's) 6th Marine Division, just down from the north, seemed comparatively less difficult. It remained on the west coast facing the East China Sea, where the Asakawa and the Asato, another river farther south, rimmed some three miles of relatively flat land.

Most of the 6th Division began the May 11 offensive a day earlier in order to cross the Asakawa and some fairly open ground to the main fortifications. For G (George) Company of the 2nd Battalion, 22nd Regiment, May 10 started in the predawn darkness, at a point where the Asakawa was shallow enough to wade across. G–2–22, comprising green men and savvy veterans of earlier Pacific combat, was a typical Marine company typically convinced it was far better than typical. Its young commander, Captain Owen Stebbins, had fought on the Marshall Islands and Guam after graduating from Officer Candidate School. Having been wounded on Guam, he was as relieved as anyone at the ease of the company's landing on L-day and relatively painless April in the north.

Good-natured Stebbins, who'd played football for Fresno State College, seemed to take everything in stride. Admiring him for his combat experience and fairness, his men were confident that "nothing ever fazed him." But after crossing the Asakawa in the morning's dense fog, he was no less amazed by the scope and skill of the Japanese preparations than Paul Dunfrey had been.

"Their camouflage was so superb even in fairly open territory that some of my men were hit by machine-gun fire from five yards away. And in the back because they had the terrific discipline to hold their fire until our patrols passed. Or until our men came almost right up on top of them—so near they couldn't use mortars or grenades to knock out the machine guns or get back the wounded, who were just too close."

When two of Stebbins's three infantry platoons were pinned down almost immediately, he was faced with one of the decisions that torment company commanders in the field. A scout cut down by a hidden Japanese machine gun lay within yards of it. Stebbins felt he couldn't attack the emplacement with grenades or mortar fire, because his man might be alive. He risked using his binoculars, whose glint in the sun now rising over the Japanese position would make him a special target. From two hundred yards away, he saw the body wasn't moving—but still hesitated to use heavy armament until he could be sure.

Now entered the element of chance that always determined life and death on the line. A medical corpsman who'd already saved several men by braving pinpointed hostile fire crawled out to rescue the scout while the machine gun still chattered. The wounded man *was* alive, because he happened to have fallen into a crease in the ground, where further bullets whizzed over him— but now killed the corpsman.

When Stebbins later had time to think beyond the demands of the field, he saw that twist of fate as yet another confirmation that combat was a constant roll of the dice. "The element of luck is enormous. One guy's miracle is the next guy's death."

Two long days later, Stebbins's company was again pinned down by heavy, accurate fire from a hill in its path. It had been assigned a platoon of tanks to attack with it by Lieutenant Colonel Horatio Woodhouse, the commander of the 2nd Battalion. After encountering increasing fire as they neared that hill, the four tanks waited some eighty yards back. Stebbins himself was in an unprotected observation post some three hundred yards forward of the company's command post, where First Lieutenant Dale Bair, the executive officer, or second in command, was positioned with the machine-gun officer. Stebbins's 1st Platoon was on his right, the 2nd on his left, and the 3rd in a reserve position, just behind the company command post. Dashing to consult with him in his observation post, Second Lieutenant Edward Ruess reported that heavy fire had pinned down his platoon, the 1st, and was inflicting casualties. He hoped the tanks would help.

Rising for a better look at how they should use the terrain, Stebbins was quickly hit by three machine-gun bullets. He would recuperate for several months in a hospital and then go home, whereas the same burst that raked his little observation post, no doubt aimed at him, the officer, killed his runner—by that time, the single surviving rifleman in his forward observation post. His other runners had all been hit earlier.

Meanwhile, Ruess had sprinted back to his men, dodging, ducking, and hitting the ground every ten yards. Platoon leaders were the officers who stood or crawled beside, or in front of, their men in battle. Known as one of the best, Ruess was virtually idolized by his men for his leadership. Two days earlier, Stebbins had noticed a dirty bandage the lieutenant was trying to conceal. Shot through the hand the day before, shortly after crossing the Asakawa, he went without treatment in a battalion aid station because he wouldn't leave his men when things were getting difficult. Stebbins also knew Ruess would never let his platoon stay pinned down long, which is why the captain had chosen it to lead the way onto the troublesome hill ahead. Fearless, "tiger-quick" Ruess liked to fix the positions of machine guns that were pinning down his men by showing himself to draw their fire. But this hill had too many concealed machine guns firing too great a volume of fire. Trying his daring move again, Ruess was killed.

The body of the runner who'd been killed beside Captain Stebbins tumbled into a decline. Unable to find his walkie-talkie radio, the captain crawled toward the rear until he was spotted by one of the tanks. The captain radioed the company command post, and stretcher bearers were dispatched to bring the captain farther back. While he was being bandaged, he told Lieutenant Colonel Woodhouse, who'd run back from his battalion's forward observation post, that the tanks were needed quickly.

Woodhouse took First Lieutenant Bair, who replaced Stebbins as company commander, to where they could coordinate another go at the hill. Runners were sent to inform the three platoons to ready themselves for a tank-supported attack to be led by Bair. The obstacle had to be taken quickly. Its fire was holding up the entire advance in the area.

Casualties among the lieutenants serving as platoon leaders had been especially heavy in the two days following the crossing of the Asakawa. Stebbins had also lost the leader of his 3rd Platoon on that same advance—to mortar fire in the morning fog of May 10. His place was taken by Platoon Sergeant Edmund De Mar, the Brooklyn boy who'd ventured a spell in Miami before enlisting in 1940. Now twenty-five years old, De Mar was called not Pops, like so many men over twenty, but Mommy, thanks to his regular admonitions to his teenage charges during their training. "Do I always have to be a mother and father to you?"

When the runner arrived with the message from Bair, Mommy was in a protected little position near the company command post, several minutes' run behind where Captain Stebbins had been hit. Despite the delay during the previous hours and the casualties to the company's two other platoons, the new obstacle gave no indication that it would be uglier than others in the two-mile lake of fire since the Asakawa event. The "prominent hill," as the Americans referred to it, stood beyond a slight draw that formed a corridor leading up to it. A similar rise called Charlie Hill had fallen the day before to the 1st Battalion, after a day and a half of a tank and infantry assault supported by naval gunfire. There was no reason to expect the new hill, barren except for a few scrubby trees, to be more difficult. De Mar, studying it again from a few hundred yards north, saw it as "just another lump, a brownish incline with a little knoll on top."

G Company's return to combat had been hard. After suffering only two battle-fatigue casualties during its weeks in the north, it lost nine men to exceptionally heavy artillery, mortar, and small-arms fire in just two days in the south, including five killed on the first day alone. De Mar's 3rd Platoon had escaped from one action only with the aid of a smoke screen. But the company would soon look back to those two days pushing south to here as almost easy going. At least everyone could still keep track of the killed and wounded.

Actually, De Mar was reassigning the functions of the missing men in his weakened platoon when the runner arrived with the order to meet with Lieutenant Bair for coordination. De Mar had twenty-eight men left of a full complement of forty. According to the plan, they would be joined by nineteen men still fit for action from dead Ed Ruess's 1st Platoon and be supported by the tank platoon. The hill had to be taken quickly, because its machine guns and mortars were badly chewing up everything in sight, including other companies.

The tanks were waiting in a depression not visible from the hill. When Lieutenant Bair gave platoon Sergeant De Mar and the replacement for Ed Ruess the plan of attack, they took the usual precaution of squatting far enough apart so that one mortar round couldn't hit them all. They were eager to learn one another's names to avoid calling out "Lieutenant!" or "Sergeant!"—another way of making themselves priority targets for snipers. The plan was straightforward: De Mar and his men on the left, Bair and the reduced 1st Platoon on the right, and the tanks moving out at the same time, while a machine-gun section would give additional fire support as they advanced.

The tank commander wanted assurance that he wouldn't be left "high and dry." Tanks were a great advantage to the infantry they supported, and the American 10th Army had vastly more of them than the Japanese 32nd Army. But enemy fire of such intensity and accuracy turned even the best American Shermans into a danger, too, as targets for concentrated salvos. Veterans learned to control their first instinct to crouch behind them for protection and to mistrust the false sense of security they provided.

Especially when antitank guns and other armament zeroed in on their whistling and clanking, the instinct of troops at their sides was to scramble as far from them as quickly as possible, leaving them vulnerable to dreaded Japanese infantrymen with satchel charges.

Against powerful defenses, therefore, tanks needed the protection of infantrymen as much as infantrymen needed the extra punch from tanks. De Mar urged the lieutenant in command of those four Shermans not to worry: "We'll stick to you like flies on shit." They synchronized watches. Jump-off time would be 1600 hours on a signal from Lieutenant Bair.

De Mar returned to his platoon and gave the word. Final preparations were made for the attack. Waiting was a miniature prelanding limbo, the men hoping the moment would come soon and that it never would. De Mar worried about them, about the steady Japanese fire from both flanks, and about communications because his radio had been knocked out. It would be nice, he mused, to be somewhere else. At 1600 hours, the lead Sherman's hatch cover closed and it started off with the 3rd Platoon.

It was only minutes to the hill. Starting the climb, De Mar and the others suddenly saw it was thick with guns. Tank fire had ripped down camouflage, exposing dozens, maybe hundreds, of emplacements now showing gun barrels and muzzle flashes. They didn't yet know that some of the most damaging fire pouring down on them was from other hills. De Mar had no time to look at anything other than his men, some of whom were already down. The tanks were being hit just as fast by concealed, expertly placed mines and antitank guns. Two were put out of action almost immediately.

The crest was only a few hundred yards away. Hoping audacity would compensate for their lack of deception, the two platoons charged straight up and reached it, but with a much-reduced complement. Bair spread his remaining dozen-odd men into shell holes, but the Japanese fire was so intense and the American already so diminished that the lieutenant, his radio communications also out, sent a man back to report that G needed help to hold the summit. Racing and dodging down, that messenger could see little movement among De Mar's group, which was "getting the hell beaten out of them."

Nothing De Mar had seen in combat, let alone in films, had prepared him for such concentration of incoming fire. It very quickly killed many of his men and left others unable to function as fire teams. Soon only a handful remained unhit, most prominently Bair. The big, burly first lieutenant was a man of few words who, like Ed Ruess, had been among the noncommissioned officers selected for officer training as the Marines' need for more officers to replace casualties grew. He presented a fine target—but also served as an inspiration to the men—as he tried to see to the wounded and rally the others. He motioned to De Mar: something about one of the disabled tanks. Then he was violently spun around and De Mar saw a large chunk had been ripped from his upper leg. But powerful Bair picked up a .30-caliber light machine gun from alongside its two dead operators, threw a belt of ammunition over his shoulder, and, like a John Wayne character, laid out lead in the enemy's direction—one of the directions.

It wasn't long before he took a second hit, this time in the arm cradling his machine gun. The lieutenant continued producing covering fire so that some men could crawl to help others who'd been wounded going up the hill until his third hit, in the buttocks, sent him spinning out of sight.

De Mar quickly threw some grenades and started crawling toward Bair. Then he felt as if someone had taken a log from a fire and slammed it with all his might into his leg. He went down flat and couldn't get up. Still down, he saw one of his 3rd Platoon men spring up and bang on a disabled tank with his rifle, after which the crew fired furiously for a moment—against what looked like "thousands of Japanese coming at us," as a crew member would later put it—until they ran out of ammunition and escaped through the tank's emergency hatch. Other tank crews continued firing although their vehicles were burning, then leaped out to help wounded riflemen.

There was no place anywhere to make a stand. Much later, in the sweet luxury of being alive to remember, De Mar would quip it was a situation from which General Custer would have cut and run. Dirt had jammed his rifle. He had no cover or protection. Knowing a sniper was poised somewhere on his left, maybe the one who'd already hit him, all he could do was hug the ground for all he was worth. He heard cries—from about ten yards away, he guessed—from a private named James Davis, whose size had earned him the nickname "Little Bit." Strong and tough nevertheless, Davis was only eighteen years old and his wounds were obviously very bad; he was crying for his parents to come get him. De Mar grunted for him to shut up: Any noise there would probably be a fatal noise. When Davis eventually did fall silent, De Mar hoped it was because he'd heard him.

Disabled in the extremely precarious position on the crest, De Mar thought of his own parents. He looked at his watch. It was 1645 hours. Forty-five days, not minutes, seemed to have passed. Now no Americans at all seemed still to be firing, and he could see none except dead and wounded. "What am I going to do?" he asked himself, trying to stay calm. He decided to wait, head as flat on the ground as he could push it. It would soon be dark.

His leg was numb and he'd lost a lot of blood, but he knew he could crawl. A figure slithering down the hill in the dark would most likely be finished off by his own troops, who would take him for a Jap, especially at night when they were the only ones to move. He didn't even have that night's password. But those were problems for later; now he could only lie where he was, still surprised and dismayed by the dense, accurate Japanese fire from big guns, small arms, hand grenades, and mortars.

Some time later, he heard a whisper. "De Mar, you hit bad? Can you crawl?" Although he didn't recognize the voice of the man risking his own life for his, the sense of comradeship gave him an incredible lift.

"Can I crawl?" he whispered back, his head still half buried in the mud. "I can crawl back to the States."

A good smoke screen was laid down—from smoke shells fired by the surviving tanks, De Mar would later learn. He started down. Someone joined him from behind and cut off his pack to ease his crawling. Finding a little ditch, he squeezed into it for cover and kept crawling until his hand touched the body of a rifleman from his platoon—who had a bullet hole between the eyes. He tried to pull the body with him, but the helper behind urged him to just get down off the hill for now. Although it would have been a four-minute stroll from summit to bottom, the incomprehensibly intense enemy fire made their progress painfully slow.

Soon he came upon Lieutenant Bair, badly bleeding from his wounds but trying to get his machine gun operating. De Mar tossed him his pistol because he believed he had some hand grenades left for any Japanese who might try to hurl satchel charges against the tank he hoped would take him back. Reaching it, he saw Little Bit's body lying alongside, where it had been pulled by Jim Chaisson, the man who'd run to the command post for reinforcements, then run back up the murderous hill to help his buddies. A tank man quickly dressed De Mar's wound, but Mommy refused to move until all known wounded had been brought down from the hill.

Then he was hoisted up onto the turret, where another wounded man was soon placed beside him. Recognizing the youthful voice of the "tanker" who'd rescued him from the hill, De Mar took out his battle dressing, leaned toward him, and asked where he'd been hit. Five fast rounds cracked out. Four hit the "expeditionary can"—five gallons of spare water or oil on the turret inches from De Mar's head. The fifth hit his savior behind the ear, splattering blood and brains all over De Mar. Gripping the now grievously wounded boy as the tank roared off, he reached for his grenades and found he had none; his pouch had been shot off.

When the tank made it back to Fox Company's command post, the young tank driver was dead. A sergeant asked how things were going. "Pretty rough on that goddamn hill," answered Mommy, not suspecting how much rougher it would become. The full strength of the defenses was still beyond his imagination—or that of any American, including General Buckner.

Those were the first assaults on Sugar Loaf Hill, as it would be christened two days later (when Lieutenant Colonel Woodhouse would call it by a name he'd used for objectives during training exercises on Guadalcanal). No more were made that day, for the battalion commander, now aware that the objective was far more difficult than originally believed, withdrew G Company and called for air strikes. Starting the next day, the sequence of attacks became so confused, with so many Americans cut off from their units, that it was impossible to keep track of who reached the summit before he fell.

Besides, holes from both sides' shelling were so large that men who crouched in them couldn't see members of other units, yards away. What was known for certain was that five of De Mar's 3rd Platoon were killed and ten wounded on May 12, a casualty rate of 50 percent. Other platoons lost even more men. On May 14, G Company's three rifle platoons with their machine-gun sections had to be consolidated into a single platoon—whose lieutenant would be killed that night. Sustained losses like this would quickly prostrate the 6th Division.

The 6th Division was up against the Sugar Loaf, main western anchorage of the Shuri line, where there took place a combat not exceeded for closeness and desperation . . . by that at . . . Iwo Jima or any other.

—FLETCHER PRATT, MILITARY HISTORIAN

[Sugar Loaf is]the most critical local battle of the war . . . the blood-
iest battlefield in the world.

— *NEWSWEEK,* MAY 21 AND 28

The hated hill looked to most Americans less like anything involving sugar than a rectangular loaf of coral and volcanic rock. Stebbins and De Mar weren't alone in wondering how such an object, seemingly less significant than the Kakazu Ridge finally taken by the Army, could cause such slaughter. To the 6th Division staff, it was merely a minor midway station wanted as a platform for fire support against a higher hill called Kokuba about a mile farther south.

Sugar Loaf's three hundred or so yards of frontage rose abruptly to a height of sixty feet from an area of plain before it, an unhappy feature to those who had to cross that open country, about the size of six football fields. The hill itself was low enough, especially in relation to the others in view of it, including the Shuri heights, to appear almost negligible—a "pimple of a hill," as one Marine would call it forty years later, still trying to fathom how it could have been so evil. A young man in the good shape of all infantrymen could run to its crest in three or four minutes. Yet it would cost more casualties than any other single Pacific battle, on Iwo Jima or elsewhere.

The next assaults were prompted not only by the continued need to take the hill for the sake of the advance but also to stop its defenders from rolling hand grenades down on American wounded lying at the base. But "shot-to-shit" G Company was losing its power to attack on its own. Of the 215 men with which it had started on May 12—down from a full complement of about 250—only seventy-five, including just three officers, were fit to fight by nightfall.

The summit was reached again the next day, but rapid counterattacks drove the attackers off. On May 14, Sugar Loaf became the focus of the entire stalled division. The 22nd Regiment was ordered to take it before nightfall at any cost, but more Japanese artillery from Shuri and deadly fire from unapproachable anti-tank guns repulsed every attempt. All approaches to the hill that gave the slightest protection of defilade were covered by intense mortar fire.

In the late afternoon, the commander of the 2nd Battalion ordered the remnants of G Company to try again, this time together with F Company. When the force of 150 reached the base of the hill two bloody hours later, 106 had been disabled, together with three of their four supporting tanks. Amazingly, the intensity of the mortar and machine-gun fire seemed to have increased.

Although riflemen normally carried almost two hundred rounds in their rifles, belts, and bandoliers, the counterattacks from the reverse slope and flanks depleted their supply in minutes. The open killing field was now littered with smoking hulks of tanks and casualties who couldn't be recovered while it was still more or less light: Snipers were everywhere. But twenty-six men from a supply echelon now arrived with replenishment, and Major Harry A. Courtney Jr., the battalion executive officer (or assistant commander), had an idea. Courtney had spent the day and previous night with the forward units to bolster their morale after the loss of so many of their senior officers, especially G Company, which, after the wounding of Stebbins and Bair, was under its third commander. Now he formed up the new arrivals with the survivors of F and G Companies. Pressed against the base under devastating fire, the twenty-eight-year-old major told the group that he wanted volunteers for a banzai of their own: Otherwise, the Japanese would be down with a counterattack in the morning. "That hill's got to be taken and we're going to do it. What do you say?"

All said yes, and they stormed up after dark, comrades near the base braving continuing fire to collect the dead and wounded from the earlier attacks. At the same time, the exchange of grenades near the crest was at such close range that members of Courtney's group could hear Japanese grunting as they tossed theirs uphill. When Marines answered, their grenades raised so much dust that the hill slope was obscured. The dust turned to mud when a drenching rain resumed a few hours later. Then the rain of Japanese grenades and mortars grew more accurate. Courtney was killed by one or the other shortly after he reached the crest. (He would be one of four 6th Division Marines awarded the Medal of Honor, three posthumously; Dale Bair received the Navy Cross.) The leadership passed to Ed Pesely, another first lieutenant up from the ranks, who'd taken over F Company earlier in the day when its commander was shot in the hip. The thinning force dug in and threw grenades to try to avert an imminent counterattack by Japanese seen gathering in the light of illumination shells fired by American ships.

A Japanese grenade in a steady barrage of them shot fragments into Pesely. Bleeding from the chest, he radioed Colonel Woodhouse, who told him to try to hang on; he'd get as much fire as he could from every possible artillery battery, Marine and Army. The lieutenant colonel stayed on the radio with him all night, calling in coordinates for that artillery. Shortly after dawn, a handful of survivors—some fifteen of the sixty men who had stormed the crest with Courtney—withdrew, slightly protected from the severe Japanese fire by a morning mist.

One of the lucky fifteen was Wendell Majors, a G Company rifleman who realized sometime after midnight that he was the only man left alive on the hill's left flank. Private Majors began inching closer toward what he hoped would be friends in the center when a Navy star shell burst into light overhead. He dashed for the cover of a shell hole, jumped in, and felt a searing jolt. A bayonet fixed to a rifle, one of many weapons abandoned in earlier seesaw charges by both sides, had entered the back of his right thigh and was protruding from the front.

Another lucky one was Irving Oertel, whom De Mar had given command of a machine-gun platoon in the emergency of the soaring casualties. "Guys were all over the place, wounded, bleeding, dead—and the living could hardly move because you simply *couldn't* without getting hit.... Then it got dark and I stayed [below the crest] all night because the air was still really thick with Japanese fire. The platoon was down to a few men. We just didn't have any guys left."

Those who *were* left had reached the limit of endurance. Corporal Dan Dereschuk had been assigned to protect the right flank with two machine guns and eight G Company Marines—all sunken-eyed with exhaustion after five days with almost no sleep since crossing the Asakawa. The corporal had actually fallen asleep while digging his foxhole the previous night. He was even more spent now, and his face ached from shrapnel wounds suffered the previous day, but there could be no sleep. Mortar fire knocked out one machine gun and steady firing burned out the barrel of the other. Dereschuk's eight men dwindled to three, one alternately crying out and moaning from a stomach wound, which brought more grenades down on the three survivors. But they managed to evacuate at dawn.

After the seesawing of May 14, the 2nd Battalion was a skeleton and the entire 22nd Regiment was down to 62 percent of combat efficiency. May 15 was no better. The pitch of that day's fighting probably exceeded any in the division's history. Furious artillery and mortar barrages met the units that moved out early in the morning. The Japanese counterattack that had driven the last of Major Courtney's group from the hill pushed forward until early afternoon, retaking some precious ground just north of it. By the end of the day, the 2nd Battalion had to be withdrawn because it had taken more than four hundred casualties, almost half its normal complement. (Owen Stebbins's G–2–22 was down to one officer, a lieutenant who'd become the company commander, and a scattering of enlisted men.) Further reduced by sickness and exhaustion, the battalion could field 282 effectives out of its normal complement of roughly one thousand men.

Two boys had returned to combat that afternoon, their wounds from up north patched on a hospital ship and in Hawaii. Not finding their unit before dark, they tried to wait out the night in the safety of a cave. But since all were too packed with other Marines sheltering from the fire to squeeze in, they lie down just outside one of them, under a tepee formed by two huge rocks. A shell found its way even into what seemed that perfect cover and killed them before they could rejoin their buddies.

Only the Shuri Line, in general, has been more studied by military analysts than its Sugar Loaf segment—attention well deserved, for the skill and sweat of Japanese groundworks were in dramatic evidence here.

The terrain favored them almost by the nature of things; defenders almost always fortified the high ground, toward which attackers had to fight from below, along predictable routes. In this case, the Japanese had a better view of the attackers than usual, especially from the Shuri heights that dominated the entire area. Their cave exits on the rear slopes and the flanks as well as the forward slope allowed defenders protected from American shells to rush out to counterattack Marines who had reached the summit—and in force, because the unusually elaborate network of tunnels provided safe access for reinforcements. In addition, their machine-gun emplacements, hidden mortars, and other defensive arrangements had been sited with particular care, probably under General Cho's personal direction.

The crux was that Sugar Loaf Hill, or Heights 51.2, as the Japanese designated it, didn't stand alone in the defensive scheme, although the Marines began by attacking it alone. Much to the contrary, it was one component of a triangular system including Horseshoe Hill on the right and Half Moon, or Crescent, on the left. Those two formed a funnel for pouring dense fire down on

Sugar Loaf, especially on every square yard of the summit whenever Americans approached it, as Sergeant De Mar and those who followed him discovered. The chance of surviving without a hit was measured in minutes rather than hours. Additional heavy artillery from the Shuri heights behind Half Moon was less accurate on individuals but more devastating to groups. More voluminous and more accurate than any previously encountered in the Pacific, the linked fire also ravaged troops attempting to flank Sugar Loaf from either side. And since many of the mortars were on the reverse slopes of Horseshoe and Half Moon, they were largely protected from American artillery and mortar fire until Sugar Loaf could be taken.

Few Americans there, as elsewhere in the best Japanese positions, saw the defenders at all. "We were fighting an underground enemy the whole time," one of them realized after catching on to their strategy. But the Americans could advance only by showing themselves. "Hell's half-acre"—the flat, bare ground beneath Sugar Loaf and the other hills—exposed them to simultaneous crossfire from the several interlocking sources, unseen and unreachable positions causing half to three-quarters of the American casualties.

"At first we were totally unaware of the power of the whole defensive line and Sugar Loaf's part in it," Captain Stebbins would put it with restrained regret. "It took several days to begin grasping the extent to which it was fortified with pillboxes, tunnels, mazes, and interlocking automatic weapons. It took another day before the mutually supporting system would become apparent: the key to the defense of that whole side of the island."

From the air, the full line bore a resemblance to a series of spokes radiating down and out from the hub at Shuri. Sugar Loaf was at the end of the one that reached farthest toward the western coast and Naha. That made it the key to the barrier protecting both Shuri and Naha, and explained Cho's personal interest in the preparations there and special reinforcements now ordered by Ushijima.

The American response was less well-conceived. "No matter how heavy the supporting fire," a historian of Pacific combat has put it, "a moment arrived when men had to stand up and run across naked ground into a level stream of bullets." But that moment might have been better chosen than on Sugar Loaf, whose punishing triangular "fort" was further argument for devising something more imaginative than the 10th Army's bludgeon; for outflanking by the line with a second landing in the far south, as General Buckner's critics advocated. However, the pain at Sugar Loaf and almost everywhere else in the Shuri Line evidently didn't prompt the commander to reconsider.

A few infantrymen in the fighting units began to wonder, when off the line for breaks between their maulings, why they seemed to be fighting a Japanese fight, almost hand to hand, despite their huge advantage in equipment and firepower. The much-vaunted, perhaps congenitally overoptimistic American intelligence had again failed, in this case to give unit commanders like Captain Stebbins and Sergeant De Mar any idea of the deadliness of the Japanese preparations.

Japanese forward observers happened to use Hill 51.2 for spotting during their months of artillery training. Thus, their knowledge of the terrain was such that "they often didn't have to adjust because they fired on the right spot the first time.... We couldn't have done them a better favor than attacking there," according to General James Day, who fought on Sugar Loaf and studied it during many later tours on Okinawa. "They had us beautifully zeroed in." Sergeant De Mar knew that without later study. "It was like target practice for them from all those damn hills. They had every foot covered with grids." Above all, it was pounding from Shuri's big 150-millimeter guns—hardly seen before in the Pacific—that made the battle horrendous for the Marines.

As the crow flies, Sugar Loaf was about a mile from the 32nd Army headquarters in the tunnel deep beneath Shuri Castle. The battles being waged simultaneously along the rest of the eight-plus miles of the main Shuri Line—separate pitched battles into which Buckner's general offensive had broken down almost immediately—were equally ferocious, though they seesawed less between attack and counterattack. The Shuri Line was accomplishing for the Japanese much of what the French had hoped from their Maginot Line, and that was far more Ushijima's feat than Imperial General Headquarters', since their support of him had been minimal for a campaign of such importance. Clinging to their fundamental belief in attack, IGHQ had resisted the Ushijima-Yahara strategy of a war of attrition fought from underground. Besides, they had already decided that the Tennozan of Tennozans, for which all possible arms and equipment had to be husbanded, would take place on the mainland. Thus, the Shuri Line was essentially the 32nd Army's own creation.

Almost a quarter of a million men faced each other there: "two great armies," in William Manchester's telling image, "squatting opposite one another in mud and smoke ... locked together in unimaginable agony." In the deepest combat, Manchester continued, battalion frontage (the length occupied by the battalion's thousand-odd men) was approximately eight hundred yards. "Here it was less than six hundred yards ... about eighteen inches per man." The military analyst Thomas Huber would agree. "The fighting on Okinawa had features that were all its own, but even so its dynamics bore a startling resemblance to the fierce no-man's-land fighting of World War I."

Almost without exception, the Japanese had constructed a fortified position on every hill and ridgeline, with other positions heavily covering their approaches. Taking each little knob and crease, even when only ten yards away, was an operation in itself. A rear-echelon Army colonel who visited one of the line's easier sectors during a relative lull in the fighting was almost as overwhelmed as a civilian would have been.

> There is nothing colorful about such an engagement. The rapid staccato of machine gun fire continued along with the crack of .30-caliber rifles and carbines. The plop of mortar shells as they left their muzzles punctuated the incessant hail of other hardware. The whole valley was covered with a thick pall of smoke that completely obscured the sky overhead .... On the road, several hundred meters away, stood one of our disabled tanks that could not be recovered due to the enemy artillery and mortar rounds falling in the vicinity. The burst of our own artillery shells was clearly discernible as they landed on the hill in billows of flame and smoke and the whistle that accompanied them and then the boom of the guns in the rear. Our ears were filled with the din of battle and the smell of gunpowder penetrated our nostrils with a burning sensation. This, however, was almost overcome by the stench of rotting flesh while the sting and stickiness of the flies became almost unbearable. The ... dirty, slimy troops around us seemed somewhat oblivious to most of these happenings, only concentrating on their particular job.

It was no miracle that two such congregations of men could cause each other so much torment. By that time, both had absorbed lessons that made the fighting harder. The Americans, among other things, had learned how to keep getting water and supplies to the front so their men could stay there. The Japanese had learned that the banzai attacks to which they'd resorted on other islands were far less effective than the methodical warfare they were waging here.

Despite the Marines' conviction that they were being used for "target practice," the Japanese agony was greater than theirs. Sugar Loaf's defenders were remnants of the 62nd Division, which had opposed the American attacks in most of the south, reinforced by the 15th Independent Regiment, airlifted to Okinawa the previous July to supplement the 44th Independent Mixed Brigade that had been largely lost on *Toyama maru*. Led by a highly skilled colonel named Seiko Mita, the 15th Independent Regiment was also suffering heavy losses. But the Sugar Loaf complex had to be held as long as possible, and Ushijima committed some of his last reserves of well-trained infantry troops to reinforce the defense during the night of May 15. They included a farmer named Masatsugu Shinohara.

When the Americans had landed, Shinohara was stationed about fifteen miles east on Tsuken Island in the Pacific. Tiny Tsuken controlled the entrance to large Nakagusuku Bay, which the invaders needed for an anchorage and landing supplies. Some 250 Americans set out in ten yellow rubber boats to take the little dot on the morning of April 6, roughly when *Yamato* was setting out for Okinawa. Its little garrison had a field gun, two heavy machine guns, and four mortars. As the enemy boats approached, Shinohara, leader of a mortar section, chased them off with some deadly rounds, after which American bombs shook the island for days, preparing for a second landing led by amphibious tanks. Of the defending force of sixty, twelve survived to follow their orders to find a way to rejoin the rest of the regiment on Okinawa. Crossing the fifteen miles in diminutive fishing boats, they snuck through the American force already controlling the Okinawan coast where they landed.

On Sugar Loaf's rear, southern slope, Shinohara and other Tsuken survivors crept through trenches to carry mortar shells to their positions. To avoid the enemy observation planes that seemed to be always hovering over them, they worked at night and tried not to move in daylight except to fire their mortars. Their rations consisted of dried biscuits only. They had no sleep during their seventy-two hours on or beside the hill.

Although the prodigious defensive works and their firepower dismayed the Americans, the Japanese saw themselves as children fighting giants. Still, Hill 51.2, the anchor for nearby Shuri, had to be held, no matter how impossible that seemed. Some remembered the feats of arms, courage, and endurance on the 203 Heights, a key hill in the high ground around Port Arthur that the Japanese had simply *had* to take in the 1905 war with Russia—and did. Few hated the Americans now; there was no energy for that. But all knew the enemy, as obsessed with Sugar Loaf as he was, must be killed because failure would lead directly to the loss of Okinawa, then the same kind of vicious assault on the homeland. Meanwhile, short rounds from the heavy artillery at Shuri inevitably killed many Japanese too. When Shinohara was at last withdrawn from Sugar Loaf, fifty-five of the original Tsuken group of sixty, including its commander, were dead.

The Americans, even those who had landed on Okinawa loathing everything Japanese, retained no more energy than their enemy for the luxury of hatred. "We were past that, past bitterness. This was simply the ultimate athletic contest that you had to win. A contest with literal sudden death and no overtime."

The same machine gun that got Captain Stebbins got me too. . . . I don't know what happened to the other guys because the concussion busted my right ear drum and I couldn't see or hear for a couple of hours.
—MARVIN ZIMMERMAN

When you got to the top, the Japs were just waiting for you and cut loose; all hell was being kicked out of our units. I was very, very lucky, one of the few to come down—by crawling over bodies.
—JOSEPH BANGERT

A buddy and I were told to man a machine gun about 30 yards away. . . . A mortar and hand grenade barrage interrupted us about halfway there and pinned us down. . . . A grenade went off

*in front of my face and blew my helmet to the back of my head. . . .
I don't know if I'd been unconscious for any length of time. I looked
over at the machine gun we were headed for and saw two dead
Marines by it and thought . . . if we do get there, we'll be two more
dead Marines. . . . Suddenly I heard a "poof" behind me. I turned
around and saw that my platoon leader, a first lieutenant, was killed
instantly by a direct mortar hit and the body was a black hulk. A
little later, a Marine ahead of me began calling for a corpsman. I
found out later the corpsmen were all dead or wounded. The Marine
finally gave up calling and crawled [out]. . . . As he passed, I saw
that his right foot up to the middle of the calf had been blown off.*
—Declan Klingenhagen, about some thirty minutes
on the morning of May 15

After ninety-six hours, most Americans were too depleted to
remember what happened with much clarity. Some could hardly
tell in which direction they were looking. The mental exhaustion
led to many extra casualties, because not enough adrenaline continued pumping to maintain the concentration that would have
prevented stupid mistakes.

Most of the 22nd Regiment was approaching that state on
May 16, which some felt exceeded May 15 as the 6th Division's
hardest day of the campaign and the war. Several companies of
the 29th, including Dick Whitaker's, had recently joined the battle. Units of both regiments launched a general assault on the hill
from the front and both flanks, and were met by crippling defensive fire. Replacements had replaced replacements, and reformed
units were again so badly shot up that some survivors had to take
their organization into their own hands. The day's huge losses had
again produced no territorial gain.

Before dark on that May 16, Anthony Cortese of Company
I–3–22 ran to the top of a little hill called Chocolate Drop and
looked at Sugar Loaf through his lieutenant's binoculars. He
"couldn't believe what I saw; it was covered with dead Marines.
A few enemy too, but mostly our guys, maybe a few hundred in

my view alone." Cortese also saw some Japanese rebuilding their positions and ran back to tell his lieutenant that Sugar Loaf had to be softened up with more artillery before they went in. "But the next day, up we go into the slaughter, just like the others."

That next day, three battleships moved in close to blast Sugar Loaf, Horseshoe, and Half Moon with their heavy guns while aircraft carriers launched waves of bombing strikes. Then all three hills were attacked. Cortese's company of 245 men ended with three fit to fight. Two of them, including Cortese, quickly set up a machine gun to stop a counterattack until yet more reinforcements could be rushed in.

Dick Whitaker was told his go at Sugar Loaf was the eleventh. When his stint unloading invasion supplies on the landing beaches ended and he was assigned to F Company, 29th Marines, Private Whitaker was made a helper in a machine-gun squad, charged with lugging ammunition to the gun and protecting it with his rifle. Both his cans of .30-caliber ammunition, carried in addition to his pack and his own M1 ammunition, weighed about twenty pounds. But the hill seemed to him, as to all the others in the previous ten or so charges, almost insignificant in size, especially in its present blackened, denuded condition.

His platoon began attacking it shortly after seven o'clock on the morning of the seventeenth, single file, Whitaker third in line. Mortar fire cascaded on the little column as if the Japanese had been preparing for them alone throughout the night. Running, panting, sweating, thinking of nothing, not even of what his body was doing, Whitaker pushed forward and upward as if the absurdity were happening to someone else. Three squads with three water-cooled machine guns followed a lieutenant whose name he couldn't remember, the young replacement having appeared only hours before to take over the platoon.

The attack plan—to move right at the crest—never had a chance. Whitaker couldn't tell where the bullets and shells were coming from, only that he now understood the expression *withering fire.* As the men neared the crest, enormous and stunningly accurate fire from mortars, machine guns, and rifles deluged them, shaking the ground. When they reached it, they were showered with hand grenades from unseen positions on the reverse slope.

The next minutes seemed years. At the crest, the platoon couldn't unlimber their guns. Even if the right targets could have been found, it was impossible to set up the machine guns because each move out of a shell hole or scar in the ground brought another deadly burst of fire. Whitaker's gunner was hit. The new lieutenant was killed four steps in front of him. When the platoon finally did manage to set up despite the casualties, it was so outgunned that the men hardly knew where to shoot. Desperate nonstop firing burned out the barrels of all three machine guns. Whitaker realized that even if they somehow held on, the Japanese on the reverse slope would continue pinning them down indefinitely. He was frightened out of his mind yet impervious to fright because the scene was beyond his ability to grasp.

Down the line from him, more men kept getting hit as they sought cover until someone, Whitaker thought a sergeant, yelled, "Let's get the hell out of here!" But getting out would prove harder than getting up. Whitaker and another private named John Senterfitt picked up their gunner, groaning from a bad stomach wound, and tried to take him down to safety. Fierce mortar fire resumed the moment they started. Panting from the strain and from exhaustion, they took a measure of refuge in a shell hole. Other men passed them, carrying and supporting their own wounded through the smoke. "Corpsman!" they yelled. "*Corpsman!*"

A corpsman was found only when the two crawled to the bottom and across a portion of the open-killing area to the marginal protection of the back of a small elevation north of the hill. Without glancing back, Whitaker carried the noise of Sugar Loaf's ferocious fire in his ears. It was not yet 8 a.m. on the fifth day at the hill. His fifteen minutes going up, taking fire, and coming down had been beyond belief. It would later strike him that "war is hell" was a silly metaphor because "no one has been to hell with the possible exception of Dante." He would prefer "hell is war"— but such conceptual notions did not come to him in the filth and fear themselves, when nothing mattered that wasn't immediate, instant. One of Ernie Pyle's last observations on Okinawa was that "life up there [at the front] is very simple, very uncomplicated, devoid of all the jealousy and meanness that float around a headquarters city." Men continued worrying about their buddies after coming down from Sugar Loaf. *Did we get everyone off? Did we leave anyone up there in that hell?* Slowly, immense relief that his duty there was over for now began washing over Whitaker, together with a vague hope he wouldn't have to go up again. It was up to his officers to think and to order that the hill must be taken. He only felt profoundly happy to have made it down.

Attack, counterattack, attack, counterattack . . . each time units were pushed back, it was with many or most of their men killed or missing. The wounded were pulled into craters until corpsmen or fellow fighters chose a time to risk slipping out to them. Scatterings of unhit men left behind in holes fell asleep from exhaustion that conquered even fear of their hopeless situation out there all alone. Part of F Company would go up again, but without Whitaker's decimated platoon. Later on May 17, E Company of the same 29th Regiment was driven off three times, the remnants by bayonet charges. Although a fourth attempt might have succeeded, their ammunition was exhausted and too few men were left to spare help for the wounded.

The Japanese didn't know the attackers could not persist much longer because no more replacements were available. But their own casualties had been so heavy that the general in command of the defending force doubted he could hold on another day. Assembling the last of his reserves from the caves of Horseshoe and Half Moon, he told them that fresh troops would arrive in three days; meanwhile, they must defend Sugar Loaf to the death. After dusk, he sent them to reinforce the shredded units there.

But Americans had taken enough of the little rises to detect their movement. No fewer than twelve battalions of Marine artillery fired violently on the intended reinforcements, probably killing and otherwise disabling all but a dozen. (In all, 6th Division artillery fired 92,560 shells in the Sugar Loaf engagement.) That helped quicken the end for the Japanese the following morning, May 18. The commander of D–2–29 Company sent half his men around the right side of the hill with tanks. When they had engaged the defenders' attention, he sent the other half, also with close tank support, around the left flank. That turned out to be the final charge. The 1st Marine Division's taking of Wana Draw and Wana Ridge at last had silenced some of the artillery fire from there, two miles northeast. Here, enough damage had been done to the Japanese guns on the triangle's other two hills to enable the tanks to work their way ahead while eighty men from D Company ran up the forward slope to the summit.

Although six tanks were quickly knocked out, the other flankers encircled the hill from both sides and fired into the Japanese positions on the reverse slope while the infantrymen showered them with grenades. An hour of savage fighting followed, desperately brave Japanese squads attacking with satchel charges. By then, the defenders had been weakened enough for the Marines to properly dig in. By nightfall, the organized defense system had at last been cracked, after the hardest single battle in the Pacific War and, by some measures, the hardest for Americans anywhere in World War II.

The next day, General Shepherd, commander of the 6th Marine Division, received a dispatch from his immediate boss, a Buckner subordinate.

RESISTANCE AND DETERMINATION WITH WHICH ELEMENTS
OF YOUR DIVISION ATTACKED AND FINALLY CAPTURED SUGAR
LOAF IS INDICATIVE OF THE FIGHTING SPIRIT OF YOUR MEN
X MY HEARTY CONGRATULATIONS TO THE OFFICERS AND MEN
CONCERNED.

That night, a newly deployed Marine sat in "one of the deepest foxholes I'd ever seen," atop Sugar Loaf. Now that there was time to look, Naha's smoking ruins, only two miles southwest, could be seen from the crest. The stench of Japanese corpses, piles of which had been collecting for days—and of American ones too—was "indescribable." His own squad was down to four men. Flares from nearby warships "kept the area as light as day, all night long. We lost many men that night and the next day."

So did other American units; the battle still wasn't over. Sister companies D and E of Whitaker's F Company took heavy casualties on May 19 and 20 from fire from Sugar Loaf's rear slope as well as neighboring hills. "Taking a hill was a very loose term there," Whitaker's company commander would explain, "because our men hadn't gone inside it, where many Japs were still fighting from all those caves.... My own company had a night of terrible casualties after Sugar Loaf was officially secured. There seemed no end to it." Certainly not the night of May 20, when a machine-gun squad was included in reinforcements sent out at 10 p.m.—one of the rare American advances after dark—to support an infantry company that had suffered heavy casualties repelling a counterattack. The squad's sergeant had just managed to find cover in a trench when "all hell broke loose between Sugar Loaf and Horseshoe Ridge."

General James Day's studies of Sugar Loaf during his tours of duty on Okinawa—most notably forty years after the battle, when he would command all U.S. forces on the island—were prompted by his old fighting days, when he, a young corporal, was wounded on the hill. Day would conclude that more men were killed per square foot there—mostly in the open-killing area beneath the hill—than anywhere else, including the larger and longer battles. The profusion of casualties stunned even the toughest veterans. Nearly three thousand were killed and seriously wounded, roughly the same as on all of Tarawa and more than at Casino, and up to 50 percent more than the worst battle for a single position on Iwo Jima. An additional 1,289 men were lost to sickness and combat exhaustion—but the numbers can't convey their effect upon the survivors. There was little hyperbole in a Marine's lament that "battalions melted away, companies vanished."

Parts of four battalions were mangled. Several rifle companies ended with a dozen men from their normal complement of roughly 250. In two, not a single officer or staff noncommissioned officer survived. In many others, privates ended in command of their shattered platoons. In Marine Evacuation Hospital Number 2, four or five men receiving transfusions in shock positions on litters learned they were their entire rifle companies' only known survivors. Medical personnel observed that their dismay was exceeded only by that of the green troops who'd still been in boot camp on L-day, seven weeks earlier, and were introduced to combat at Sugar Loaf.

So many tanks were knocked out that some companies alternated crews on the remaining ones. In the infantry, eleven of eighteen company commanders, including Captain Stebbins, had been killed or wounded. Scarcely an original platoon leader escaped. Mommy De Mar was G–2–22's only exception, and he was a substitute. "For the men who'd been pushed into this fierce cockpit for eight days," a survivor would remember, "it seemed like an eternity."

SIX.

Crash Boat

George Jepson and Earl McCandless

THE JAPANESE ATTACK ON PEARL HARBOR ON DECEMBER 7, 1941, changed an American generation forever. Young men and women starting their lives, whether in the labor force or attending colleges and universities across the country, suddenly found themselves in the nation's armed services or working in wartime industries. Personal lives were on hold for the duration.

Although storm clouds had been on the horizon since the late 1930s, and Great Britain had been fighting for its very life against Nazi Germany, Americans had gone about their business, hoping to avoid war. While politicians debated a position of isolationism, and President Franklin D. Roosevelt found ways to support the British, there were strong signals that Japan was moving toward armed conflict with the US.

The air raid on Pearl Harbor, Hawaii, brought everything into the open, and sixteen million Americans faced the greatest challenge of the twentieth century. By early 1942, America was beginning to respond. Lines formed at recruiting stations as young men enlisted in various branches of the military.

Earl A. McCandlish was working in New York City, waiting for a US Navy commission to be confirmed when the war began. "Greetings" from Uncle Sam in early 1942 superseded his Navy application, and he was soon wearing an Army uniform, completing Officer Candidate School in Virginia.

As war engulfed the globe, aircraft flew over vast stretches of the oceans en route to targets and returning to bases. Rescuing downed pilots and flight crews at sea was a significant challenge. Unfortunately, there was little agreement among the services as to who was responsible to oversee air-sea rescue and how to carry it out. Surface vessels of all sizes, submarines, and amphibious aircraft worked to recover downed pilots and aircrews without a clear plan of operation. Patrol boats of assorted sizes and converted military and civilian vessels were used, but these were not explicitly designed for the task, and each had its weaknesses.

In 1942 and 1943, a program to build air-sea rescue craft called "crash boats," officially designated as aircraft rescue vessels (AVR), was started. A standard design for a sixty-three-foot boat to be used by the Navy, Army, and Coast Guard was developed by a young naval architect named Dair Long who worked for the Miami Shipbuilding Company. Construction of the swift, sleek boats began in shipyards across the country.

At the same time, officers to command these vessels and crews to operate them funneled into training programs at the Higgins Boat Operators and Marine Engine Maintenance School in New Orleans. Instruction revolved around classroom sessions and hands-on experience aboard boats on Lake Pontchartrain and in the Gulf of Mexico.

US Army Air Force (AAF) Lieutenant Earl A. McCandlish arrived at the Higgins School as an instructor commanding the P-100, a cumbersome 110-foot-long antique from World War I, designed initially as a minesweeper. By autumn 1943, he was assigned command of a new AVR 63, then under construction at the Fellows & Stewart shipyard in Wilmington, California, near Long Beach. Along with his first permanent crew, he climbed aboard a train and headed west.

The new crash boats were developed along lines similar to Navy PT boats, though smaller in length by some seventeen feet. Designed for speed and maneuverability, they were outfitted with medical facilities for treating rescued pilots and flight crews. These boats also carried twin .50-caliber machine-gun turrets flanking the bridge and a single .50-caliber weapon in the stern cockpit.

Although designated as rescue boats, they also were frequently used as gunboats in both the Pacific and European theaters during the war. With graceful lines, they were pleasing to the eye and a joy to operate, skimming along at speeds over forty knots, powered by two Hall-Scott 630-horse engines. Their maneuverability was an asset in performing rescues and combat operations.

Earl McCandlish would command the P-399—later named the *Sea Horse*. By VJ Day in 1945, the *Sea Horse* had plucked more than thirty airmen from the sea. Among the crew was George L. Jepson, father of author George Jepson.

Over a period of approximately eighteen months in the Southwest Pacific, the P-399 endured nightly Red Alerts (Japanese air attacks), survived typhoons, searched for and rescued downed Allied flyers, dropped agents on enemy-controlled islands, and provided humanitarian aid to Filipinos.

According to Lawrence (Bud) Waggener Jr., who skippered the P-401 called *Gung-Ho* in the 15th Emergency Rescue Boat Squadron, the *Sea Horse* was the most decorated AAF rescue boat to serve in the Pacific.

SANSAPOR

On November 2, we arrived in northwest New Guinea to cover flights from Sansapor, Noemfoor, and Middleburg Island before moving to Morotai a week later. In August, Operation Typhoon secured the Allied operations area on the Vogelkop Peninsula from the Japanese.

With the Allies controlling the area, General Earl Barnes had a new airstrip built for his P-38 fighters. The air group would provide cover for the Morotai Task Force in a month and a half. He selected Middleburg Island near Cape Sansapor, and the Seabees and other engineering construction outfits went to work.

Clearing coconut trees and dense undergrowth from about 140 acres of the 240-acre island opened up land for a runway. Bulldozers moved nearly two hundred thousand cubic yards of jungle topsoil and sea coral to prepare a solid base. Large backhoes with tank treads dug more than forty-five thousand cubic yards of coral from the island's reefs at low tide.

After leveling the land with a heavy roller, they laid the final landing surface, more than five hundred thousand square feet of steel matting, to complete the base. This tremendous effort provided General Barnes's 13th Air Force Task Force and the 13th Fighter Command with an airstrip to carry the air war to hundreds of Japanese airfields, including the next big leap to Morotai, three hundred miles to the north.

By the time we arrived, the airfield was fully operational.

The P-399 covered the 42nd Bombardment Group B-25 flights from Mar, Noemfoor, Sansapor, and Middleburg Island. Flying cover to the Celebes and Molucca Islands for these bombers were P-38s from the Eighteenth Fighter Group. Some of these roundtrip flights covered more than two thousand statute miles—the most extended fighter missions of the war.

The 347th Fighter Group was eager to operate from this new base—the most advanced in the Southwest Pacific. They faced the fierce defenses of Japanese planes and antiaircraft batteries; they had a severe flight problem because they couldn't stay over their targets long enough to conserve fuel for return trips to Klenso and Mar.

Belly tanks attached to P-38s increased fuel capacity but also cut down on the bomb and ammo capacity because of weight limitations. Many planes returned to Klenso with only a soda bottle full of petrol remaining in their tanks. Ground crews and mechanics sat on logs along the strip, sweating out the return of their pilots. Cheers erupted when their planes touched down.

The 13th Air Force Liberator bombers flew missions from Noemfoor to destroy one of Japan's most crucial wartime possessions: the oil wells and refinery at Balikpapan on the eastern coast of Borneo. Each bomber carried 3,500 gallons of high-octane gasoline (more than eleven tons). Strike planners had to reduce the amount of ammunition planes carried by half to stay within weight limits. Bomb loads were about 2,200 pounds. All of the fuel, ammo, and bombs brought the Liberators' load to about six tons, which was overweight.

To get their planes off the ground, pilots had to taxi to the end of the runway, lock their brakes, gun the engines to near maximum rpms, and, with full throttle, literally lift this burden slowly into the air. They cleared the end of the runway, with their retracting wheels about six feet above the water level at high tide and, with a prayer, coaxed these huge, overloaded planes into the air.

We stood by holding our breath. Engines were laboring as the planes slowly gained altitude and then set their course, hoping to dump their bomb load on the target and return safely to base. This process continued, plane after plane, every ninety seconds until seventy-two Liberators were in flight formation headed for Balikpapan in the early morning darkness.

At the target, Japanese ack-ack sprayed shells at them, and enemy fighters were constant threats to the unescorted Liberators. The fierce Japanese defenses didn't save Balikpapan. After five such raids by the 13th and 5th, the oil refinery and installation were no longer considered primary targets.

Although we were only on station at Sansapor for a brief time, we were glad to be on the flight line, doing air-sea rescue work— our primary mission. The crew was at its most productive, busiest, and satisfying level. They were happy to be in action, even though it was often life-threatening.

We experienced Japanese bombing raids by Betty and Judy aircraft, and we patrolled near the shores of occupied islands exposed to enemy gunfire. Baker said, "Their aim is so poor they couldn't hit a barn with a handful of rice." Charlie barges were formidable and we never challenged the thick hulled vessels with their greater firepower.

Over the months, our boat carried out many other assignments between patrols, such as carrying sick and wounded to station hospitals, moving threatened islanders from one island to another, and transporting medical and surgical supplies from back base warehouses up to local surgical units.

One physician, a top-notch plastic surgeon whose practice was on Park Avenue in New York and charged ten thousand dollars per operation, offered me a free nose job after we had delivered their supplies so quickly. I was invited to their unit when they didn't have surgery scheduled, but I turned it down. Later, the recipient of two broken noses, I was sorry I hadn't accepted.

We took out command officers and engineers—the latter for offshore inspections—and welcomed convalescing and off-duty pilots who had a non-flying day to sail with us and, as they put it, "just to get off the rock." They relaxed. But no one after Guadalcanal tried to use the P-399 for recreational purposes. They were too busy fighting a war.

Morotai

On November 7 we arrived at Morotai, barely six weeks after the 31st Division, and the 126th Infantry Regiment, 32nd Division, had surged ashore, catching the small Japanese force by surprise and forcing their troops away from the southern coast. A secure perimeter defense protected the base against the Japanese.

Meanwhile, the island was developing into a significant Allied base. Construction units immediately built airstrips to handle the 13th Air Force and Royal Australian Air Force aircraft. Two airfields were ready for use in October. Morotai played a vital role in liberating the Philippines during the remaining months in 1944 and 1945.

More and more units were moving three hundred miles north to the island, including the 38th Fighter Group. Our assignment was to cover the Pitu fighter strip and patrol the strait between Halmahera and Morotai. Our anchorage and dock were off the northwest corner of the airstrip, with facilities for unloading Liberty ships, but most ships came into the east side of the island off the Wama bomber strip. Johnny Cranston's P-406, another sixty-three-foot crash boat, was assigned to Wama Strip.

It was easier to cover flights to the north (Philippines) and west (Halmahera and Celebes), because of our proximity to the airstrip.

When we arrived, there were about thirty-seven thousand bypassed Japanese across the Morotai Strait on Halmahera, and approximately two thousand troops were cornered in the mountainous center section of Morotai by units from the 31st Infantry, which had a perimeter set up north of the airfields.

Japanese soldiers made several attempts to float on a log from Halmahera to central Morotai. Our orders were to stop any migration of these locked-in troops. PT boats also patrolled this area and were sinking enemy barges attempting to transport supplies to Morotai.

Morotai was reputedly the most bombed island in the Pacific. Air raids were almost continuous on some days, and there were always two or three raids each night. Sometimes there were as many as five raids by Japanese Judys and Bettys attacking the airstrip at Pitu. Betty bombers, with their high-whining engines, also raided at night. Zero fighters came in low to strafe shipping in the harbor. Allied troops onshore and ground crew personnel had dug foxholes and covered them with coconut logs.

The *Sea Horse* tied up on the end of a long floating dock, or, if the docks were loaded, we anchored away from the pier. We watched the raids from our deck. There was no place to hide. We manned our twin-turret .50-caliber machine guns but had to be careful. We didn't want to hit another ship in the harbor. Morotai had an effective ack-ack defense and on most evenings our crew sat on the roof of the sickbay and watched the show.

Anticipating night raids from the Japanese, we sent up a couple of Black Widow night fighters who climbed to high altitudes and attacked the Bettys or Judys from above. One night, the anti-aircraft guns were pumping away and just missed one of the night fighters. We had our short-wave radio on, and a voice yelled, "Hey, guys, knock off shooting at me! I'm on your side!"

A bomb striking a little close was unsettling. The power of those five-hundred-pounders exploding a couple of hundred yards away would scare anyone. You couldn't help but wonder if the next one might be right in your lap. The happy thought was that you would never know if it happened. But the Good Lord protected us.

The controllers in the Pitu tower were the best of any we had worked with at other bases. Together we completed many good rescues. The professional level of tower operators throughout the South Pacific was extremely high, but we seemed to hit it off with the Morotai operators. Mission times and courses were always on target, given to us early enough in the morning or sometimes late in the evening.

The first week at Morotai, while patrolling around the north end of Halmahera, we were given grid coordinates for the approximate location of a ditched B-24 Liberator. We wound up the *Sea Horse* and headed at full throttle for the coded grid area.

The P-399 could fly. We arrived at the spot, which was only a quarter of a mile off the shore of the island occupied with Japanese. We were within small-arms range from the coastline. The coastline was also an area where the Japanese hid their cleverly camouflaged barges during the day. You could look straight at them through binoculars and still not see them.

There was no air cover above the crash site to spot for us, so we had our binoculars trained on the calm sea searching for the downed aircraft. Finally, after we had sailed around the point of the island, Baker spotted the plane near a cove with the crewmen hanging on to the partially submerged fuselage and wings. We exposed ourselves to enemy fire, as we had no choice. These airmen had to be removed from the downed plane and soon.

We backed in alongside the plane and three air crewmen jumped from the wreck and scrambled on board. The pilot, navigator, and gunner had all been injured when the plane hit the sea but had been able to get the hatch open and, with their Mae Wests inflated, had floated a short distance away from the wreck. The plane was about ready to sink, engine nacelles down first.

We lifted them aboard in the wire litter and carried them to the sickbay and the stern cockpit where Baker examined them and kept them covered while we dried their uniforms on the cockpit awning. All during the operation, I held my breath, expecting gunfire from the Japanese. We were sitting ducks, but luck was with us.

The *Sea Horse* headed for Pitu docks. Barzow called operations to request the base hospital have ambulances standing by when we docked. They were there, along with a doctor and two nurses who took over from Baker. Each member of the Liberator crew thanked us before going ashore. We told them thanks weren't necessary. Like them, we were just doing our job.

Jep recorded each rescue by painting a hash mark next to a small parachute with a seahorse floating under it on the flying bridge's starboard side. Our numbers were rising. We surmounted lack of sleep, malaria, and the bad seas, which were frequent, to work together as a smooth, precision-working team. There were no typhoons or terrible storms during this period.

Because of the long flights north from Morotai to Japanese targets in the Philippines, and west to Borneo and Celebes, more and more planes suffered damage from enemy action. Fuel supply was a significant factor in their safe return to Morotai. Planes ditched and pilots bailed out.

A call came in one afternoon after a fighter pilot radioed a "mayday" to Pitu tower. They gave us the approximate grid coordinates. A choppy sea was running and visibility was marginal as we sailed to the estimated position of the ditched pilot. We began a "square search." Because visibility was poor, we set a course to the west, one-eighth mile, then traveled one-eighth mile south and the same distance due east.

In the search area, we only found a couple of floating coconuts. They looked like heads sticking out of the water, even when we were within fifty feet.

We extended our search to one half-mile, north, west, south, and east. We were trying to calculate the pilot's possible drift if he was in a one-person yellow life raft and extended our courses in that direction. On the third change of square search distances, Jep was up on the mast and spotted the pilot about one hundred yards off our starboard bow.

Barzow radioed Pitu tower with our ETA, so an ambulance and medic could be standing by on the dock. We sailed to the windward side of the pilot and the crew prepared the wire litter. Baker and Jep got in the water, lifted the man onto the litter, and hoisted him aboard. The flyer knelt, said a brief prayer, and thanked God for the Navy. We didn't tell him we weren't Navy. In his early twenties, the pilot was in shock after being tossed around in the sea for a couple of hours, thinking about shark attacks. In all of our seagoing times, we never heard of a shark-biting incident.

Baker took the young pilot, a major, down to the sickbay, gave him an ounce and a half of Old Taylor bourbon, removed his wet clothing, and wrapped him in a Navy blanket. We wasted no time in getting him back to base.

In a letter dated November 26, 1944, Jep wrote to Joyce about another rescue, "One of the fellows we picked up had been in the water sixteen hours and within a mile of [Japanese-] held islands . . . when we got him aboard he fell to his knees and said a prayer. It made me feel very good . . ."

Now and then, operations loaned us to other units. The Dutch East Indies needed a small gunboat to drop native scouts on Halmahera's northeast shore, which was occupied by some of the nineteen thousand Japanese troops bottled up on the island.

The drop point on Halmahera was about twenty-six miles from Pitu dock on Morotai. The mission was difficult because the scouts were being put ashore in early morning hours, requiring complete silence and secrecy—no lights, no sound. The Dutch briefed us on how to carry out the mission. Their interpreter went through the procedure with the scouts, who had done it many times before, for our benefit.

The scouts were small, young, and in tip-top condition. They were only about five foot two, an ideal size to move like shadows through the island's undergrowth, spying on the enemy.

Our departure time was 0300 hours. The moon-phase was critical and planned by the Dutch for our departure to be favorable. Bright moonlight would have been disastrous. Each of the three scouts had a carefully prepared backpack, complete with a nylon strangling cord and other support and protective items, including a big knife, but no gun. There was enough food to last them three days and nights. When the scouts got ashore, their officer told us that they would conceal themselves where they could watch the daytime military activity. At night, the three scouts moved over the camp area and airstrip, returning to their hiding place during the day.

Our navigation had to be exact. In the darkness the shoreline loomed black and foreboding. I cut the port engine, but even with the starboard engine at near idle it still sounded like a rumble of thunder.

As we neared the drop point, the crew helped the scouts inflate their small, one-person rubber rafts. Bake was on the bow with our lead line, taking soundings and relaying the depths in a whisper to Whitey, who relayed them to Barzow and me. Ron was in the starboard gun turret in case the twin .50-caliber machine guns were needed.

When we were about fifty yards off the murky shore, about two fathoms over the coral bottom, we helped the scouts into their rafts and handed them their paddles. I held up three fingers and then pointed down, indicating we would be back in three early mornings. They nodded.

I looked at the shoreline and selected a spot with two trees that I was sure I would recognize on our return trip. We had a small flashlight to return their screened signal when we were ready to pick them up. They quickly melted into the darkness of the island night. George was going nuts about the big engine idling for so long, but I couldn't turn it off because it would roar when restarted.

I slowly backed the *Sea Horse* into deep water and swung around, moving at the lowest possible speed until we were out of hearing distance. Only then did George start the port engine, and I wound up the starboard engine. We covered the twenty or so miles back to our dock in quick order.

Coming into an anchorage or dock at night is always tricky. Everything looks different. Thank goodness the glow of a new day was brightening the east, but there was a groan from the crew when I told Jep we would get underway as usual for the morning flights.

I managed a two-hour nap before George started the engines. I woke up smelling the fresh-brewed coffee Ronnie was making in the galley, just outside the door of my quarters. Later, the weather was good and the sea quiet. I took time to swing by the shore where we had dropped off our native scouts.

Air raids were incessant. Every night the Japanese sent over at least one flight of bombers, and they often would come in low over Halmahera during the day to bomb the airstrips. Incoming afternoon flights could only land if the strips were damage-free. Otherwise, they had to try and make it to Sansapor.

Over two months we sweated out more than one hundred raids, and the Japanese weren't dropping geisha pillows, either. We were all weary from the night work as well as the ups and downs of the night air raids. We weren't getting enough sleep.

Before we were due to pick up the native scouts, we ran into a little excitement.

BATTLE OF GALELA BAY

On December 13, a beautiful tropical morning, four light-green P-40 Kittyhawk fighters from the Royal Australian Air Force 80 Squadron took off from Morotai on a routine mission to strafe Japanese positions on Halmahera across the Morotai Strait. As the squadron struck targets along Galela Bay, anti-aircraft fire hit the plane flown by Flight Sergeant James Lennard.

At approximately 0905 hours, Lennard crash-landed his damaged aircraft on the beach a mile north of Galela Village. Severely injured, the twenty-year-old Aussie pilot took refuge under the left wing.

Thirty miles to the north, the *Sea Horse* cruised along on calm seas off Halmahera's north tip, a routine patrol. Some of the crew were still in their bunks catching up on sleep when our call letters crackled over the radio from Pitu Tower at 0935 hours. Responding to the base, we received the aircraft's approximate location.

The *Sea Horse* bolted ahead while Bake called general quarters, knowing the area bristled with Japanese troops and gun emplacements. All hands, a little bleary-eyed, were up and working at once. We closed on the plane's reported position in about forty minutes, preparing to go ashore in a rubber raft.

Jep was on watch, looking to spot the wreckage. Suddenly he turned to me on the bridge and said, "Skip, we've got trouble." The plane was lying about ten feet from the water's edge, right under Japanese guns.

Six.

As we neared the upper end of the beach at 1020, a Navy PBY circling the area started to land near shore, seemingly unaware of the heavy concentration of Japanese guns protecting the nearby Galela airstrip. As the plane was about to hit the water, the pilot gunned both engines and the Catalina climbed back into the air, alerted by Pitu Tower to the danger.

The RAAF pilot, who appeared to be injured, was visible under the wing, so I circled toward the beach. The Japanese opened up on us with 90-mm antiaircraft guns depressed to cover water approaches. Out of the corner of my eye, I could see tall geysers off our port beam. "Those aren't fish jumping," I yelled to Jep. I zigged and zagged but soon realized that the shots were going over our head as we neared shore. We were safe from the big guns as long as we were close to the beach.

Barzow called Pitu Tower and informed them we were out-gunned and requested air cover while he provided Morotai with a play-by-play description as the battle developed. The tower responded that the 38th Air Group would cover us and "stand by," adding that the whole island was listening to Barzow's description of the radio attempt on the tower radio.

Within minutes, eight P-38 Lightnings from Pitu roared in, strafing the shore batteries and Japanese riflemen moving toward the beach. I spun the *Sea Horse* around and headed out to sea. It was apparent that approaching the beach in a rubber raft was impossible. So, Jep and Whitey, our two best swimmers, volunteered to swim ashore to bring the Aussie pilot back to the P-399. They put on their Mae Wests under blue shirts, an attempt to hide the yellow vests, and Baker tied an one-third-inch line around their waists.

Then we made a starboard strafing run on the trees and foliage behind the beach, after feinting a movement out to sea. Suddenly the unthinkable happened—our port engine conked out. I needed its reverse to keep us from washing up on a very unfriendly island. George was back on Morotai with an infected foot and our substitute engineer was of no help. About fifty yards from the beach we went aground in the sand. Jep and Whitey dropped off the stern where they weren't visible to the Japanese and started for shore.

The P-38s continued low-level strafing runs while Bake, in one of the turrets, and Ronnie, on the bow, laid down withering fire with our twin .50-calibre machine guns. As Jep later wrote to his father, " . . . the boys on the boat were giving them hell. You should have seen the cook on the bow guns out in front of God and everybody . . . really pouring the lead."

Snipers targeted Jep and Whitey when they were only ten yards from the boat, but they continued toward shore where they could see the pilot lying alongside the fuselage. Then all hell cut loose with heavy enemy fire, so we backed out of the sand, picked up Jep and Whitey, and retired to open water where the P-406 came alongside. Warrant Officer John Cranston and his engineer, Warrant Officer James Gray, climbed aboard the *Sea Horse*.

It was apparent the Japanese were using the pilot to decoy us into a trap. The fighters kept ground troops away from the RAAF plane while we called for Navy PTs to lay a smokescreen and bring additional firepower. By the time PTs 162 and 365 arrived, we had the port engine running again with assistance from Cranston and Gray, who helped keep the *Sea Horse* off the beach.

A new plan conceived in consultation with Pitu Tower and the PT skippers called for the PTs to launch smoke mortar shells onto the beach to shield the P-399 from the Japanese. PT 162 made a strafing run and drew heavy fire, while PT 365 stayed offshore with seven crewmen suffering with shrapnel wounds from enemy fire.

These PTs had been battle tested over many months, moving from the southern Slot up the island chain. In early August 1943, PT 162 was the boat closest to John F. Kennedy's PT 109 when it was rammed by the Japanese destroyer *Amagiri* in the Blackett Strait during an ill-conceived mission.

The smokescreen was successful, and the *Sea Horse* moved toward the beach, again going aground on a sandbar. Jep and Whitey went back in the water and swam toward shore. When they were within fifty yards of the beach, they observed that the tide had risen. The plane and pilot were nearly awash and there was no sign of life.

At the same time, the Japanese launched a mortar barrage. Jep and Whitey, growing weary, attempted to inflate their Mae Wests. Jep's worked, but Whitey's didn't, so they swam back sharing the good one. Once we pulled them back aboard we retreated across the danger line, averting enemy fire.

It was a sad and disappointing ending to the mission. Barzow reported the situation to Pitu, and the P-38s returned to base. With only one fully functional engine, I requested that we return to base, which was approved. We were still eighteen miles or so from Morotai when a lumbering LCM, with a drop bow, was spotted coming toward us. Clinging to the metal grill on the drop gate was Lieutenant Colonel Wallace Ford, our squadron commander.

The *Sea Horse* eased alongside the LCM, and he clambered aboard. Ford said he had been listening to the Galela Bay battle, and it got so exciting that he decided to come over to see it, but his boat was too slow. The colonel congratulated everyone who had a part in the attempt to save the Australian pilot. When we finally tied up, I commended all hands for their courage under fire. Begging off mess, I went to my quarters, flopped on my bunk, and suddenly became extremely frightened, reflecting on the day's events.

The next morning George hobbled aboard, mad because he had missed the fun. A couple of weeks earlier he had stepped on a sea urchin and his foot had become infected. It only took him about fifteen minutes to identify what the trouble had been with our engine—the distributor rotor had cracked. He had a spare, and the Hall-Scott was soon purring like a kitten.

We fueled and arranged for John Cranston's P-406 to cover both Wama and Pitu airfields, allowing us to rest, re-arm, and make minor repairs to the hull.

Two days later, Jep wrote to his father: "I was wondering just how I would feel in combat, and I found out. I was scared as hell. And I don't think there was a man on the boat who didn't feel the same. We've got a damn good crew, and I would go through hell and high water with any man." He continued, "We were all talking last night about how lucky we were. And this morning, I found a bullet hole in one of the turrets. That was the only scratch we got. I also had to do my laundry if you know what I mean."

The same day, we cleaned our guns. There were about six inches of empty shell casings in the gun turrets.

Early the next morning, under cover of darkness, we picked up the scouts on Halmahera. We had little trouble finding the cove for the rendezvous. As we quietly coasted in, I had the queasy feeling that the Japanese had us in their sights and expected them to flash a spotlight on us. But there were just two little screened blinks from the scouts, which we returned, and soon we made out their dark shadows paddling out of the blackness. Once they came aboard, we roared out of there—mission accomplished.

On Christmas Eve, we received a call in the afternoon that a fighter was down in our sector. We headed out and followed our normal search procedures, eventually locating the general area where the plane ditched, but all we found was the pilot's parachute. It had been a rough few days for rescue attempts.

BAKER'S RED HAIR

Most of our missions were within two to three hours of sailing time from Pitu, along the flight line toward the Molucca Straits, northwest of Morotai. We requested that the P-399 be permitted to anchor off a small island named Rao, near the north end of

Morotai. It was volcanic, covered with palm trees, and had a small lagoon that provided shelter from northeast winds.

We checked with the 31st Division Intelligence and our squadron headquarters and learned there was a small Malaysian population on the island. These people had initially migrated from Menado, Celebes Islands. When the Japanese invaded there, they moved to Ternate off the west coast of Halmahera and finally to Rao Island. About 150 people, including children, had banded together. Many of them were related. They had moved from island to island in small boats.

These were cultured Malaysians living in a village called Leo-Leo. Their leader was Philip Tambariki, who had been a schoolteacher on Menado, Celebes, before the war disrupted their lives. They brought along seed, chickens, and pigs; built homes; and created gardens. The island provided fruit, vegetables, and fish.

Overall they were living pretty well. The village even had a Singer sewing machine (vintage 1930) with needles, shuttles, thread, and repair parts. They appeared to be healthy, but most suffered from malaria. Some of the children spoke excellent English.

The first evening we anchored in the lagoon, Philip Tambariki, his brother, and a friend came aboard to visit. He told us the latest history of his group and offered to teach us the Malaysian language. Jep, Barzow, and I accepted. Philip told us to get magazines such as *Life*, *Saturday Evening Post*, and others that we could obtain from Special Services so he could use the pictures to teach us the Malaysian name for items and objects.

His lessons helped us to better understand the islanders in the Malaysian areas. Our knowledge of his language, along with often-used phrases and greetings, was limited, but it came in handy, even in the extreme southern Philippine Islands, where some Malaysians lived.

After the day's patrol work was finished, Baker would keep busy visiting the village, where there were many malaria cases. He took a quinine and atabrine supply and often sat with individuals helping them through their high fever. He also treated and bandaged cuts.

The villagers loved Bake for his kind and professional way of caring for their sick children. They also loved his red hair and that he made them laugh, even though they had come through tough times.

Bake's red hair also created a problem. As we traveled throughout the South Pacific, the crew knew that women were attracted to his red hair, even to the point, in several cases, where their husbands asked if Bake would give their wives a redheaded baby.

These Malaysian villagers had close family units and were better educated than some of the islanders we had encountered. They didn't ask Bake for a redheaded child, but the attraction to his hair was noticeable. He always requested that Ron or Barzow accompany him to the village, riding shotgun just in case. Islanders' fascination with Baker's red hair began on one of the Solomon Islands when they would gather around him in awe.

In the Melanesian Islands—the Solomons, New Georgia, Bougainville, Treasury, and New Guinea—many men tried to dye their black hair red. It was a long and challenging procedure. They pulverized coral and seashells to make a paste, which they baked to produce a robust and caustic lime (calcium oxide). They mixed this with birdlime, juice extracted from ground up wild lime tree leaves, and lime juice. Working with a friend, they usually made enough paste for two heads.

As soon as the mixture was ready, they packed it on each other's hair, let it dry until it became hard as cement, and left it on their head for many weeks. When it came off, if all went well, there was a distinct reddish hue to their formerly jet-black hair.

Red hair made the wearer a significant person in village social life or the island's government. Eventually the red faded away, and it was necessary to repeat the process. New Guinea was the last island where I saw "lime heads."

SIX.

Despite his red-hair problem, Bake was able to do many good
things for the Malaysians, in the small amount of time available.
Spending so much time in their homes, he spoke more of their
language than Jep, Barzow, and me.

We shared fish with the village by chumming for them in the
lagoon when the water churned with yellowfin, sea bass, small
sword, and tuna. George would drop a grenade in the water and,
presto, Leo-Leo, and the *Sea Horse* had a fish feast. Clawless
Pacific lobsters were particularly tasty. In return, the villagers
brought us fruit, eggs, and vegetables.

Sailing out of Rao Island a couple of times a week made
duty easier because we didn't have to head out to the flight line
so early. We got better sleep but were still awakened every night
by bombing raids. It was easier to get supplies and gasoline when
we docked at Pitu. It also allowed Baker to check the stateside
Liberty ships that had just arrived, identified by brand new paint
jobs, to see if he could trade for food.

One day Baker heard that two new ships were unloading
on the east shore docks, trading targets for stateside food, and
he asked me to drive him over. I had a borrowed jeep, so Bake,
Ronnie, and I drove up the sand road along the north side of the
Pitu airstrip.

We had driven about halfway around the strip when we spotted three Japanese soldiers walking out of a side path. When they
saw us, they threw their arms in the air, and I pulled the jeep over
to them. I unholstered my .45-caliber Colt pistol, and they went
down on their knees, heads lowered. Baker and Ron motioned for
them to get up. It seemed as though they thought we were going
to cut their heads off, probably as their officers had warned them.

Baker pointed for them to head down the road. We walked
them to the camp's stockade at the end of the strip, where guards
took custody.

Along the way, guys came out of their huts, laughing as we
passed. The Japanese were wearing US Army-issue shirts and

134

pants, likely stolen off clotheslines on night trips into the camps foraging for food.

The Japanese soldiers were tired, I guess, of living in Morotai's interior jungle with no food and cruel, sadistic officers. They had probably decided to end it by surrendering to the evil Americans. I'm not sure, but I believe we were the only gunboat crew to capture three Japanese prisoners onshore, without firing a shot.

When we reached the island's east unloading docks, Baker told Ron and me to stay in the jeep while he went aboard the shiny, newly painted Liberty ship to trade for food with our Japanese invasion money. He had six bills. I reminded him we had three cartridge boxes full and asked why not give them a handful of the stuff in exchange for some meat. "If I take only a few with me, they'll think they're scarce, hard to get, and worth more," he said. "I'm only going to show them one to start."

Ron and I watched him go aboard. Shortly, he appeared on deck with someone in a white apron who looked to be a galley worker. They leaned over the rail and I could see Bake letting him sneak a peek at the "rare" Japanese invasion bill. They went inside and soon after, Bake returned to the jeep, all smiles. He told us about all the goodies he had procured for two of the Japanese bills.

The first bill was for the food. The second was to pay a Liberty ship crewman to get the four boxes of food off the ship and into the jeep without being detected. The boxes came off the ship so quickly I couldn't believe it. The galley hand put the four boxes in a large crate, took it over to the crane operator, and gave him the other Japanese bill. With that, he lowered our goods to the dock near our parked jeep.

The place was so busy with cargo coming off the ship that no one noticed our box. Ron and Baker put it in the jeep's rear, and off we went.

When we got back to the *Sea Horse*, we discovered that the boxes contained pure gold—frozen meat, including pork chops, hamburgers, bacon, and chicken, plus real potatoes, ketchup, mustard, mayonnaise, and a variety of canned vegetables. The crew was as happy as clams at high tide. Morale leaped 300 percent.

During the rest of our assignment at Morotai, Bake and Ron swapped Japanese junk invasion money for food, beer, and tobacco, sharing our newfound wealth whenever possible.

The Japanese had a lookout station and radio transmitter on the north end of Morotai that was tipping off their airfields and other targets whenever our planes took off on strikes. Morotai defense decided to close it down and sent in a company from the 31st Division. After they cleared the area, Signal Corps headquarters requested we take a few of their officers up to inspect the station.

They told us later that they were surprised at the high-tech equipment and were shocked when they found a primitive example of our transistor tube. The Allies believed this important technology was secret. The Japanese were not inventors, but master copiers, and had a well-devised spy network to steal inventions. Every Japanese Zero had an American Delco electrical system and many other parts manufactured using our processes.

On the return trip from the Japanese station, we brought a few seriously wounded Japanese and some of our casualties to the base hospital. One of the Japanese died on the way back. It took a long time to get the smell of death off the *Sea Horse*'s deck. The Japanese prisoners received the same medical attention as our men at the base.

While we were still at Morotai, we learned that the *Sea Horse* crew had been awarded medals by the War Department for bravery in action during the Galela Bay rescue attempt.

Colonel Ford had put this request through channels, with many endorsements, including the Royal Australian Air Force. The Far East Command liked our actions because it supported cooperation between countries and services in the Southwest Pacific. Of course, we did it because that was our mission, regardless of under which flag pilots flew.

When asked to submit a list of our crew present at Galela Bay, I added John Cranston and James Gray. Each had taken a significant risk in coming aboard to assist us on deck and in the engine room while we had two men in the water.

Jep and Whitey were awarded the Silver Star for "gallantry in action." Baker, Ronnie, Barzow, Cranston, Gray, and I received the Bronze Star for "meritorious achievement."

On the day of the award ceremony in March 1945, I went into shock when the crew informed me they didn't have starched parade clothes or shoes. They didn't have shoes because regular-issue footwear, made with heavy leather, wasn't fit for deck use. We had requested canvas deck shoes, but supply turned us down. When the crew received the leather shoes, they cut the tops off, leaving the bottom and a small strap across the instep. The shoes were cooler but didn't qualify for an inspection by an Air Force general and his staff.

I told them to request new shoes, shirts, and pants from supply. Failing this, they had to borrow shoes from the ground crews at Pitu airstrip. Lacking new shirts and pants, they were to take their own to the hospital laundry for a quick ironing job. Bake issued Japanese invasion money to grease palms at supply, shoe borrowing, and the laundry.

They were all back in a few hours, all set with everything but insignia. Sewing stripes and unit patches on their shirts slipped our minds. So they wielded needles and thread like crazy. A quick inspection showed they could get through an hour-long ceremony if the command didn't look too closely. Ronnie and Chaney were in a lot of pain because their borrowed shoes were too small. They went barefoot and carried the shoes until we fell in for the awards.

I enjoyed hearing praise from my peers for the P-399 and its crew. It was a day to be remembered.

On December 7, 1991, fifty years after the Japanese sneak attack on Pearl Harbor, I called members of the *Sea Horse* crew and pledged to wear the Bronze Star lapel pin on my jacket in their memory.

While we were still at Morotai in the Netherlands East Indies, bombing raids on the Japanese positions in the Philippines continued to increase. We were a lot busier responding to distress calls from pilots.

Early one morning before dawn we received a report that a fighter pilot had crash landed forty miles from shore. Already on the flight line, we started our search pattern and three hours later we located the airman in his small rubber raft. He was nibbling on a cracker and reading his handbook *How to Survive in the Jungle.*

This kid was one relaxed flyer, shading himself from the sun with his parachute while he held his handbook with one hand and wielded a fishing pole in the other. If we hadn't arrived so soon he would have been just fine. He was all set with provisions—two canteens of water, rations, a medical kit, signal equipment, a compass, revolver, and Dutch currency.

"I've been expecting you fellows," he yelled, "but you're just too late for breakfast." Climbing aboard the *Sea Horse* with a smile, he remarked, "I don't suppose anyone remembered to bring my mail."

On another routine patrol, this time with an AAF news reporter and the cook from a visiting ocean liner as our guests, we picked up a fighter pilot returning from a raid in the Philippines who crash-landed in our sector.

As we returned to base, the cook was panic-stricken when he realized his ship had embarked for the US, leaving him behind. Not so funny for him were the keys to the captain's pantry clinking in his pocket. The cook had permission to accompany us on patrol, but his ship sailed unexpectedly. Attempts to contact the P-399 by radio had failed.

So we chased after the ship, which had a two-hour head start. The *Sea Horse* climbed up on the plane and we caught up with the liner, which stopped and lowered a rope ladder to our deck. The cook climbed upward to catcalls from his shipmates lining the rail and the severe glare from his captain.

An officer on the bridge with a bullhorn, speaking slowly, said, "Thank you *Sea Horse* for your delivery service. The next time you borrow the captain's cook, consider him a gift."

Fighters seemed to be regularly dropping into the sea between Morotai and the Philippines. Another day we received a distress call that a pilot was ditching about forty miles from our present position.

Three hours later we spotted a life raft and the pilot. Tears ran down his face as he stepped aboard the *Sea Horse*. "When I saw you coming, I got down on my knees and thanked God for the Navy," he blurted.

Jep shook hands with the young flyer and said, "Lieutenant, add a P.S. to your prayer and say a good word for present company, this is an Army boat and crew."

Embarrassed and blushing, the pilot replied, "Did I pull a boner, if *I* were you, I'd toss me back to the fishes."

TASK GROUP 78.2

By April 1945, the war had moved north into the Philippines. General MacArthur made good his promise to the Philippine people on October 20, 1944, wading ashore on Leyte Island after his troops had landed. "People of the Philippines, I have returned!" he declared in a radio broadcast.

In January 1945 MacArthur's forces landed on Luzon, the main Philippine island. A month later Corregidor was recaptured and Japanese forces on Bataan were isolated. Manila, the Philippine capital, toppled in March. Sadly just one-third of the men left behind when MacArthur was evacuated to Australia in 1942 had survived the war.

"I'm a little late," he said, "but we finally came."

With fewer bombing raids flown out of Wama Drome, Morotai, we weighed anchor at Rao Island and returned to operate full-time out of Pitu.

The last night at Rao we all went ashore for a farewell party. Baker and Ronnie brought three large cakes from the enlisted men's mess on Morotai (using some of the Japanese invasion money), which was a tremendous treat for our Malaysian friends. As we were leaving we exchanged addresses with Philip Tambariki and his friends and swore we would write after the war. We never did write, but that was the nature of wartime promises.

Our crew, particularly Bake, had made good friends of these people. They were just like families around the world, no matter how remote—a mother with a sick child, a child without the support of a parent, a father with a hungry family. Families everywhere face life much the same.

The next morning we were out on the flight line at sunrise and never saw Rao again. Our work continued as before, until one day, out of a clear, blue sky, while we were on patrol off north Halmahera, operations radioed a coded order moving us at once. I was stunned because I hadn't made provisions for a change of station. We were low on water, gas, and food.

The order directed the P-399 to overtake Amphibious Task Group 78.2, which was bound for Mindanao in the Southern Philippines with the 24th Infantry Division and Headquarters X Corps under Major General R. B. Woodruff, Major General F. C. Sibert, and Vice Admiral A. G. Noble. General MacArthur's orders were to clear Japanese troops from the island.

The operation wasn't necessary because the forty-three thousand enemy soldiers had been bypassed, contained by twenty-five thousand guerrillas under Colonel Wendell Fertig, a former civilian mining engineer. The guerrillas controlled about 95 percent of the island. There was no valid military reason for a large, powerful invasion force to hit Mindanao. It was merely an action undertaken to fulfill MacArthur's promise and please our Philippine friends (and the Moros, who hated the Japanese).

"I shall return," MacArthur had said. And he did.

TG 78.2 sailed south from the central island of Mindoro. It looped around the Zamboanga Peninsula where the second part of the invasion force, the 31st Infantry Division from Morotai, under General C. A. Martin, joined it.

TG 78.2's destination was Malabang, Parang, and Cotobato, on the west shore of Davao Peninsula on the Moro Gulf, Mindanao Island. The invasion force left Mindoro on April 11, 1945. We weren't aware of it because it sailed under blackout and the 31st Division loaded on Landing Ship Infantries (LSIs) and Landing Ship Tanks (LSTs) on the east shore of Morotai. As a result, we didn't see it sail north so we were surprised to be ordered to join TG 78.2.

I called the crew together and explained what I knew. I said all we could do was follow orders, overtake the task group, tie up to a larger ship, and hitch a ride to Mindanao.

The *Sea Horse* could fly, and with it kicking up a rooster tail it didn't take us long to spot ships in the task group on the horizon. Approaching the trailing vessels, I maneuvered the P-399 alongside an LSI, which permitted us to tie up to their stern. They threw us a light cable and George cut the engines. Ron prepared a meal, and we stretched out and relaxed.

It didn't last long. Barzow received relayed flag code signal for the P-399 to report to Rear Admiral Noble's flagship, USS *Wasatch*, a Mount McKinley–class amphibious command ship. General Sibert of the 31st Division and General Woodruff of the 24th Division were also aboard. They had a decision to make.

On the day of TG 78.2's departure from Mindoro, they received an intelligence report that the Mindanao guerrillas, under Colonel Fertig, had cleared the town and airstrip at Malabang of Japanese. The area was now under their control. Since April 3, Colonel Clayton C. Jerome's Marine Air Group

Zamboanga (MAGSZAM), flying SBD Dauntless dive bombers and F4U Corsair fighters, had launched air strikes against Japanese positions from the Malabang airstrip.

When this news reached Generals Sibert and Woodruff aboard the *Wasatch*, and General Eichelberger on the cruiser *Montpelier* with Admiral Riggs, a decision was made to change the invasion plan under strict radio, signal, and visual security. While the fleet was en route to the invasion objective new orders were prepared for distribution to the task group.

Wasatch signaled us to come alongside. I spoke with George and Jep, telling them I didn't know what to expect but that we would do our best. George wasn't sure we had enough gasoline to carry out an extended duty but said he and Whitey would monitor both tanks' fuel levels.

Jep removed the LCI's cable and yelled to the seaman on the deck that we would be back. My first job was to find the *Wasatch* among the waves of ships. It was still light enough to read masthead signal flags, and Barzow made sure he knew what a commodore's flag looked like so we could pick it out at the van of TG 78.2. The *Sea Horse* weaved through the task group to the *Wasatch*, which Barzow and Jep picked out of three large ships near the van.

On the way we made emergency preparations. Should we start to run out of gas, two lines were ready to throw to the nearest ship. Blackout curtains on the main bridge maintained the security blackout should light for reading maps or charts be required. The companionway hatch was to remain closed.

I eased the *Sea Horse* up on the *Wasatch*'s starboard beam. We were about twenty feet away but we could feel the wake. A staff officer yelled to us through a bullhorn, maintaining radio silence and a light signal blackout. With a heaving line, he tossed down a leather shaving kit, a separate packet with our orders, and another box containing maps. The orders specified directions for delivering orders to ships in the task group and included a map showing each ship's location in the task group.

The deck officer shouted, "Good luck, Sailors!"

"We're going to need it," I muttered to myself.

Looking at the sixty-plus ships making up TG 78.2, I realized this was one hell of a job. A multimillion-dollar, combined-services invasion defended by over forty-three thousand Japanese troops was ahead of us, and an air-sea rescue gunboat was delivering the plan to liberate it with a shaving kit.

Jep had several heaving lines with monkey fists onboard should we lose the one tied to the kit. I maneuvered the *Sea Horse* to the eastside of the fleet, where destroyers were protecting the cargo and troop ships from the Japanese submarines they believed were trailing us. I carefully read the instructions and studied each ship's location in the task group.

There was no way I could memorize the names and positions of so many ships. We would have to do this one at a time. We would locate a ship on our list, then deliver the orders while Barzow prepared the next ship's name and location.

I wondered what the hell would have happened if we had not been available at Morotai to deliver the command's change of orders to TG 78.2. Why was an AAF air-sea rescue boat, rather than a Navy gunboat or PT, ordered to perform this crucial mission on which the orderly invasion of Mindanao depended? We were flattered that command, which had assigned the task to the P-399, had confidence in our ability to perform. Maybe it was our Galela Bay record.

The destroyer USS *Flusser* was close by, so we approached its starboard beam. Jep put their new orders in the shaving kit and tossed the heaving line to an officer on the deck. He removed the orders and threw the bag back to our foredeck—so far, so good. Baker successfully heaved package two to the second ship and retrieved the line. Ron took a try at it and did fine.

SIX.

We moved from vessel to vessel—LCIs, cruisers, destroyer escorts, and the US Coast Guard Cutter *Spencer* with General Eichelberger onboard. Admiral Noble later moved his flag from the *Wasatch* to the *Spencer* for the offshore fighting in Davao Bay. Finding a Coast Guard ship that America equated with protecting our vast coastlines in a battle zone was surprising. But it probably was just as eye-opening to the *Spencer* to find an AAF air-sea rescue gunboat working the night shift for TG 78.2 between Morotai and Parang, Mindanao.

Working in and around the fleet was not too difficult during the late afternoon hours, but this changed after dark when large ships loomed out of nowhere and appeared too tall for us to reach with a heaving line. There were a few misses with the monkey fist and we had to toss it again, but the crew kept at it.

Pale light heralded a welcome beginning to dawn. As visibility increased, we took short cuts around ships, often barely missing their intimidating bows. The helmsmen aboard these vessels must have cussed us out. I was glad there were no carriers or battleships in the fleet. I don't think the crew's pitching arms could have tossed a heaving line that high.

Carriers were not needed in this invasion because Colonel Jerome's MAGSZAM had swept the skies of Japanese aircraft on Mindanao.

There were reports that the Japanese lacked pilots, and their maintenance and repair crews couldn't keep their planes in the air. They had pulled back their best air squadrons from Indonesia and the southern Philippines to protect Japan. Command knew that the 347th P-38s stationed at Morotai could provide support if needed.

Our last delivery was to Lieutenant Colonel Robert Amory, who commanded the Army's 533rd Engineer Boat and Shore Regiment landing craft flotilla. After the war, Amory served as Deputy Director of the Central Intelligence Agency from 1952 to

1962. The amphibians would go ashore in waves after the naval bombardment known as a "Spruance Haircut."

Spruance Haircuts were so named because of the appearance of coconut groves after the palm fronds at the top of each tree trunk were scissored off by five- and eight-inch guns from Admiral Raymond Spruance's cruisers during the pre-invasion bombardment of an island's shoreline. The accuracy of the ships' guns from miles at sea was incredible. They aimed at this level to hit installations and airfields built inland, away from the coconut groves along the shore. The frondless tree trunks sticking up at the same level resembled a crew cut when viewed from the sea.

I asked George if we had enough gas to report to the *Wasatch*. He said it would be close, but we could try. If we ran out maybe we could hitch a tow from our old friend Lieutenant Bob Pickering, commander of a squadron of 110-foot gunboats (PGM's). Bob was the skipper of the PGM-4, which had accompanied the *Sea Horse* south from the Treasury Islands to Kiriwina Island in a raging typhoon earlier in our South Pacific duty. During our deliveries we had pulled alongside PGM-4, but it didn't ring a bell until we finished. It would have been good to wave to him.

Low on gas and with a tired crew we pulled up to the *Wasatch*. I yelled to the deck officer to tell the commodore that we had delivered orders to the entire task group. Jep threw back their "10-million-dollar" shaving kit and we sailed back to our tow, the LCI. Just as we grabbed the cable, the engines coughed and sputtered like we needed gas.

I told the crew I was proud of their work, assisting in the joint command's gamble. Jep set single watches until the task group reached Parang. I went below but don't remember falling into my bunk; I was exhausted.

It was April 17 and it seemed as if I had barely dozed off when Barzow, who had the morning deck watch, woke me and said that Vice-Admiral Riggs's cruisers and destroyers were sailing into position to bombard Parang and Cotabato. Jep had somehow gotten us tied up to a small supply ship loaded with the Corps of Engineers material for bridges. Thankfully we were a long way from the shoreline and the rolling thunder of the big guns.

Assault waves landed on their assigned beaches without opposition and moved steadily inland. In the days ahead, gunboats commanded by Lieutenant Bob Pickering and Captain Rae Arison supported troops going up the treacherous Mindanao River.

Using our intercom radio, George and Barzow located a high-octane gasoline barge attached to PT Squadron 24, and we made the short distance to it. George said he was amazed that we had a few drops left to get there. We took on all they would give us at that time, about two hundred gallons. While we were pumping gas, with the red "Baker" flag on the yardarm, Barzow relayed a radio message from the commodore, requesting P-399's skipper to come aboard the flagship.

As soon as we completed refueling, we approached the *Wasatch* and requested permission to come aboard. Jep and George came with me. Admiral Noble gave us a hearty welcome and we saluted in our best military manner, something with which we had little practice. He and his executive officer were cordial and flattering about our successful mission, but there was no written commendation to my commander, Colonel Ford.

The exec asked if we needed anything. I explained that we had left Morotai without prior notice and didn't have time to refuel or secure food, supplies, and water. I told him we already owed a chit for two hundred gallons of 110-octane fuel. The admiral ordered his supply officer to write the necessary chits for us. I put the three separate orders in my shirt pocket, thanked them, saluted the ensign, and left.

After circulating through the supply ships, we found the one listed on our chit. I went aboard and spoke with the officer of the day, who directed me to the issuing officer. I gave him our chit, and he looked at me, taking in our AAF insignia and my crushed cap, shrugged, and said, "Where do you want us to put this?"

I pointed to the starboard side and we walked over to the rail. Looking down on the P-399, he started to laugh, really laugh. Supply officers didn't usually laugh. Then he said, "The commodore gave you a chit for a destroyer escort ration supply, which weighs several tons. If I gave you all of this we'd sink your boat, but maybe we can work something out."

The Navy can always work something out and did. The supply officer gave me the fleet number of a ship that would take aboard the entire ration issue and then dole out what we needed, including meat, fresh vegetables, coffee, tobacco, and 3.2 beer. He said that he had watched us deliver orders the night before and was glad to help us.

Later that afternoon, the destroyer escort's skipper gave us our share and there was a grand celebration aboard; but, I didn't think we could sail with the boxes and crates stacked all over the deck. We could only take a small amount of frozen meat because we only had a small refrigerator. The destroyer escort allowed us to come by each day while we were at Parang to pick up what we needed.

The shorefront at Prabang took on a fresh look, with newly repaired docks. The unloading of materials and personnel continued. Trucks, tanks, and troops moved across the island up the Mindanao River, following the first wave.

We lost track of the Davao inland war when we received orders to support Colonel Jerome's MAGSZAM, which had been flying out of Malabang airstrip since April 3 after guerrillas cleared the area of Japanese. We reported to Colonel Jerome at about the same time the 24th Marine Air Group F4U Corsairs flew into Malabang to provide close air support for the Army action around Davao and against the forty-five thousand Japanese troops that were cut off inland.

The crew wondered what this would mean for us.

SIX.

THE PHILIPPINES

The sail along the Mindanao coast from Parang-Cotabato to Malabang was smooth and relaxing. The second-largest island in the Philippines was also one of the most rugged. It had a dense forest of mahogany, banyan, sandalwood, and on the coast, cypress trees. The lumber business was its most important industry, next to the manufacture of sisal rope.

Inland there were marsh and grass areas, and many lakes, especially Lake Lanao in the north-central part of the island. Its coast is typical of the Philippines, with small towns and villages where coves provided good anchorages.

Mindanao has a strange shape, with three peninsulas in the southern part, one tipped by Zamboanga on the southwest and twin capes bordering Davao Bay. The vast, island-dotted expanse of the Moro Gulf lies between Zamboanga and Davao.

The population on most of the southern islands included Spanish-speaking Filipinos and Asiatic Muslim descendants called Moros. There had been, and still is, an extremely hostile relationship between the two, with many local wars and conflicts, mostly religious but some over land possession and living standards. A third group in the population, Melanesian Negroid people, lived in the inland mountainous regions.

As we made landfall at Malabang, Barzow reported in and told them we were standing by, monitoring the flight operations radio channel. I officially reported to MAGSZAM headquarters the following morning.

Three beaches designated during planning for the invasion were available: Red, White, and Blue. We chose to anchor off Blue Beach. The downside of this decision was that it was much farther away from the airstrip, but the advantage was that it was mostly sheltered from the weather by a small, fertile, palm-covered island containing freshwater streams.

This island had a small village, and we could hear the voices of the children at play from our anchorage. We made two attempts to anchor because the coral bottom kept breaking off. I planned to request an old aircraft engine to drop at our anchorage so we could fashion a makeshift mooring buoy.

The next morning, Jep dropped me off at the small Malabang dock. We didn't tie up because it was busy and crowded with fast supply vessels. I located headquarters and reported, feeling the amicable atmosphere compared to the other installations where we had worked. These Marines were friendly and extremely helpful.

After leaving Colonel Jerome's office, I arranged for supplies. The Marine Air Group ground crew told me where to contact the tankers that would come down to the Malabang dock to refuel us. Not surprisingly, vehicles were difficult to come by, which meant walking from Blue Beach to camp if we were at anchor—a distance of half a mile.

I walked the jungle path along the shore from Red Beach to Blue Beach to check it out. It was very primitive. Even in the middle of the day, covered with a leaf-and-vine awning, it was shadowed and hot. You could sweat a quart just standing there. Finally, I reached Blue Beach and stood on the shore waving to the P-399, which was anchored fifty yards out. After a time, the watch saw me, and Jep came for me in our black, rubber raft with an outboard motor.

"What was the crew doing up on the bridge?" I asked Jep. He said the watch didn't see me at first because they were busy watching village families taking their daily bath in the freshwater stream flowing into the sea, opposite to our anchorage. "Watching people take baths?" I asked. Staying silent, he brought the tender into our boarding net. By the time I came aboard, everyone had dispersed.

During mess, Jep said he wanted to check out the freshwater stream above the village laundry and bathing area where the crew could enjoy freshwater baths. The next afternoon, after patrol, Jep and Barzow took the tender over to the small offshore island to investigate the river gushing into the tidewater about a hundred yards from the nearest hut.

The two of them were gone about half an hour and returned with a report about the swimming and bathing pool with a thirty-foot waterfall pouring into it. Jep set up a lottery to determine who would be the first to enjoy this welcome treat.

Villagers bathed at the mouth of the stream, pouring water over their heads and bodies using half of a dried coconut shell. Village men, except for the elderly, bathed early in the morning. Women and children bathed the rest of the day. Most brought their laundry, washing in the brackish water at the stream outlet and beating it on large stones worn smooth after hundreds of years of use.

We were off patrol the following day. Leaving Bill Chaney on watch, the rest of us went ashore with towels and soap. It was a lovely tropical spot. Tall coconut palms surrounded the glen on two sides of the pool and a beautiful, splashing waterfall on the inland side. A rim along each side of the top of the fall went back to a slope of tree-covered hills.

In minutes, we jumped into the crystal clear, crisp, fresh water. After a bath and a swim, I was toweling off when we heard a woman laugh. All of our eyes looked up, searching the rim along the falls. So help me, the entire village was peering down on us. As we were nude, instinct caused us to jump back in the pool, but the funniest sight was Baker trying to hide behind a young tree, with a trunk the size of a one-inch manila line.

The villagers laughed and enjoyed looking at us, perhaps because of our bare white skin, which contrasted with our deep tans. Once again, we dried off and dressed. As we prepared to return to the P-399, a few villagers came down and asked for our soap. I nodded, and the crew gave them the bars we had with us.

They were friendly Moros. Both the women and men surrounded Baker. Not surprisingly, they liked his ginger hair. As we were leaving, they gave our raft a friendly shove. When we returned to the *Sea Horse*, Ron, Barzow, and Baker took Whitey over for his turn under the falls.

Security at operations told me to make sure we had an adequate watch on deck. This precaution was to protect against the possibility of a Moro activist attempting to come aboard to get our machine guns and ammo and small arms. I took the advice seriously. While on watch, we had observed *proas* (outrigger canoes) with six paddlers and a couple of riders crossing from Mindanao to our small island late at night. The crew was concerned and we doubled the watch, with two men armed with pistols on night and day.

Marine Corsair and Dauntless pilots reputedly exhibited an absolute lack of fear of crashing, facing Japanese aircraft or ground defenses, ditching at sea, parachuting into jungles, or even their commanders, who, in most cases, were just like them.

I'm not deprecating the bravery of Air Corps or Navy pilots. They were no less brave or skilled as flyers. But the Marine pilot was different.

We connect the time-honored name "marine" with mud-sloshing, mosquito-fighting, jungle-crawling, and knife-wielding rifle marksmen. But we seldom link Marines with their exploits in air combat where Colonel Jerome's MAGSZAM excelled. It was an honor to work with them.

Our mission was somewhat easier because most of the Marine flight patterns were over the island's interior. Fewer strikes occurred over Moro Gulf and Davao Bay. Japanese naval activity now amounted to a few hidden barges that only ventured out at night to contact Japanese troops who had been bypassed and trapped on islands.

MAGSZAM supported the ground war around Davao and along Highway 1 and the Sayre Highway from Davao City to Cagayan de Oro and down to Sarangani Bay in the south.

The Japanese were adept at camouflaging, so finding their camps in the jungle and mountains was extremely difficult.

Pinpointing them for aerial attacks required dangerous treetop flying at speeds up to three hundred miles per hour. The skill of these pilots amazed us.

As they were returning to base they would often dive and buzz the *Sea Horse*. We shuddered when we spotted them coming down. It seemed they were never going to pull up, but they did. What worried us most was that they wouldn't know our radio antenna extended above our mast by eight feet or more. I called them on our intercom, explaining my concern, but they only laughed and said not to worry.

The pilots' blue language on the intercom was unbelievable. Headquarters always censored them for "dirty language" spoken during the serious business of giving their positions and targets, often accompanied by highspirited banter and friendly insults. Barzow, frequently listening, was always laughing. Today, I wonder what the Japanese, who tuned in to our channels, thought of MAGSZAM communications.

When the guerrillas cleared Malabang Village and the airstrip, the Marines set up a secure perimeter with guard posts every thirty or forty feet to keep out infiltrating Japanese looking for food and clothing. Real trouble developed when Moros would sneak into the Marine camp like shadows in the night while the Marines were sleeping, slip into their tents, and steal guns and ammunition. They needed weapons for their constant fight with the Filipinos.

Losing weapons was terrible, but a minor consideration if a Marine awakened and the Moro killed him. After the fifth or sixth such killing, Colonel Jerome tripled the perimeter guard and ordered them to capture, but not kill, the next invading Moros. After a week the guards seized three Moro fanatics inside the compound. Colonel Jerome had the guerrillas catch three wild pigs in the hills near the camp and bring the whole hides to him.

The following Saturday, when the colonel knew most Moros would be in their villages along Lake Lanao, he and his staff took the Moro prisoners in jeeps to Bayang. Wrapping the screaming, clawing, and twisting prisoners in pigskins and binding them securely, the Marines dragged them through the village. The Moro revulsion from coming in contact with pigskin was so great that there were no more sneak attacks on the Marine base.

E DAY

On May 8, 1945, returning to our anchorage at Blue Beach, we tied up and shut down the intercom radio from a routine patrol. Barzow flipped on our big liaison radio, with worldwide reception, and yelled, "Hey, the war's over in Europe!"

We all gathered around Barzow's radio and listened to broadcasts of the momentous VE Day story, including President Harry Truman's address to the American people announcing Germany's unconditional surrender. The president made no mention of a celebration, cautioning that, "Our victory is but half-won. The west is free, but the east is still in bondage to the treacherous tyranny of the Japanese. When the last Japanese division has surrendered unconditionally, then only will our fighting job be done."

With the battles still raging closer to the Japanese islands, we knew there was still work to be done in the Pacific, but Germany's surrender brought uplifting thoughts of the war against Japan ending.

Despite the president's somber tone, celebrations from around the world, particularly from Great Britain and Europe, poured from Barzow's speaker. We looked at each other. Savard looked at me.

"Skipper, it seems like everyone is celebrating VE Day, but us."

"Sorry, but the Three Feathers whiskey has been gone for a few months, and the corner liquor store is closed."

After a moment's pause, I asked Jep to strap on his .45 pistol.

"We'll go up to the base to see if we can find some booze at the Pilot's Club," I announced.

Jep and Baker lowered the outboard tender overboard, and we took it into Blue Beach and pulled it far up on the shore. We always hoped that an islander, especially a Moro, wouldn't steal it. Our watch aboard the *Sea Horse* periodically trained binoculars on it when someone was ashore.

We trudged up the jungle path toward the base, with spiny iguanas waddling across the sand road in several places. They were just as unhappy to confront us as we were them. They were big, and they were ugly.

When we arrived at the base, I had an idea. "Let's go over to the colonel's shack," I suggested. "Maybe he's having a VE Day party."

When we got there, all was quiet—no party. I knocked on the screen door, and there was no response. Just as we were leaving, the entrance to the Dale Hut next door opened, and a Marine major came over to inquire if we were looking for Colonel Jerome.

We told him we had just heard the news about VE Day and had come to see if we could borrow some whiskey from the colonel to celebrate. The major said the colonel had flown up to Leyte to celebrate there. And then he said, "Come on in the colonel's digs, we'll look for his liquor supply."

Entering the hut, the major pulled a footlocker from the corner and opened it up. Wow! Canadian Club, Johnny Walker Scotch, and Vickers Gin abounded.

"Lieutenant, how many men do you have in your crew?" he asked.

"Major, I haven't counted lately, but I think fifty," I responded, with a straight face.

"Fifty! Is that your boat, that pint-sized rowboat I see in Illana Bay doing patrol?"

I admitted that perhaps our crew was not quite that big, but we would take as many bottles as we could get. The major gave us four, and kept two for himself, closed the locker, and slid it back in the corner.

Stepping outside the colonel's hut, we thanked the major for his generosity. It was beginning to get dark so we headed for the base motor pool to hitch a ride back to Blue Beach. Neither of us wanted to hike back in the dark.

We each put two bottles inside our shirts, where we could fold our arms over them. There was a Marine corporal on duty, while the sergeant, already absent for two hours, finished his evening mess. The corporal said we could have a ride when the sergeant authorized it and could get someone to drive us down. While we waited, he spotted the bottles in my shirt and asked for a drink. I gave him a slug of gin.

Finally the sergeant returned and we requested a ride. "Okay, but I'll need some of that booze—now," he said.

He had a drink, sent the corporal to get a driver for us, and had another drink. When the jeep pulled up, the sergeant, the corporal, and the driver each had a drink, so I left the bottle. It was against military regulations to have an alcoholic beverage in your quarters or aboard your ship, except GI-issue beer, without special permission from your commander—a rule rarely enforced.

We drove toward Blue Beach, but near the edge of camp the driver said he was still thirsty and that a drink would help the jeep moving toward Blue Beach. So Jep pulled out one of his bottles and let the driver take a big swallow. Reaching the beach, he said he would need a few drinks to get back to base, and if we needed a jeep in the future to come and see him or the sergeant and they would take care of us. It seemed like a worthwhile investment, so we gave him the rest of the bottle.

On Blue Beach we pulled our raft out of hiding. As we approached the *Sea Horse* in the dark, we signaled the watch with our small mapreading flashlight. Jep threw our bow painter to Ronnie and we climbed aboard.

"Do we celebrate?" all hands chorused.

"We sure do," I responded. Jep and I placed our remaining bottles on the table—what a pretty sight for our crew.

Out came our best mugs. We toasted VE Day and a quick end to the war in the Pacific. We all had another drink, but, oddly, few of us wanted a third. Again, we toasted those who gave their lives for this huge victory achieved against high odds. Then I said, "Here's to Danny, now he can go home to the Netherlands, from wherever he might be, and live in peace." Everyone fell silent, and we quietly hit the sack.

The next morning the crew talked about the whiskey we had consumed the night before. Everyone agreed that two drinks had been enough. The tropics seem to make alcohol more potent and when you don't drink regularly you lose the ability to consume much. Even the low-alcohol beer issued to us every few weeks satisfied our needs.

Getting beer cold took a little time. At our bases we got to know hospital workers and pilots. Baker had useful contacts and could often get hospital ice, a rare thing in the islands.

Our connections with pilots and ground crews provided tips whenever a repaired plane was due to fly slow time at high altitudes.

We would take our beer, a couple of cases of cans, to the airstrip and a crew chief would put it in a rear seat compartment. The pilot would fly at altitudes from twenty thousand to thirty thousand feet, where it was frigid. When he landed, our beer was chilled precisely right.

You had to have someone you could trust to deliver the warm beer and pick up the chilled cans when the plane landed. Otherwise it would be long gone.

The least desirable way to cool beer was to bury it in beach sand and pour 110-plus octane gasoline over it. When the gas evaporated, it cooled the beer. The problem with this method was the difficulty in getting the gas smell off the cans. Maybe that's why many Aussie pilots preferred their brews warm.

There was no room in our tiny refrigerator for the beer—and, besides, Cookie, the galley boss, wouldn't permit it.

SEVEN.

Hell Is Green

A War Rescue

Lt. William Diebold

A GROUP OF EXCITED YOUNG PILOTS CROWDED AROUND THE desk. I tapped one on the arm and asked what all the fuss was about.

"Here!" he said and handed me a sheet of worn, dirty paper. Laboriously written in a scrawling, unsteady hand were words beginning "Somewhere in Hell . . ."

With difficulty I read the remainder of the note: "I am the pilot who crashed. I need a pair of G.I. shoes, quinine, socks, sulfa for boils and infections rotting my limbs off. I would like to borrow a blanket if you could spare one. Cold. Cigarettes would be nice. I'm ashamed for asking for so much. Thanks for whatever you can do."

The note was signed "Lt. G. M. Collins."

I could see why everyone was so excited; the note packed more wallop than anything I'd ever seen. "That was brought into an airstrip in Burma two days ago by a native," a lieutenant explained. "The native said the pilot is in the Naga Hills, in a village we think is called Geda Ga."

It was the mission, I knew vaguely, of the 1352nd Search and Rescue Squadron to which I'd been temporarily assigned to find downed airmen along the Hump route and rescue them. That's all I did know, though, for I was just this morning reporting for duty. Having arrived the night before at this jumping-off place for China supplies, I was supposed to report immediately to the commanding officer, but given the lateness a sergeant at the airfield had directed me to a hut he called a *basha* and quartered me with fifty other men.

A basha is an American hay mound with doors. The army had gone native: straw roof over a bamboo frame with woven bamboo sides and windows with nothing in them. No glass, no frame, no nothing. They could better be called square holes for ventilation. The one modern touch, cement floors, added little to their attraction. Following a long flight across half of India, I slept well enough that night, though, if I'd known what was in the books for me this morning, there'd have been little sleep.

The inevitable began to kick in when I reported to Major Roland Hedrick, in civilian life a Salt Lake City lawyer.

The major was surrounded by pilots, all talking at once. He was the boss and brains of the outfit, and the pilots were discussing with him—"arguing about" would be more accurate—the note I'd just read. To say I received little attention when I walked into this melee of men puts it mildly; penetrating that circle of gesticulating arms would have been worth a black eye at least.

A pilot near the major made a mountain with one hand, while with the other he imitated an airplane in flight. He was trying to explain how difficult it was to fly around that mountain with the objective of coming low over a native village situated on the mountain's side, near the top. He'd had to come in low over the village, I gathered, to attract the attention of any airman that might be in it. Was the writer of the note in that particular village? Nobody seemed sure.

The major listened patiently enough, but eventually he started chasing off the crowd of officers, moving them gradually toward the door and out into the growing light. One by one they left, each being assured something would be done and that he'd let them know as soon as he knew himself. Figuring he was pretty busy, I turned to leave with them, but, catching my eye, the major indicated I should stay.

"You're Diebold," he said.

So much for a slow and gentle introduction to my new job. I would soon be donning a parachute and standing terrified in an airplane door over a forbidding jungle mountain top, preparing to jump—I hoped—to the downed Lt. G. M. Collins.

Eventually, we came to the section of the country where our downed pilot was supposed to be. What a country! If a glacier made these mountains it must have been mad as hell at something. They were the biggest, highest hunks of earth I have ever seen piled in one place. When I thought of climbing around in them, they grew even larger and more formidable.

Anderson found the villages, then flew me from them to the Ledo Road, showing me the way out. It looked simple. There couldn't be more than two mountain ranges towering some two miles up apiece, or more than a hundred miles of solid jungle. Nothing to it! We buzzed the villages a couple of times, and it was some of the best flying I've ever seen done, thank God! First we dived down the side of one mountain, gaining excess air speed, and then shot up the side of an adjacent mountain. It would have been lots of fun if I didn't have to jump out of the ship on one of those shoots up the mountainside.

When I'd talked with the major, he said he hoped this second fly-over would give us an idea of which village the pilot was in, but no matter how close we came to the roofs of the houses—and the pilot came damned close—the only thing we saw were wildly waving natives. No parachute, no panel, no signal of any sort. I began to doubt if our pilot was in either of them, but the only way to find out was still the same as it was before: jump in and look.

Finally, as I knew it must, the time came to go. Pretty much at random we picked one of the villages, and Anderson described how the jump would work. He told me to stand at the rear door, and when the bell rang that was my signal to jump. The walk from the pilot's compartment to the rear of that ship was the longest I've ever made.

Sgt. Stanley Bloom from Boston, Massachusetts, helped me into my chute, showed me how to hook up to my static line, and I took my stand at the door. I could feel my heart thudding against my chest as I looked out. It was so far down to the rushing ground, and it was thick and rough. The village sat in a small clearing—very small from the airplane—but all around it was jungle. I could picture my chute being collapsed by one of the top branches of a tall tree, letting me freefall a hundred feet or so.

It seemed I stood there forever, scared to death! I was afraid even to think about it. I did think of my civilian insurance company and its directors, though. Wouldn't they be the happy lot if they could see me now? Once, back when I was a happy civilian, they insisted I stop flying because it was too great a risk for my insurance. Good God, how would they feel about this? Then the bell rang!

I had been waiting unconsciously for that sound, so it took no planned action on my part to get me out that door. I'd conquered my mind when I stepped up to it, and from then on leaping out was reaction to a sound. I'm sure of this, for I can't remember jumping. The bell rang, and the next thing I knew was the roaring of the slip-stream in my ears, the tumbling of the horizon, the tail of the ship passing overhead . . . and then the almighty jerk.

I'd learned to jump the hard way. Body position in the air was an unknown to me, so mine almost certainly was wrong. Also, my chute harness had been cinched too loose, so I got a terrific jerk. I blacked out for an instant, I guess, for the next thing I knew

I was alone in the air, all was quiet and serene, and the airplane was gone.

The feeling of elation and exhilaration that came over me when I looked up and saw that big white canopy is indescribable. The chute had opened. Oh, happy day! I kicked my legs, waved my arms, and wiggled my body to make sure nothing had been broken. Nothing had.

I watched the big plane disappearing over the far mountain with definite misgivings. It made me lonely just to see it go. There I stood in the middle of a group of staring natives . . . and all I could think to do was stare back at them.

The women wore clothes, damn it. Wrapped around their middles were long pieces of varicolored cloth. Around their breasts they wore a plain piece of dirty white cloth or another piece matching the skirt. They all wore necklaces, made of anything from animal teeth on a string to old coins or pieces of metal. The men, most of them, wore nothing but a loincloth, and others had the same wrapping the women wore around their waists.

What surprised me most was their hair. Both men and women alike wore it up, piled on top of their heads. If it weren't for the very definite outline of women's bodies, I would have been bewildered as to which sex was which. As it was, nature provided the curves.

Well, we couldn't stand there staring at one another forever, so I took an important step: I smiled. There was one old geezer the others seemed to treat with respect who I had already guessed was the head man. On top of that, he had some sort of feather in his hair none of the others had. Either the others had lost theirs, or it meant something. I gave him the old try; I smiled directly at him.

He nodded his head a couple of times and gave me what I took to be a tentative smile in return. With that, I felt on more solid ground and decided to try to get things in hand. Scattered all over the clearing were the white para-packs. Some were even in the trees at the edge of the clearing. The kids of the village were beginning to poke experimental noses into their contents, and I could picture the results if they started opening them and spreading their contents all over the area. Best to get them gathered up and at least stacked in a pile where I could keep an eye on them.

I looked at the feather-headed village elder, smiled again, and gave him another cigarette from my last pack—there were more in the dropped supplies, I knew, which was another reason to get them secured. I pointed to the various para-packs and then to one of their houses. He must have understood what I meant because he barked out some orders, and in a flash the packs were being gathered up by the natives. The chief, if that's what he was, led me to one of the houses while this was going on.

What a place those houses were. Built on stilts about ten feet off the ground, they were long, bamboo-woven things with grass roofs. In front, they actually had a porch. *Very civilized*, I thought, but later I learned the hard way about the porches' uses.

The chief and I wallowed through the mud to his house. I called it mud, with a mental frown, for surrounding the house were two or three water buffalo and a dozen or so animals that slightly resembled pigs. *Ah, the beautiful odors of a Naga village*, I thought as I followed the chief along. We entered his house via a fancy stairway made from a log with notches cut into it for steps. I wondered how my old Naga friend made it up that log on his night out; that is, if his wife gave him a night out.

The inside of the hut resembled a large communal basha, not unlike the one back at the base, though more worn with use. Several rooms ran to the rear of the shack, all connected to each other so that to go to the rearmost room, one had to walk through the sleeping quarters of everyone in the house. The front room looked like the natives' version of a living room or parlor. In the rear of the room a small fire flickered in the center of the floor on sand or something. But what stopped me cold were the decorations on the walls. On every wall hung a heterogeneous collection of dried heads. On some the skin had turned to a brown parchment-like covering. Others were nothing but the grinning, white skull. Though they were almost certainly animal skulls, one look at those and I wanted to move out of there in high gear.

Every kind of head imaginable hung in the shadows. The heads that were simply skulls really frightened me. The open holes that were once eyes, combined with the absence of any lower jaw, gave them a lurid expression. They looked as if they were smiling to me in an open invitation to join them in their vigil.

On one wall were the skulls of huge water buffalo, horns still intact. On another were the skulls of large birds, probably vultures. The long beaks protruded from the skull, and here and there I could see tufts of hairy fuzz.

What really made me gulp and thank Mr. Colt for inventing our .45 automatic were the monkey heads. I've been told since then, by men who should know, that they were monkey heads and not human. But from where I was standing they looked like the largest monkey heads I'd ever seen. They came awfully close to looking like what I thought mine probably looked like under the skin. I began to pick the spot where they'd probably put mine. At least I wanted a good spot, overlooking the porch.

The chief beckoned me over to the fire. I wasn't cold but I thought it a good idea, in view of the heads, to play ball with him. After all, I kept telling myself, I was his guest; morale and good relations, you know, are a lot of little things.

The chief sat cross-legged on the floor and motioned me to join him. He then pulled out a two-foot-long, two-inch-diameter pole made of bamboo, filled it with water, dropped in some brown stuff, put one end in the fire, and propped the other end against a forked stick. We were going to have tea, cooked in bamboo. It was almost too much. *The prisoner ate a hearty meal before . . .*

Our fire was very smoky, and there was no chimney. I watched the smoke curl up as the chief blew on the fire to make it hot. First, the smoke filtered through a series of bamboo layers hanging from vines from the thatched roof. On some layers of bamboo lay meat; on others, nothing. The ones with nothing on them, I later learned, were drying and would be burned in the fire. On the others, the meat looked delicious.

I learned later that when bamboo was used in the fire, the meat was moved out of the smoke. My first lesson in jungle lore: There must be undesirable gases in bamboo smoke. After passing over the meat and helping dry extra bamboo for the fire, the smoke curled on up to the peak of the roof, followed the peak to the end of the house, and there dissipated into the outside air. As the smoke ran along the roof it blackened the straw, or whatever it was that covered the house. Every so often a big hunk of this soot would fall down on my head and the heads of the natives, which they casually brushed off.

The chief had poured water for the tea from fat bamboo logs racked in a row behind him. These were kept constantly full by the women. The nearest water being at the foot of the mountain, they had to make that hike a couple of times a day. Coming up with their backs loaded down with water-filled bamboo gave them a beautiful carriage, and strong legs—and, as I was to learn tomorrow, made them a lot tougher than they looked.

We had our tea from bamboo cups. That tea was so strong it snarled at me as I tried to swallow it. These natives, I decided, had galvanized stomachs. The stuff tasted like boiled tobacco. Nevertheless, I nodded, smiled, and smacked my lips in evident enjoyment. This pleased the chief, I was happy to see, and he, too, smiled, smacked his lips, and said something like "Kajaiee." I treasured the word as my first. It must mean good, although at the taste of the tea, I could hardly believe it.

By this time, the natives outside had piled up all the para-packs. I stood on the porch with the chief and looked at them in dismay. There were so many and all in the wrong village, and I wished Andy hadn't been so hasty in dumping them out of the plane. How I was ever going to get them from where they were over to the far mountain where they should be was beyond me.

It was now late afternoon and too late to try and make the trek to the other village. The jungle looked tough enough in the daytime, and it didn't take a lot of imagination to guess it could be deadly at night. I went down in the mud and lifted all the packs up on the porch. I was amazed to find that one of these native boys could carry one of those packs on his back, as they had done to get them in the pile, but it took three of them to lift one up. My hoisting them onto the porch caused no end of consternation among them. It gave them a mistaken estimate of my strength, which I was to become all too unhappy about the next day on the trail. Up on the porch again, I opened one of the packs and found a couple of cartons of cigarettes. I passed a few cigarettes around to the boys who had brought in the packs. They seemed tickled as hell. It made me think of the number of servants a man could have in that country for a buck a month.

My problem was to get as much of this stuff over to the next mountain as possible. I looked at the chief, pointed to one of the packs, then to the other mountain, and made a couple of motions as if I were carrying one of the packs and walking. Then I pointed to the handful of men below us. It seemed an impossible job. Those few men could never, even if they wanted, carry all this equipment.

Evidently the chief got the idea for he smiled, nodded, said, "Kajaiee," and called one of the older boys up on the porch. They held a lengthy conversation while I stood looking, wondering what the hell was going on. At the end of the conversation, the boy crawled off the porch and, with another companion, started down the trail. Was he being sent for more help? All I could do was to hope for the best.

We went back inside, for more tea I presumed, and sat down by the fire. They did pour more tea and then sat back contentedly smoking their cigarettes. I decided there would just have to be a stop to this tea drinking; I couldn't stand the gaff. Then I remembered what Andy had said about the bottle of medicinal liquor.

After what I had been through that day I felt I wouldn't be cheating Uncle Sugar too much if I had a drink or two before dinner, so I found the bottle and did. It was damn good bourbon and was easier to swallow than the native's tea had been, but it also made me realize I was hungry.

I found some rations and started to cook a little dinner over the native's fire. I say dinner, but it consisted mostly of cereal because the rations consisted mostly of cereal. It wasn't what I would usually order for dinner, but, compared to what the Naga chief offered, the cereal looked delicious. His menu, deluxe style, consisted of monkey meat, which was cooked before my eyes. They tossed a dead monkey, whole and entire, into the fire.

The chief, after he had eaten, took out a long bamboo pipe. About a third of the way up the pipe from the bottom, an inch-thick piece of hard vine stuck out. He poured water into the mouth of the pipe, held it upright, and then lay down on the floor. In one hand he had a copper dish with a long handle. In this he put a brown pasty substance. He held this over the fire until the brown stuff came to a sizzle. At the same time he had shredded a green, folded leaf with his knife. He browned the shreds in front of the fire. When they were good and brown, he mixed the sizzling stuff into it. All these elaborate troubles were for what? Was he going to smoke the stuff or eat it?

When the mixture was cooked to his satisfaction, he put it in the vine sticking out of the bamboo. Now I was really puzzled! I've watched a lot of people smoke pipes, but this was the damnedest conglomeration of tobacco or anything else I'd ever seen. I didn't really know that he was smoking opium, but I soon guessed when I saw the beatific look on his face, the utter relaxation of his body, and the "out of this world" look in his eyes. I was surprised, but I wasn't shocked, not after these many years in the Army. Everyone had their own way of getting tight—even if this one was a bit unusual. It certainly seemed to agree with him; he looked so happy, so self-satisfied that I almost envied him. And he wasn't alone, for on all sides of me, the boys were reaching with bamboo tongs for embers out of the fire to light their own pipes. This was going to be quite a party.

I had my choice: either go to bed or have a couple more drinks of medicinal liquor. (The chief had his vice; I had mine.) This opium den held quite a bit of interest, though, so I decided I'd stay up and see how it ended. Anyway, it was darn good liquor. After a few more, the party seemed to be getting dull. Then a song, for no reason I could think of, came out of nowhere into my head, "Old McDonald Had a Farm." It seemed lively enough for the occasion, anyway, so I sang a couple of verses, and it wasn't long until a few natives began chiming in "E-I-E-I-O." Soon they were all doing it, with real gusto, and we had ourselves a chorus.

But after a couple thousand "Old McDonald"s I figured we'd disturbed the jungle enough, and I decided to go to bed. The bourbon had been so good I'd completely forgotten it was at all unusual to be singing in a shack on a mountain in the middle of the Burmese jungle with a bunch of opium-drunk natives. But at the time it all seemed rather natural.

I walked out to the porch and to the para-packs. One of those fool bags had my bed in it, but which one? I tried the one on top, and my luck was good. In it was a jungle hammock, which I'd never used, but it came with directions. The directions went something like this: "Find two trees, ten to fifteen feet apart . . ." etc. In the dark I had little desire to go wandering in the jungle looking for two trees ten to fifteen feet apart, but in the hut there was nothing even remotely resembling two trees. Then I remembered the uprights supporting the porch. *Just the spot*, I thought. As I fell down the niched log stairway and picked myself out of the mud, I decided Charlie King had been right; there had to be a better way to make a living.

With a flashlight in one hand, directions in the other, and the hammock between my legs, I tried to figure out how it should be put up. Two of these poles under the porch should do it.

The two end ropes I tied to the poles. Then there was the little matter of the mosquito netting that surrounded the hammock and attached to it. At each of the four corners the manufacturers had put a small cord. I tied these to the lattice-work the natives had covering their porch. The whole thing, as I stood back and surveyed my work, made quite a nest.

But when I tried to get into it, it wouldn't stop swinging. A zipper ran the entire height of the mosquito netting with another joining it that ran half the length of the hammock. I tried to crawl through the hole made by the two zippers and somehow made it, but when I was in, I found I'd forgotten to remove my boots. With the type of mud surrounding that hut, removing them was a necessity. I slowly reached down to get them off—a move I shouldn't have tried because I became tangled in the blankets. I guess I was twisting and turning more than the manufacturers of the hammock had foreseen, and I capsized, ending up lying on the part that should have been over my head.

It looked to me like the best thing I could do was get out and start all over, but how? The hammock was swinging furiously back and forth, tossing me around inside like a squirrel in a bag. I'll never know how I got my body out of the torture chamber, but eventually I stood in the mud and looked at the twisted, impossible mess that was supposed to be my bed.

So I started again. I had to sleep somewhere. But how was I to get my boots off and get through the hole without putting my stocking feet in the mud? I tried sitting on the edge and removing them, but it was like sitting on a swing and trying to remove one's shoes. Naturally I ended up standing in the mud in my stocking feet. By this time I was so angry I didn't care how I got into it or where I slept, on the sides, bottom, or top of the hammock. I was sweating, breathing hard, and covered with mud.

The solution turned out to be simple: I dived at the hammock's opening and made it, though it took a second to stop revolving, but eventually the hammock and I ended our struggle

HELL IS GREEN

right side up. Even so, the blankets were wound around my body so tightly I could hardly move, the mosquito netting was in my mouth, and my feet were wet and muddy. I had also forgotten to take off my web belt so my canteen was jabbing me in the back and my .45 was making a poor impression on my ribs. To top it off, I wanted a cigarette.

Slowly, so as not to upset my precarious equilibrium, I stalked the cigarette pocket with one hand, clutching the side of the hammock with the other. Somehow I got the pack out of my pocket without upsetting the whole works, got the cigarette lit without setting fire to the hammock, and settled back, exhaling a cloud of smoke and listening to the jabbering of the natives in front of their fire. It occurred to me that the bourbon (together with some of the wayward opium smoke) might possibly have contributed to my struggles with the bedding, but I dismissed the idea as unlikely.

It seemed a beautiful night now that I had stability. Surrounding our mountain were other giants of this country, each outlined in cloaks of mist and moonlight. It would have been eerie had it not been for the billion stars surrounding a huge yellow moon. It was so peaceful I almost forgave the man who had invented the jungle hammock.

On a far mountainside, a jackal raised its voice; a nearer one answered. The sound drifted to my ears out of the mist. With the flicker of the fire inside the hut and the voices of the natives, the jackal didn't scare me much. When I became convinced the animal wasn't under my bed, I relaxed again. It was still a beautiful night.

The natives continued to talk, and it wasn't long until I could recognize the different voices. The words were impossible to understand except for one which sounded like they might be trying to say, "American." I didn't care much for that; it seemed to me little good could come out of their becoming too curious about me. One voice rose above the others, and every third word seemed to be "American," and I worried a little more. The less I entered into their conversation, the better I liked it, since I could still close my eyes and picture those heads on their wall. The hair on the back of my neck crawled at the thought. I grabbed my .45 and with a trembling hand took a firm grip on it. Of course the natives were never safer than when I had that gun, but I was hoping they wouldn't know that.

As the conversation increased almost to shouting, one of the natives walked out on the porch and looked down at me. With what I hoped was a forceful voice, but was probably little more than a squeak, I asked, "Wonderful night for murder, isn't it?" The character didn't answer. He just stood there in the moonlight looking at me, the fire lighting up one side of his face.

He stared for what seemed like forever; then to my surprise came the sound of running water. I couldn't believe it, but in the moonlight I could see it was true: I was sleeping in the Naga's bathroom and this guy was using it. After the first Naga, came a long procession, all relieving themselves over my bed. I thanked the manufacturer of the jungle hammock for the tarpaulin he had put over the top; otherwise, it would have been a very damp night.

During the night, dozens of natives entered the village. The two men that the chief had sent out earlier evidently had been emissaries to other Naga villages, though God knows where they were in the jungle. The men had done their job well, though. There seemed to be an ample number to carry our equipment the next day.

One thing that interested me to no end, and scared me more than a little when I first saw it down the trail, was their version of a flashlight. Having decided I was in no danger from the natives—other than getting peed on—I was lying there relaxed and smoking. As I looked out into the darkness, I saw a small red ball bobbing and weaving in the air. The medicinal liquor had been good, perhaps even better than that, but I hadn't drunk enough to be seeing things that weren't there. But red balls don't appear for no reason. All I could do was sit up in the hammock—as much as I could sit up—and watch them approach. It wasn't really fear that made me shake, I told myself, it was only nervousness. Then, from the faint glow of the balls I glimpsed the human forms behind them. I lay back relieved, for the balls were only the glowing tips on the end of bamboo poles.

Finally I went to sleep. It was a fitful, disturbed sleep filled with little brown men looking down at me through their front porch, peeing into the night, and waving red balls in the air. I seemed to be stuck knee-deep in mud and unable to miss the man-made dew that was falling so heavily. It was not a comfortable night.

If the Naga ever went to bed that night, I don't know, but at 4:30 in the morning, while it was still dark, the women were up and pounding something I correctly guessed to be rice. The muffled thud, thud, continuous and without rhythm, would wake a hibernating bear. Shortly thereafter I heard the voices of the men and could see the brightening reflection of their fire. Wearily, I swung my feet out of the hammock, wiggled my mud-caked toes, and eased into my boots.

As I climbed the notched ladder, my eyes met a sight I won't easily forget: The big front room of the chief's house was filled to overflowing with brown-skinned Nagas, all of them staring at me. The fire behind them framed their squatting bodies and their piled up hair, with a flickering, weird background. All I could see was the glint of white teeth and the glitter of eyes. The leering, naked skulls on the wall framed them, and the air was heavy with tobacco smoke, sweaty bodies, and effluvium. Standing at the entrance of that room, I tried to smile and said my one Naga word, "Kajaiee." It worked. They actually laughed. The tension was broken. The old chief unfolded himself and came forward, took me by the hand, and led me to the fire.

My God, I thought, *not tea, not at this hour!* But tea is what the good and venerable chief had in mind. Holding up both hands to him in a negative gesture, I went to the food sack for some good old American coffee. I didn't know how it would taste cooked in a bamboo tube, but it couldn't be worse than their tea.

Taking a bamboo tube from the rack behind the chief, I poured in some coffee and water, stuck the end of it in the fire, and propped up the other end with a forked stick. At first the chief looked puzzled, then slightly annoyed until I poured him a bamboo cupful and he tasted it. His face lit up in evident enjoyment and he passed the cup around the circle of men. A few were missed, so I put another tube-full on to boil. That was a mistake. In the next half-hour, I did nothing but make coffee for the Nagas. They drank it as fast as I could brew it.

Finally calling a halt to the coffee making, I put water on to boil for cereal. The brightly colored box, proclaiming it the finest cereal in the world, was cause in itself for a murmur of assent from my friends. I cooked more than I could possibly eat since I had a feeling this was going to be a repetition of the coffee incident. It was, but I underestimated the food capacity of a Naga.

Batch after batch of cereal went down those hungry gullets. I wondered what they would have done for food if I hadn't been there to cook breakfast for them. When I finally called a halt to this noise, I sat back and contemplated them with a lifted eyebrow. I looked at my burnt fingers and reflected on the peculiarities of life. *Once was*, I thought, *the wife* . . . but, hell, that was too long ago to remember.

Still, the Naga were very appreciative and smiled their thanks. In a way, I was rather proud of having pleased and filled them, much like the hostess who has spent hours in the kitchen appreciates guests who enjoy the dinner. I leaned against the wall, lit a cigarette, and gazed with warmth upon the recipients of my labors.

But having finished his cereal and understanding I wasn't going to make any more, the chief moved to the fire and began boiling rice—and in huge quantities. It couldn't be! These people were so small and yet had eaten more per capita than is ordinarily consumed by a food-loving American soldier. The shock, so early in the morning, was almost too much. I sat there and watched with awe as those damn natives ate all that rice—and there wasn't a potbelly in the crowd.

By then, the dawn was beginning to lighten up the jungle. Red beams poured down the green mountainsides and probed the interior of our hut. In the valleys, a few trees reached through the mist they'd slept under. In the forest, the animals began to stir and yawn. The strange early morning cries of birds mingled with the dog-like bark of deer. *Soon we'll be on our way*, I thought, which proved how little I knew yet about the Nagas.

Fooling around with this and that in preparation for the day's hike, I didn't pay much attention to the chief and his men. I presumed, though, that they, too, were getting ready. But when I finally looked over at them, they were all stretched out around the fire smoking their pipes again. I went over to the chief and made signs like walking and hurry-up and pointed to the mountain he'd indicated yesterday as the one where my flyer was. To my gesticulations the old chief just nodded and smiled in a sapient sort of way . . . and continued smoking his pipe. It was most exasperating. Generations of American habit were ahead of me, which included getting a job done when it needed to be done, but like it or not I would have to wait until they were good and ready to go.

Soon, though, my friends began to stir a little. They'd started opening the para-packs, oohing and aahing at each article they uncovered, from cans of beans to a tube of shaving cream, the latter an item I could have done without. Each of the natives had a little basket which would hold, I imagined, about thirty pounds. The baskets were of a peculiar construction. The top of the baskets had two shoulder straps of woven bamboo, with another strap looping from the top of the basket through a wooden yoke. It looked a little puzzling, until they put them on their backs; then it became a sensible arrangement. They put their arms through the two loops attached to the basket and the yoke fitted on the backs of their necks against their shoulders. The end of the other loop went onto their foreheads. It looked so solid and balanced that they probably could have done somersaults without the baskets falling off.

Gradually their work grew efficient: the men formed a circle, baskets in hand, and the chief loaded them. Evidently they had union rules, though, for each man was loaded according to his size. The larger a man was, the larger his load. The chief was the big cheese, and there was little or no argument from the men in the circle.

When all of his men had their baskets full, a considerable number of things remained in the packs. The old chief went out and recruited all the youngsters, male and female, plus a number of young ladies. To all of these he gave lighter loads, but it emptied the para-packs completely.

It was a long and colorful line of porters that started down the trail. Interesting, I thought, that a complete stranger could drop out of the sky with enough equipment to fill a large truck and, merely by asking, get so much help and cooperation. So far there had been no question of payment. Either they didn't expect any or I, somehow, was supposed to know what to give them for their work.

Going downhill was fine as far as I was concerned, no effort at all. The jungle was thick, though, with brush close in on all sides and in many places overhead as well. We went through a field of grass that was at least ten feet high. I gawked so much at everything around me that I kept tripping over rocks and roots in the trail. The chief cut me a bamboo stick and, like a blind child, I felt my way along.

But if downhill was okay, the jungle nearly smothered me, and I could seldom see more than a few feet off the trail. The jungle was a solid mass of vines, trees, and brush all interlaced, forming a solid, almost impenetrable wall.

Then there were the leeches. As I walked down the trail I could see them sitting up, half their bodies waving around in the air, waiting for me to brush them with my foot or leg. When I did, they attached with such tenacity that pulling them off was a terrific job. In the first place, their bodies are covered with slime; to get a grip with my fingernails was next to impossible. Those fool slugs could crawl through the eye of a shoe or between the belt of my trousers and shirt—which some did. When they hit flesh, they sank in their jaws, excreting a fluid that frees blood of its usual ability to coagulate. Then they grew larger and larger as they drank my blood.

If, after they'd sunk their jaws, I tried to pull them off, their jaws remained, poisoning the wound and causing infection. One leech wouldn't have been hard to deal with, but the jungle was full of them, and they attached themselves by the dozens. They hung from trees, they were on the brush that whipped by bare arms on the trail, or they lay in wait in the mud. If a man should lie down on the grass for very long without taking precautions, the leeches would certainly have him.

But I only began to be aware of the leeches gradually and especially after I noticed that after about ten minutes of walking the Naga would stop and pick something off their bodies. Though I couldn't feel anything biting me, I began to look myself over. *My God*, I thought as I saw them on my legs. *I'm establishing a leech-head in Burma.* They were all over me. I tried to flick a few of the crowd off, but they'd catch onto my fingers and hang on. It was like trying to throw away chewing gum.

As I struggled, more climbed up my legs from the ground. I was being swamped with leeches. It made me almost panic-stricken; I wanted to run, to do anything to escape these weird, disgusting organisms. They turned what looked like a tropical walk in the woods into a nightmare. From there on, I, too, stopped every few minutes and pulled leeches. The natives in their bare feet and loin-cloths could see all the leeches that landed on them. Earlier I had thought of the Naga as nearly naked; now I thought of myself as over-clothed. With all my clothing, I was at a disadvantage, and it worried me to think about the leeches I couldn't see that were drinking away.

At the foot of the mountain we came to a river, a roaring torrent of water, all the more surprising because the thick growth had muffled its sound until we were almost upon it. The mountainside swept straight down to the stream, and at first it seemed impassable. But the trail had been chosen with care. Behind a huge boulder in the stream was a comparatively quiet pool, and in a second the men had stripped and were in it. The women, too, showed no hesitation as they joined in the swim.

The bath had a two-fold purpose: It was fun, and it washed off the leeches. Slightly abashed, I stripped and joined them. Women or no, the leeches had to go. When I took off my trousers I saw my legs were covered with the fat and blood-swollen creatures. The Nagas stopped their splashing and helped me pick them off my naked body. My crimson face, I guess they thought, must be getting sunburned.

By now the early coolness had passed. The sun was hot, and the cold water tumbling down out of some high place was refreshing. It was fun to stand there and watch these primitive people, unaffected by civilization, relax and enjoy themselves. But it was clear we had to move on. If the poor guy in the village we were making for was in serious shape, minutes might count. This time, though, I took a hint from these "primitives" and started out in nothing more than my shorts and boots. After all, this was their country; being nearly naked had obvious advantages.

So out of the water and up the mountain we started, and with each step uphill—and each new leech—it became hotter and hotter. The Naga are hill people, and hills are their business, but with me . . . well, hills are wonderful when you're flying over them or walking down them, but the Naga build their trails straight up and down a mountain. The trail went up in front of my face. If

I stuck out my tongue, I could have picked up a leech or two on it; and why not? They were everywhere else! I began using both hands and feet to make the grade.

For a while we followed the bed of a small secondary stream tumbling down the hill. The water rushing against my unsteady feet on the slippery rocks made walking not only difficult but hazardous. Where the bank of the stream was steepest was where the Naga, naturally, chose to climb out. We clambered along a slippery mud path for a while, sliding back half a step for every one we moved forward. Then we came to a fallen tree slanted upward across what looked like a shallow depression in the ground. Though the log's surface was covered with slippery moss, the Naga with their bare feet walked along it with ease. Then I tried it. It didn't look too bad: even if I did slide off, the ground below me was covered with foliage, or so I thought. About halfway up the log, my feet started slipping, and off I went, right through the foliage under which I expected to find the ground—but the ground was another ten feet down. The log had covered an overgrown ravine.

I landed stunned and bruised and a little shaken. My friend the chief threw me a vine and hauled me out, a somewhat embarrassed jungle novice. None of the Naga who were watching the performance laughed; I would have felt far better if they had. To the contrary, they seemed upset about the whole thing, which puzzled me. With the next log we came to like that one, they all stopped, laid down their packs, and built a bamboo railing for me. I felt rather silly but a hell of a lot safer, and I began to realize they were concerned that this big dumb American might hurt himself and ruin the whole trip.

On and on we chugged up the mountain, the hill people keeping up a running conversation as they climbed. I was thankful I was still able to breathe. Every cigarette I ever smoked came back to haunt me. The chief in front of me actually stopped once, lit an old pipe, and continued up the hill. How he did it I'll never know. The odor of that foul tobacco whipping past my nose cut down considerably on my oxygen supply.

It seemed forever, but we finally hit the top. And perched up there was a village, if I may call one house a village. I looked around for the lost pilot, but of course this wasn't the right village; we still had another mountain to climb.

By now it was around noon, and the sun was really pouring it on. The water in my canteen was about to boil—so was my blood, what blood the leeches had left me. All the Nagas jabbered to each other, and I staggered under the shade of the house. When I finally got the sweat out of my eyes enough to see, I lit a cigarette and looked around.

As soon as I did that, though, I had to pass cigarettes out to all the party. There went another pack. *The money I could make as a cigarette salesman out here after the war*, I thought as I passed them around to eager hands. Everyone quietly sat down for a smoke except one woman who stood in front of me holding a baby in her arms.

The baby was a cute little thing, except where there should have been hair there was nothing but a mass of scabs and running sores. Some of the scabs were dry and puckered and must have hurt the baby like hell. It was almost unimaginable to me, raised in America, that there should be a place where babies were raised without proper medical attention. I felt for the child and, though no doctor, thought there must be something I could do to help.

The mother handed me the baby, and, showing him a small bandage I carried that had a red cross on it, I asked the chief for the medical kit. He got the idea, unpacked a couple of baskets, and found it. First I washed the child's head with warm water and then smoothed the whole thing with boric acid ointment. I remembered that a doc had once used boric acid in my eyes, so I knew it probably wouldn't be too strong for the baby's tender skin. The salve I knew was needed to soften the scabs and relieve the pain, but that's about all I knew. I gave the mother a can of it and, through signs, was able to make her understand to put some on twice a day and to keep the child out of the sun.

All this treatment, though, must have given the Naga the impression I was a medicine man, for they all crowded around, each with a complaint. Here, I guess they thought, was a man who could help them with their aches and pains at last. My presence took on a new meaning for them, and they began clamoring for attention. Being human, I couldn't resist the temptation; also, I figured I could at least help them more than if they had no treatment at all. Naga after Naga came forward, many with the same trouble, infected leech bites. They were rather vicious-looking things in their later stages. Some of the holes looked like volcanoes and bore down to the bone. I opened each one with a sterilized knife, swabbed it clean, applied sulfa powder, and wrapped it with a bandage. I was doubtful about how much good I was doing, but it was at least an effort in the right direction. They all seemed satisfied with my treatment, though, for they went away smiling.

So far, I had been the great white savior that is until a case appeared that stopped me cold. A woman made her way over to me. She tapped her chest below the breast and grimaced. She was older than some of the girls and rather heavy, and her trouble might have been any number of things. But so as not to lose face with my new crowd of patients, I put on my best professional air: I thumped her chest with one hand tapping the other, put my head down as I had seen doctors do, and listened with an intent expression. Actually I couldn't hear a thing except one hand tapping the other, but I could see the Naga watching in wonderment.

After three or four thumps, I raised my head as if I had found the solution, a smile of assurance playing around my mouth. But the solution I'd found was to my trouble, not hers, for my eye had caught the caption on one of the bottles in the medical kit. It said "bicarbonate of soda, peppermint flavored." I solemnly unscrewed the top, handed her a couple of tablets, and told her to chew them by putting an imaginary pill in my mouth and chewing vigorously. The old gal put the two I'd handed her into her mouth and chewed. The effect was immediate: After rice all her life, the peppermint must have tasted swell. Her face lit up with evident enjoyment. From there on, after she told the rest, I had a dozen cases of chest pains, and my bottle was soon empty.

Other cases came forward as well—various infected cuts, punctures, and sores, and I fixed them all up, one after another. I was making friends by the dozen, and, frankly, I felt sorry for them. And, curiously, I began feeling friendship toward them as well. The fact is, I was learning to like these people. I liked them for their toughness and their willingness to help, for their friendliness and enthusiasm and quickness to smile, and for the way they trusted this oversized American stranger who had entered their lives by dropping out of the sky.

Eventually, we started out again. Though I still felt the urgency of getting to the pilot, by now I wasn't in so much of a hurry. My muscles ached, and my head swam. The thought of another grueling climb like that last mountain nauseated me. But off we went.

What goes up must go down, thank the Lord, because for us it was now down, but so steep and muddy that I spent most of my time sliding on what was left of my undershorts. The stones didn't bother my posterior much; it was the sharp roots that did it. Still, we made good time and soon reached another river. This one wasn't as large as the last one, but it was just as welcome. To the natives, who obviously knew this stream was coming, the trip down didn't seem so bad, but to me, who could see another half a day ahead with nothing but leech bites and the sweltering heat, it seemed longer than it was.

We shed our clothing again, and in we went. I took a moment to look at my feet, though, and they seemed like bloody stumps. Blisters everywhere. Then, when I jumped into the pool, damned if I didn't get almost swept downstream with the current. Going under, I grabbed the nearest hand. When I got back onto my feet and blew the water out of my lungs, I was able to mutter a meek "kajaiee." I looked at the person whose hand I had grabbed and who was now holding me up, and my face turned crimson; the big strong hero had been saved by a gal half his size . . . and she wasn't hard on the eyes either. Mumbling at the vagaries of fate, I felt like a country bumpkin, but she smiled at me as if she saved stupid Americans every day. I smiled back . . . and we began to pick leeches off each other. It was fascinating, too, to see where a quick-eyed girl with nimble fingers could think of to look for leeches. I was becoming accustomed to this primitive way of life and began to think it an inviting way to live.

The stream, of course, was at the bottom of the mountain we'd just descended, but to me it had been the top of the day. But from here on it was up, up, forever up. I was so slow that even the women, burdened as they were with packs, pulled away from me. I just couldn't keep up. No longer was I walking: stumbling and struggling were more the words for it. Climb a hill for an hour, most of us can do, but when it comes to climbing them all day— give me a streetcar. Two hours after we left that stream, I was about finished. I kept thinking of Rudyard Kipling's poem "If." The line kept running through my head—"And so hold on when there is nothing in you . . . you'll be a man, my son!" Hell, I didn't have anything in me now, and I didn't care if I ever was a man. All I wanted at that point was to lie down and die.

I thought I was beginning to imagine things when I heard the sound of airplane motors, but I wasn't. I grabbed the little radio and lay down on the ground and started calling. An opportunity to rest my weary bones is about all it meant to me; I was so exhausted I'd almost forgotten why I was in this hell. I was so hot, so tired, so wet from sweat it had become a battle just to keep moving.

The cool, firm voice that came out of the set brought me around a little. It was Andy. "Where the hell are you, boy?"

"You've got me," I answered. "But where I am is hell sure enough, though I haven't been introduced to Satan yet."

"Well, get on the ball, Diebold. You haven't got all day, you know."

The injustice of it, I thought. He sits up there in a nice cool cockpit in a blue sky I can barely make out through the foliage, turning a wheel, and telling me to get to work. I counted to ten and then answered him. "Give us four more hours, and I should be with the body, I think."

"Four hours. Okay, we'll be back then, but hurry up."

I was so mad at the absurdity of it that I beat the hot, steaming jungle floor with my fists while the chief, who had come back down the trail to find out what the fuss was about, clucked his disapproval. Andy had only been riding me, but it was tough to take at that point. It was just as well that I didn't speak the chief's language, for I'm certain if I had I would have been in for a fatherly lecture on temperament.

Wearily we ploughed ahead. My throat was raw from the quick gasps of hot air. *Somewhere this God-awful churning of the legs and sweat in the eyes must end*, I thought.

It was unexpected when it happened. Around the corner of some heavy brush, they came into view, the most beautiful sight I'd ever seen—two Naga houses. To me, instead of being surrounded by mud and filth, those two huts seemed made of ice cream and peppermint candy. There's no describing what reaching the ultimate goal is like when everything inside you tells you that you'll never make it. It's like a gambler raking in an unbelievable pile of winnings. Home never looked better.

I staggered to the nearest log, slumped down on it, and simply stared at those huts. They were only a hundred yards away, but I didn't think I'd make it even that far. Tomorrow, the day after, or a thousand days after that, I didn't think I'd be able to move again.

But when I'd regained my breath I thought better of it and made my way up to the largest of the two huts. On the porch stood a wrinkled old man, a welcoming committee of one. My native friends were standing below the porch looking at the old man, and all were talking at once.

As I approached, the jabbering ceased. I stood with the crowd and looked at the old man, too. "We're in the wrong village again," I moaned. "Not that. I simply can't go any farther." The old man spoke a few words to me, none of which, of course, I could understand, and then he motioned me up on the porch. I climbed the notched log and entered the house after him. As tired as I was, I was getting excited. Was he there?

I peered into the dimly lit front room. Over by the fire I could see the outline of a form stretched out on the floor. I walked over to it, afraid of what I might find, but he was there, lying by the fire, the back of his head toward me. But was he alive?

He twisted around, and I saw his face, and tears were running down his cheeks. Neither of us said a word. I knelt beside him, and we gripped hands. It was impossible to say anything; I was too choked with emotion. I tried an experimental smile, but it was forced, for even though he was alive I thought even now we might be too late. He looked to me as if he were on his way out of this lovely world of ours as he lay there softly sobbing.

He was covered with dirty pieces of cloth, so all I could see of him was his face; but that was enough. It told a horrible story of suffering and starvation and exposure. His beard was long and tangled, his hair spread like a woman's on the log he was using as a pillow. The bones of his cheeks stood out in ugly relief below yellowing, bulging eyes. He spoke, through cracked, fever-ridden lips. "Thank the Almighty. You've come."

I spoke with all the unfelt confidence I could muster. "Right you are, lad, and a couple of doctors will be here in a minute. We'll have you running as good as new in no time and out of this fire trap in a jiffy."

He smiled at my slang, and I realized it must have been a long time since he'd heard any language but Naga. He closed his eyes and gave a long sigh. I was afraid this was it, but then he opened them again. "Have you any food?"

"Coming right up," I answered. "Would some nice warm cereal fit the bill?"

"Of course," he said and closed his eyes. I have never made cereal faster. As I cooked, I could see his hands; they were nothing but bones covered with a layer of skin. He was a human skeleton.

When the food was ready, I fed him. All he was able to take were a few spoonfuls and a couple of sips of tea; he was exhausted from the effort. He seemed to go to sleep or he was in a coma, I couldn't tell. I lifted the dirty burlap the natives had covered him with for an examination. He opened his eyes again when I did this. I hoped my face remained normal when I looked, but my stomach turned inside-out. He was all bones, and his legs and body were covered with huge, ulcerous sores. He was looking at me hard, and I had to say something, so I smiled and said, "Prickly heat, eh?" It was a poor attempt at humor, but he managed a feeble grin.

This boy needed a doctor in the worst way. I began praying for the rescue ship to come. This was too much for my first-aid knowledge of medicine. I replaced the sacking and started talking to him, anything to make him feel better. It seemed to help. As I talked, I could see him improve . . . or at least to become more alert. It made him feel safer. Another American was there, he was rescued.

He told me, in a weak voice, that his name was Greenlaw W. Collins (he actually gave his middle initial) and that he was from New Orleans. I took up the conversation and talked about New Orleans since, luckily, I had been there. He liked to hear me talk of his home, it was easy to see. He mumbled in the middle of one of my sentences that it had been his first Hump trip and his last, he hoped. I assured him he was on his way back to New Orleans as of right now.

"I was flying a pea shooter"—a fighter—"and had engine trouble," he said. "The plane went into a spin, so I had to bail out. I landed in a tree and lost my jungle kit, so I had no food. I followed a river I found. How long I don't know, but it was over three weeks."

Out in this country for more than three weeks without a knife, a compass, food, or anything. This boy was tough, and then some.

"The natives found me going down the river and brought me on a litter up here. Don't know how long that was, I lost track of the days. On the way down that river, I slept on rocks in the middle of the water to get away from the leeches and the animals. My shoes wore out, and the rocks cut my feet to ribbons. It was tough going at times. The natives here have been trying to feed me. It's pretty awful stuff, monkey meat and rice and then rice and monkey meat. I just sorta lost my appetite, I guess."

No wonder, I thought, remembering the smell of burning hair before the meal at the other village. A piece of soot fell from the roof onto his face. He raised a shaking hand and brushed it off.

"Did you get my note?" he asked.

"Yep, that's why I'm here."

"Never thought you would. I thought sure I was a goner. You know, it took me a whole day to write it."

Talking was an effort, and he rested a bit. He closed his eyes, but in a moment he spoke again.

"Didja see those sores on my legs?"

"Yes."

"Well, once they got me here I kept 'em open with a native knife. I thought I had better keep them running. That was right, wasn't it?"

"Perfect. You'll be up and running in a week."

"Thanks," he said with a wry smile. I wasn't fooling him, I could see that.

He told me a little more, and I learned other details later, like his eating bamboo shoots, bitter berries, and even leeches! He talked about the soaking rains, using his socks as gloves and wrapping up his head at night to escape the mosquitoes and crawling pests. In that fetid, humid jungle, his boots rotted and started to fall apart. And most of all he mentioned the cold, how awful cold the nights got, and the terrible, solitary loneliness of that sea of green.

But mostly he seemed to drift in and out of focus. There was no doubt his had been a close thing. What I was worried about was that it was a close thing still, that if we didn't get help there soon, he might not make it.

Then I heard it—the search plane approaching the village. It was faint at first, but in less than a minute it sounded as if the pilot had brought the plane right down in the hut with us. Collins heard it, too, and looked at me.

"Here come your doctors."

I went out on the porch and turned on the radio. Andy's voice came over the ear-phone. "Air rescue calling gravel shuffler. Air rescue calling gravel shuffler."

I was in no mood for jokes right then. "Yeah, this is gravel shuffler, and we need medical help down here as soon as you can get it."

"Stand by, Diebold," he answered. "I've got the docs on board, and they'll be right down. How bad is he?"

"He's not too good. Tell them to bring the works as far as equipment goes. And may they be young and strong, for this is no country for the feeble."

"Will do," Andy answered. "And they look pretty big and strong to me."

The plane circled around, and I knew just how those two medicos felt as the big C-47 skimmed down the side of the far mountain. It shot up the side of our mountain and over the village and then a parachute blossomed from the rear. It was exciting to watch from the ground and not a little satisfying. But then the wind caught the falling chute, and it disappeared over the far side of the mountain. I wished the boy luck and then turned to the chief and pointed in the direction the chute had gone. He immediately sent two of his men on the run in that direction.

"Pretty lousy aim," I radioed Andy. "It shouldn't take more than two days to find him out there." He deserved that dig after the gravel shuffler guff he'd been handing me.

Andy didn't answer. Around again came the plane, and the sprawling, tumbling figure of a man flew out of the cargo door of the ship. The figure tumbled and fell straight down, but the chute didn't open. It was free fall, no paratrooper chute! I could see the doctor's arms flailing in the air as his hand grasped for the ripcord and missed. My knees turned to water as I stood there holding my breath. I didn't want to look, but I couldn't tear my eyes away. The sensation of helplessness was awful.

It seemed almost too late when he finally found the ripcord and the chute opened. The canopy streamed out and snapped open above his head, and a split second later he hit the ground. As I ran to where he hit, I hoped and prayed it had opened in time to break his fall. I expected to find him with his hips driven up between his eyebrows. As the natives and I approached on a dead run, he slowly sat up and shook his head.

"My God," he said to no one in particular, "I thought I'd had it."

The doc had landed in soft mud at least six inches deep, the chute slowing his fall and the mud cushioning his landing. That was all that saved him from being seriously injured. He was a big man, over six feet with wide, husky shoulders. After I helped him to his feet, he stuck out his hand, and we shook. His fingers were long and narrow but strong. He had a grip like a vise. This must be the surgeon, and did we need him! "My name's Spruell," he said, "although it was damn near mud." We both laughed in relief. "Bill to my friends. I'll look after the patient. You had better try and find our friend. He's somewhere over in that . . ." He waved his hand in the general direction the other chute had fallen.

"The natives have already gone after him," I said. "Don't worry, they'll get him. They've been a big help. Come on, I'll take you to see Lieutenant Collins. He needs you fast, and I'm not foolin.'"

Suddenly I remembered the radio. Andy's voice squawked out at me, "Get on the air, gravel shuffler, get on the air, will ya' before I have to bail out and find out what's goin' on."

"Everything's going to be all right, Andy," I said as the major and I walked toward the hut. As I spoke, I saw the figure of a white man with some natives come limping out of the jungle above the village. "Everything *is* all right," I corrected. "Everyone accounted for and unhurt as far as I can tell."

"Whew! I'm sure happy as hell about that. They had me plenty worried."

"Don't think for a minute they weren't worried, too."

"Right," he said. "Is there anything else you want?"

"Better stick around for a few minutes until the doc takes a look at Collins. He may need more supplies than we have here, although I can't see what it'd be except a kitchen sink or something."

"If he wants one, tell him we'll drop it."

Around us the natives had gone wild. This was too much for them, a big noisy airplane swooping over the mountain, men dropping from the skies all over the place.

Inside the hut, the major took a quick look at Collins while I laid out the medical supplies dropped to me the day before. The major rummaged through them. "Tell them all I need is some glycerin."

I told Andy who radioed back, "O.K., I'll be back with it in the morning. Good luck, old top."

Up the notched log came the other parachutist. We shook hands, and he introduced himself as Captain "Sandy" Morrissey from Milwaukee, Wisconsin.

The two doctors went immediately to work on Collins. I watched them start to give him blood plasma, and though I wanted to help they didn't seem to need me. Then I thought I'd better be paying off the natives who had helped bring the stuff over from the other village; they might want to go home again. I opened the pack I'd carried and took out my bag of silver rupees. I went down the ladder and tried to hand each of the natives a couple, but they wouldn't take them from me. Instead, they pointed to the chief, so I turned to him and gave him a handful. He took them, went around to each of the natives, and handed them one apiece, then he handed the remainder back to me, keeping one himself.

One rupee, about thirty cents American for all that work. I handed the chief back the extra rupees, enough for another round, and motioned that he give them to the others. Everyone looked highly pleased. Sixty cents for all that mountain climbing burdened down with heavy packs, and they considered it high wages. *What a place to retire*, I thought.

EIGHT.

Gunslingers

The Pilots Remember

James P. Busha

LT. COL. ROBERT J. GOBEL
31st Fighter Group, 308th Fighter Squadron, 12th Air Force

By the time I arrived in the MTO, I had over 240 hours of fighter time in Curtiss P-40 Warhawks and Bell P-39 Airacobras. I had dueled fellow squadron mates over the well-protected and Axis-absent skies above Panama. I thought the P-40 was a great block of concrete with wings on it, but given a little time and opportunity, I thought I could do all right with it. The Airacobra was another story.

I was young and naive and christened with the title "fighter pilot." I thought the P-39 was a good plane, but at the time I just didn't know any better. It had some very tricky flight characteristics to it and you had to honor those if you wanted to stay alive. In retrospect, I was glad I didn't have to go up against the highly maneuverable Bf 109 with it. Actually, it was a greater danger to American pilots than it was to the Germans. In fact, years after the war, I had mentioned to Luftwaffe ace Gunther Rall about my flying the P-39 in training. Gunther smiled at me and said, "We [the Luftwaffe] were very familiar with the P-39; we loved them!"

When I was deemed combat-ready, with no actual combat, I was shipped overseas. Shoehorned aboard a Liberty ship full of other combat-bound servicemen for twenty-one days, we bobbed on the Atlantic Ocean, dodging U-boats, until I finally arrived in Oran, Algeria, in early 1944. From there I was sent to the 12th Air Force fighter training center at Telergma, which was the former home of a French Foreign Legion outpost. Unfortunately, we were not living the comfortable high life as our brother pilots were in the European Theater of Operations (ETO). About the only thing we did have in common was our great affection for flying the Spitfire.

I had just been assigned to the 31st Fighter Group, 308th Fighter Squadron of the 12th Air Force. Our group along with the 52nd Fighter Group was to receive training in the Spitfire Mk V in preparation for our role as a close air support unit flying Spitfire Mk VIIIs and IXs. The Spitfire was a recognized front-line fighter and a proven combat veteran. For me the Spit was a true joy to fly—light on the controls, very nimble, and highly maneuverable—very different from anything else I had flown previously. It turned on a dime, and it was easy to see why the Brits loved it.

The only issue I had with them was that they had short legs: We couldn't carry enough fuel to carry the attack long distances. Although the cockpit was snug, I felt as though I was an extension of the airplane. Inside the cockpit the layout was a little different than the American fighters I had flown. Instead of a straight stick, the Spit had a lovely loop control that took no time getting used to. I was elated at flying the Spitfire and looked forward to the day I would fly it in combat.

Unfortunately, that day never came. After receiving 20 to 25 hours of familiarization time, our group of recently trained Spitfire pilots was moved to the home of the 31st Fighter Group at Castel Volturno. It was a very short stay. Without warning, we were removed from operational flying, told to turn in our Spitfires, and transferred to the 306th Fighter Wing of the 15th Air Force. We were also told that our new combat assignment would now be bomber escort, and we would be flying an airplane that was a cousin to the Spitfire called the P-51 Mustang. Although the Mustang was faster than the Spitfire, it was not quite as nimble.

It was fun to fly while it lasted, and I will always have fond memories of the Supermarine Spitfire.

Lt. J. D. "Jerry" Collinsworth
31st Fighter Group, 307th Fighter Squadron, 12th Air Force
Tunis, Algeria

When the group switched over to the Spitfire Mk IX from the war-weary Mk V, it changed our squadron's whole outlook on life. The new and improved Spitfire made me turn from a defensive mind-set to an offensive one. The Spitfire Mk IX could still out-turn the Fw 190, and in some cases, we could still outclimb and outrun them as well.

Most of the time, though, it was the Germans who were on the run! I went from horrifying and scary looks in the cockpit to beating and thumping my chest in triumph as we tangled with the Luftwaffe over the deserts of North Africa.

On May 6, 1943, I was in a flight of four Spitfire Mk IXs cruising over Tunis, Algeria, at 10,000 feet. Leading our finger-four formation was our squadron commander, Maj. George LaBresche. I had flown a Spitfire Mk V with Major LaBresche on one of the missions over Dieppe, France, in August of 1942, where we both barely survived by the skin of our teeth.

Times had changed and we were now itching to fight. It didn't take long to find a scrap to get into as my wingman, Johnny White, spotted a pair of Fw 190s above us. After receiving the okay from the major to attack them, Johnny and I pointed the noses of our Spitfires skyward and went tearing after them.

Johnny and I were a great team, and we always knew what the other was thinking as we closed in to attack. I got behind the number-two Fw 190 and gave him a short squirt of machine-gun and cannon fire, until I saw his canopy come off, and then I stopped firing and watched him bail out. I broke to the right to clear my tail and continued through a full 360-degree turn. I looked for Johnny but I couldn't find him anywhere, as the sky was empty except for the billowing white parachute a quarter-mile away.

Seeing no other German airplanes in the area, I decided to go back and give this guy in the parachute the once-over. As I closed in on him, hanging in his straps, I pulled some power back on the Spitfire and stared at him through my open canopy. This guy had just made me one step closer to becoming an ace, so I wanted to thank him. I placed my thumb on my nose and moved my fingers back and forth, waving at him. It was a hell of an insult to him, but I'm sure he was glad I wasn't shooting at him as he hung helpless in that parachute.

After I had my fun, I split-assed out of there and headed for home.

Pilot/Officer John Keller
680 Squadron RCAF
PRU Spitfire Mk XI

I had great sympathy for the poor British during the dark days known as the Battle of Britain. Reading about their plight, I wished that I could do something good to help instead of attending those lavish parties that they were giving at Harvard while I was there as a senior. I had taken a short course in something called the Civilian Pilot Training Program in 1940 and became immediately interested in flying while at the controls of a J-3 Cub.

Although I was desperate to join the fight, I knew I didn't have enough money to get to England. I did have enough to get to Canada, however, which was only a hop, skip, and a jump for me. I dropped out of Harvard in late 1941, ran to Canada, and joined the Royal Canadian Air Force (RCAF), training with them for ten months. One of the airplanes I trained in was ironically called the Harvard, the Canadian version of the AT-6. In November of 1941, I got married and then two weeks later I was on a troopship bound for England.

When I arrived in England I was told there were no aircraft for us; they were all in the air currently defending the British Isles. We were "volunteered" to go to the Middle East, where allegedly aircraft would be readily available. I embarked on a long two-month trip that took us around the Cape of Good Hope up to Egypt. From there I was sent out to Libya to an advanced landing ground. My further flight training became all fouled up due to one Desert Fox—Gen. Erwin Rommel and his Afrika Korps, as they pushed us backward for two months, losing one airfield after another.

Although I had earned my wings and was deemed a fighter pilot, I was stuck shepherding a petrol bowser to the Nile Delta. From there I was shipped up to Syria and met a delightful chap named Geoffrey Morley-Mower who became my instructor as I acquainted myself with the Hawker Hurricane.

I really thought the Hurricane was a dog. It was very clumsy and very difficult to fly, but it won the Battle of Britain. The Spitfire had a much better public relations team and received all the credit for saving Old Blighty, but it was in fact the Hurricane that saved the day. I never flew the Hurricane all that well even though I was offered a choice when I completed my training: fly a Hurricane on the deck with 40mm cannons sticking out of the wings, or fly as high as I could up at altitude with nothing in the wings for protection and only a couple of cameras stuffed inside the fuselage as part of the photoreconnaissance unit (PRU). I chose to be on the deck, but my instructors must have seen how I handled a Hurricane, so they sent me up high, unarmed and very afraid.

I joined 680 Squadron and stayed with them for the rest of the war. I was introduced to the Spitfire Mk I and II, which I thought were beautiful airplanes, one in which I thought I could cope, and manage quite well. Sitting in the cockpit, your shoulders were only about an inch away from both sides, and it felt like you were part of the airplane—an integral part, if you will. In the air it was a delight to fly. It had a lot of power, even though it was the same Merlin engine that was in the Hurricane: a 1,655-hp Rolls-Royce. The "poor" bloody British had no extra money for joyrides or extra engine hours, so I really didn't get much time flying for the fun of it.

Our training field in Beirut was interesting, to say the least. We had two runways that formed a big X. One was concave and the other convex, which made for some very interesting landings on my part—but I survived. Every hour was mainly spent flying over occupied Europe. In reality, I only had 15 to 20 hours of Spit time before I was sent out on missions over Europe doing photographic reconnaissance.

Most of my flights departed from Libya, flying over the north coast of Africa out over the Mediterranean and then photographing the airfields, marshaling yards, and harbors of Greece and the surrounding islands. For almost all of my PRU flights, I was operating at between 25,000 and 30,000 feet or above, unpressurized, unarmed, and shit-scared!

We started out with the Mk I Spits and ended up with the Mk XI. The Mk XI was my favorite, of course; it was a pure delight to fly, as it had a retractable tail wheel and it was supercharged. You would be happily cruising along at 12,000 or 13,000 feet and the supercharger would kick in and give you a great big boost in the tail as you slammed back in your seat while your airspeed jumped another 20 to 25 miles per hour.

Our 680 Squadron was a wonderful outfit, full of nice guys, made up of all kinds of nationalities, including Tasmanians, Australians, Canadians, and this one lone American—me! Our Spitfires matched our pilots in the unit: we were not a very pretty bunch. Both men and airplanes were downright filthy looking.

Below all the dust and dirt was a dark blue fuselage that was chipped and dented. Our Spitfires weren't fancy looking, but they sure could go high!

Thankfully we had nice long runways both in Cyprus and Libya as our Spits operated from Lancaster bomber bases, and it felt like extra security to land and take off from these. We carried two F24 Fairchild cameras weighing 21 pounds apiece that were behind the cockpit, embedded in the fuselage. To operate them we had one little control on the dashboard where you could turn the camera on and vary the interval between each picture, so almost every spot on the ground was taken twice from a different angle. That way the analyzers could do stereoscopic views of the ground.

The interpreters used to work far into the night interpreting our images and gleaning wonderful amounts of information about the ships being loaded, how many fighters and bombers the Germans had on a particular airfield, or what kind of supplies were in the marshaling yards. This intelligence proved invaluable to mission planners, as our bombers would return to where our lone Spits had once been.

In all of my eighty-one missions, I was only shot at twice over Crete when the German flak guns targeted me. The scary part is, when you are all alone you know exactly who they are firing at!

On another trip when I was returning from a recon over Europe, the engine suddenly began to run rough. It felt as if it was shaking the Spitfire apart and I could barely maintain my altitude. I was concerned that I was going to have to set in down in the drink with a swim in the Mediterranean. Thankfully the northern coast of Libya was now underneath me, so I switched off the engine and was shocked to see what was staring at me from out in front of my nose. Lo and behold, there was one foot missing off one of my wooden prop blades and two feet off another blade. I didn't recall being shot at, and the only way I can account for the damaged blades was because of icing—or gremlins!

Cold temperatures were always an issue, and one of the problems with carrying these bloody cameras up so high was that half of our heat had to be pumped in the back to keep the camera toasty warm while we as the pilots were freezing!

Most of my flights were 3.75 hours, and that was about the duration. With only 270 imperial gallons of fuel in the wings, we couldn't fly much longer than that. On one trip I clocked 400 mph coming out and 400 mph coming back—a tailwind each way. Who could ask for anything better!

The only defensive weapon I carried was a Very pistol to shoot flares up if we had to bail out over the Med and paddle around in my dinghy. When I flew my missions I usually wore a bright red shirt, for a couple of reasons: One was as a good luck charm, and the other, more important reason was the fact that if I ever went down in the sea, I was hopeful the air-sea rescue chaps would spot me a mile away—and that the Germans were color-blind!

The only German aircraft I had encountered were below me, as I took photos of them at their bases. Thankfully they didn't have good radar; otherwise, they would have been up there waiting for us and we would have been as helpless as church mice surrounded by a bunch of ravenous alley cats. The Me 109 was a fearsome opponent and quite deadly for any PRU pilot.

I had the opportunity to transfer into the United States Army Air Forces (USAAF) and wind up who knows where and flying who knows what. I had been flying high over Europe every two or three days, in an airplane that I thoroughly enjoyed and was with a group of men that were a delight to be with on a daily basis. Needless to say, I never made any application and let the deadline lapse.

After the war, as a reward for serving with the RCAF, they sent me a check once a month so I could apply it to my schooling back at Harvard. But my personal reward had been even greater: being allowed to fly a Spitfire.

Lt. Peter A. McDermott, USAAC
71st Tactical Reconnaissance Group, New Guinea

I guess you could say I really paid for my sins at an early age—all because of my "big Irish mouth." I was kicked out of a Liaison Squadron in 1943 and sent to a newly established home for troublemakers and wayward pilots—the Tactical Reconnaissance Group (TAC/RECON). There I was introduced to the most God-awful airplane, the Bell P-39 Airacobra. To be brutally honest, the Cobra had its fangs removed and was more or less a "paper tiger" in the sky. The P-39 was outclassed by just about every airplane the enemy had. Having no class myself, though, I felt right at home in the little fighter, and exploited its limited strengths in combat.

On paper, the P-39 seemed like a first-rate fighter. With a huge 37mm cannon sticking out of the nose along with two .30 caliber machine guns and an additional pair of .50 caliber machine guns in each wing, the Cobra should have had a deadly bite. Unfortunately, it turned out to be more of a dog with an intermittent bark and very little bite. First off, the cannon was a complete joke; it seemed that it worked one out of ten times in combat. With a thirty-round capacity we were lucky to get a few rounds to fire before it jammed on us. Combat was a serious matter, but it was comical to be flying in trail behind other P-39s on a strafing run as the pilots flew all over the sky trying to stay on target and charge the cannon at the same time.

I watched as guys around me pounded their fists bloody on the charging handles trying to get that damn cannon to fire—hell, I've got scars of my own! Thinking back on it, I wish I would have spent more time with the armament people to learn more about what made this popgun tick. Thankfully for us, though, we never encountered any Japanese fighters over New Guinea where we were based. With our limited fuel range and lack of altitude capabilities, we couldn't fly far or high enough to engage them even if we had wanted to. Most of our missions were down low anyway, strafing Japanese ground and barge targets. The P-39 was definitely in its element at these treetop levels; even if the cannon didn't work, those machine guns could tear the enemy apart.

On a few occasions, we even went so far as to turn the P-39 into a dive-bomber. We would strap a 250-pound bomb to our belly and stagger up to 14,000 feet where both airplane and pilot were out of breath. Leveling off, we simply pushed the nose over and rode the Cobra back down, releasing the bomb over the target. We got pretty good at it and hit some of our targets most of the time.

The flip side of flying this low, however, came at a very high price. We lost most of our guys in combat from the accurate flak and ground fire we encountered on these missions. Make no mistake: The P-39 could take some hits—it just couldn't take a lot of them. I must admit that although I was a harsh critic of the Cobra's fighting abilities and considered it a miserable mutt to fight with, the P-39 was a loyal dog; it always brought me back home in one piece.

Capt. William B. Overstreet Jr., USAAC
357th Fighter Group, 363rd Fighter Squadron

When the war broke out in December of 1941, I knew the only way I could do my part for the war effort was to become a fighter pilot. The only problem was that I had to survive flight training in order to make it safely into combat!

I began flying the PT-17 Stearman in California at an air base run by the world-famous aerobatic champion, Tex Rankin. Tex's attitude on flying must have rubbed off on my instructor, Carl Aarslet, because he challenged me right out of the chute.

I only had a few hours of stick time in the Stearman when Carl grabbed the stick from me while we were on a downwind leg to land. He flipped us on over, shut off the engine, and yelled through the Gosport tube, "Now you land it." Instinctively I quarter-rolled the PT-17 into a left turn, lined it up with the runway, and greased it on the mains—after a few bounces, of course! Carl was testing me to see if I would panic or if I had what it took to become a military pilot. I believe Carl directed me down the right path in becoming a fighter pilot. Everything I learned about unusual attitudes was later put to the test when I climbed into the cockpit of a P-39 Airacobra.

I honestly loved the looks of the P-39. It was really a beautiful airplane, very modern looking, especially with a tricycle landing gear, a rear mounted Allison in-line engine, and cockpit doors that looked like they belonged on a car. I rather enjoyed flying the P-39, but for some strange reason it didn't like me very much; the P-39 kept on trying to kill me! It probably didn't help that the CG (center of gravity) was way off. With the engine situated behind the pilot, a 37mm fully loaded cannon sticking out between your legs, and a propeller driveshaft, it always flew out of balance. Heck, it was so sensitive that it would sometimes fly off on its own whenever it felt like it. Usually we could correct its gyrations, but sometimes it totally ignored the guy behind the windscreen throwing the stick all over the place, trying to keep it from wandering off on its own.

When I joined the 363rd Fighter Squadron in Santa Rosa, California, they had just returned from shooting up and bombing the deserts near Tonopah, Nevada. I heard wild stories from some of the vets of the squadron, including my good friend, Bud Anderson, telling me about the bad vices of the Airacobra—tumbling, to be exact. Some of the guys recited a lyric they used to put to a song that went like this, "It'll tumble and spin and soon auger in!"

Fortunately I was young and foolish and couldn't wait for my checkout. Most of my early flights were led by Lloyd Hubbard, who was not only a real good stick but fearless as well. He would take our flight of four P-39s on some low-level work, and at times it felt like we were only inches away from going underground!

And if that wasn't excitement enough, he would lead us up near San Francisco where we played a game of follow the leader, looping the Golden Gate Bridge. Of course we received complaints from the locals, but with a war going on you could practically get away with most anything.

Looping a bridge in a P-39 was really fun, but the fun soon faded away on one particular flight in late June of 1943. I had been out practicing aerobatics—loops, rolls, and tight turns. I must have done something to make the P-39 mad at me, because all of a sudden the Airacobra began to tumble. No matter what direction I threw my stick in—right, left, forward, or rearward—the P-39 ignored my imputes. It was time to bail out. We had been warned, of course, about not pulling the ripcord too soon—so we didn't hit the stabilizer on our way out—but at the moment it was mere trivia, because I was having a hard time getting out. Try as I might I couldn't budge the cockpit doors because of the building pressure against them.

As I squirmed around inside of the cockpit, trying to figure a way out, I was able to shoulder one of the doors while pushing the other one with my knee. That seemed to work, and I was able to pop a door off. I squeezed out of the tumbling P-39, waited a second, and pulled my ripcord as soon as I was clear. I felt a violent tug of the chute as it blossomed above me and a few seconds later my feet hit the ground. The P-39 had beaten me to the ground by mere seconds because when I landed, I was surrounded by cannon shells and my bent propeller—everything else was twisted metal.

The next day I hunted down my parachute packer and thanked him for a job well done.

I would be far from the last guy to bail out of a tumbling P-39 in training. Unfortunately, some guys weren't as lucky and were unable to get out in time. The P-39 was definitely a tricky little fighter with some unique quirks, but it taught me how to become an aggressive fighter pilot, and the tactics I learned from flying the Airacobra kept me alive over the skies of Europe.

Col. Kermit E. Bliss, USAF, and
Lt. Col. John S. Blyth, USAF

The Allied ground and air commanders knew early on that in battle, the person or "team" with the best set of eyes held a decisive advantage over their opponent. Target selection, bomb damage assessment, troop movements, and current, up-to-the-minute information on what the enemy was doing and where it was hiding was placed in the hands of a shadowy group of pilots known as the PRU—the Photographic Reconnaissance Unit. In order to be accurate and successful on these missions, the air corps needed a plane that was fast, stable, and maneuverable, one that could reach high altitudes while penetrating deep into enemy airspace. They also had to fly these missions unarmed and alone. The pilots of the 7th Photo Group, 14th Photo Squadron, stationed at Mount Farm air base in England, blindly put their faith and trust in a Reverse Lend-Lease aircraft the British painted baby blue.

The needs and wants of the air corps came in the form of a battle-tested proven fighter whose lineage was flown by so few for so many during the Battle of Britain. Removed from these aircraft were guns and British roundels, replaced by gas, American Stars and Bars, and cameras.

Hidden under a coat of powder blue paint was the unmistakable elliptical wing that supported a graceful and streamlined fuselage that housed its "heart and soul": a 1,655-hp Rolls Royce Merlin engine. The Mk IX and Mk XI Supermarine Spitfires became the Blue Eyes of the 8th.

When I was commissioned in early 1942, we had a choice of fighters, medium and heavy bombers, and something called PROTU. Someone in our group asked the lieutenant in charge what that last choice meant. The lieutenant scratched his head for a minute and said out loud, "Protu—protu? I don't know; must be some damn Indian name!"

No one signed up for this mysterious, unknown acronym, and that gave the air corps a problem. There were a certain number of bodies that were committed to be sent to PROTU, so a well-proven, scientific solution was devised: Everyone whose last name started with A, B, or C was quickly volunteered.

As part of the 14th Photo Squadron, I was sent to Colorado Springs, Colorado, where I began training in Lockheed P-38s and found that PROTU meant Photographic Reconnaissance Operational Training Unit. Instead of guns and cannons, I shot with cameras. After almost a year of high- and low-altitude photo reconnaissance training over the United States, we were deemed combat ready and sent to jolly old England.

For the next ten months I flew alone, unarmed and unafraid (?!) over flak-infested enemy territory in F4 and F5 Photo Recon Lightnings, taking pre- and post-strike photos for 8th Air Force Bomber Command. I also did a lot of aerial mapping over the Continent in preparation for the invasion. The P-38 was a stable camera platform, but when loaded up with gas and film, we couldn't get to higher, safer altitudes, trying to avoid German fighters and flak.

Bomber Command also wanted intelligence on German factories and other industrial targets located deep inside the fatherland. The P-38 was stretched to its limit on range and altitude capability. We knew we could get to the targets okay, but on some missions, with the throttles to the stops, we didn't think we could make it back to England with both motors turning. P-38s didn't float very well in the English Channel either!

Our British counterparts held the answer to our dilemma. The Brits had been flying Spitfires all over German airspace at such high altitudes and they never really had trouble with the Luftwaffe. At altitude, the Spitfire sipped gasoline compared with the gulping gas consumption of the Lightnings. And yet, as the Spitfire burned off fuel, it flew higher and faster.

Another great advantage the Spitfire had was it had parts made out of fabric. German radar had a hard time detecting it compared to the 19,000-pound all aluminum-skinned P-38s that seemed to attract every flak gun we overflew. Most of the planes lost in our group fell to German 88s and their accurate flak barrages.

The Spitfire was a delight to fly. Each Spitfire we received from Vickers was a handmade piece of art, and, of course, each one flew differently. The Spit was very agile and required little stick movement to get it to do what you wanted. You just simply thought about it and it moved. With the guns removed and two K-52 cameras installed in the fuselage, I took one up to see how high I could get it.

Filling up both wing tanks and strapping on a belly tank, we were theoretically 2,000 pounds, overloaded for takeoff on those little bitty donut tires. If you blew one on takeoff, you were certain to become a torch burning bright on English soil. Directional control was crisp and coordinated as I lifted off from Mount Farm.

The golden rule in reconnaissance was that you fly if it's clear over the target area. It didn't matter if our base was fogged over, rained on, or snow-packed, as long as the other end was clear, or at least predicted to be. By the time I left our base and was over the Channel, I had hit 30,000 feet and was still indicating 100 feet per minute. I passed through 37,000 feet and with a kick in the tail from the jet stream I was zipping along on my way to Germany.

Eighty percent of the 8th Air Force intelligence for Bomber Command came from photo recon. We went in first and took pictures of target possibilities. With hard evidence inside our cameras, the intelligence people evaluated the photos to see if they were suitable targets. Working factories, marshaling yards, aerodromes, V-1 sites, and anything else of interest were photographed by our unit.

After the target was selected and the bombers sent on their way, we hung in the background to await the devastation and destruction that would soon follow. Orbiting at well above 30,000 feet, my cameras froze a moment in time as smoke and dust cleared over the target area. Sometimes the bomber pilots didn't like us too well.

The bomber boys would come back from a mission and report "We really clobbered it! Scratch one factory!" Unfortunately for them, on some missions their eyes or nerves played tricks on them and their reports did not add up. After their B-17s and B-24s were long gone, we would fly over the craters and take pictures showing where they had blown up a bunch of woodcutters' huts and potato patches. Our photos didn't lie, which meant those poor SOBs had to go back and fight their way through swarms of Luftwaffe fighters and black walls of flak. War is hell.

Col. Philip R. Adair
80th Fighter Group, 89th Fighter Squadron, 10th Air Force

By the time I graduated from high school in Oklahoma in 1940, at the ripe old age of nineteen, I could see that the United States was going to get dragged into a world war. I had grown up in a farming family during the Great Depression and had felt the terrible hardships it caused us firsthand. The effects of the economic devastation continued to linger throughout our state. Finding a good-paying job—or any job, for that matter—was like trying to find fertile soil in the ravaged Dust Bowl.

I tried to join the army at Fort Sill and asked about becoming a pilot. A lieutenant with a very sharp tongue shot me down right away. "Sonny boy," he said, "you got to get yourself two years of college first and then *maybe* we'll talk to you."

I was as depressed as the red clay soil under my feet but was determined to earn my wings. I moved to Wyoming, found work, and enrolled in the Civilian Pilot Training Program (CPTP), earning a private pilot's license in a 50-hp Piper Cub with no brakes and a tail skid.

A week later the Japanese bombed Pearl Harbor, and I got the impression from the army recruiter I visited that if a fellow could see lightning and hear thunder, then they would gladly take him!

By September of 1942, I was a green second lieutenant flying P-47 Thunderbolts with the 80th Fighter Group out of Mitchell Field, New York. In the air the P-47 was stable and solid and an all-around efficient gun platform. But once you pulled the power back, the Jug was more like a homesick brick and came down fast.

In February of 1943, I had flown my P-47 for the last time in stateside training as I watched the Jug I was to fly in combat being loaded aboard a ship that would cross the Atlantic, bound for England. I looked forward to flying and slugging it out with the Luftwaffe as the rest of the 80th Fighter Group prepared to join the fight in Europe. Unfortunately, the military brass had other plans for our group, and I would not see my beloved Jug for a very long time.

General Hap Arnold gathered our group together in the middle of the night and informed us we would be embarking on a very important mission, one that was vital to the war effort. At that time, he couldn't disclose our final destination. He did tell us that we could forget everything we knew about the P-47 Thunderbolt and instead look forward to our new mount—the Curtiss P-40 Warhawk. There wasn't a guy in the room who didn't have a shocked look on his face!

The P-40 Warhawk was definitely lighter and slower, and carried a lot less firepower than what we had been used to in the Thunderbolt. I found the P-40 to be a good, honest, and reliable fighter in the air, but it was short on range and was a slow turner.

In less than a week's time we hurriedly trained a total of 25 hours in the air on our new fighters before we abandoned our cold-weather gear and left for parts unknown.

After fifty-three days at sea on three different boats, the 80th FG finally landed in India. By the time we arrived in late 1943, the Japanese had been fighting, conquering, and expanding their empire southward since 1937. They had set their sights on Northern India and were already in control of the Burma Railroad by the time we arrived.

It was tough going for the US, British, and Chinese composite forces on the ground as they tried to halt the advancing Japanese. Most if not all of their supplies—including ammo, fuel, and food—were sent up north by air over the "Hump" (Himalayan Mountains) in C-46s and C-47s. Our main job was to protect the Hump route from Japanese fighters that prowled over the thick green Burma jungles, looking for an overloaded, unarmed transport to shoot down.

I was assigned to "D" Flight as its commander, with three other P-40s assigned to me. To signify our 89th Fighter Squadron, we painted our spinners blood red and had a large, white-colored skull painted on both sides of the nose. We knew the Japanese were superstitious and somewhat afraid of anything that resembled death, so we added an extra surprise for them. Because we flew a lot of dive-bombing missions in support of the ground troops, we installed an 18-inch air-raid siren on our bellies and turned it on when we went into our dive-bombing attacks. We called this the "Banshee Wail," and it scared the hell out of the Japanese!

I personalized my P-40 with the name *LuLu Belle* after a girl I had known back in the States. I was also an old car nut and loved the cars from the early 1930s. As a tribute to my passion, I had brought along a can of whitewall paint and painted my main gear and tail wheel tires. I now had something no other fighter pilot had: a customized P-40 Warhawk!

Superstitious or not, the Japanese Zeros were still a constant threat. On many Hump escort missions, they would zoom up, give us the once-over, and hightail it out of there. It wasn't because they were intimidated by us; it was because they had strict orders to leave the fighters alone and attack the transports. They couldn't afford to take a chance of losing one of their fighters because they also had a long supply line to protect.

If a Zero did decide to tangle with us, however, we had been given specific instructions never to try to turn with him. Our instructors said we had two good chances: One was a good chance of being shot down, and the other, with so much dense jungle and rugged terrain, a good chance of never being seen again.

Although we were given the title of fighter pilot, I dropped more bombs than engaged in dogfights with other airplanes. We went after the Burma Railroad, a vital Japanese supply line. We attacked road convoys, airfields, and troop camps. But my favorite targets were bridges. We worked with A-36 Apaches and B-25 Mitchell bombers as we went bridge busting. It must have been a helluva scare for the Japanese on the ground when we pushed our noses over and that God-awful sound of our air sirens strapped to our bellies began to wail! Once the bombs were gone, we dropped down and did some strafing as well.

We had a few things in common with the Japanese—mainly, that our living conditions were nothing to write home about! We lived in tents that housed an assortment of mosquitoes and other bugs. Our rations were meager at best. Hell, the Chinese were fed better than we were. When it didn't rain, it was damn hot. And to make matters worse, we had to endure the constant assault from jackals in our tents at night. Somehow we managed to get along and survive.

But I almost didn't on a mission I will never forget.

On December 13, 1943, I had just completed my forty-third combat mission—a three-and-a-half-hour patrol over the Hump route, with no Japanese aircraft encountered. Our four-plane flight had just landed at Nagaghuli Airfield, and the place looked desolate, with all other serviceable P-40s off on other missions.

As soon as I shut down *LuLu Belle*, my crew chief, Carol Peake, began servicing "his" airplane. I walked to the alert tent 100 feet away and waited for the rest of my flight to come back in. I had just laid my head back on the couch and started to relax when all of a sudden the alert sounded.

I took off running for the flight line. Sergeant Peake had hit the electric start and the Allison engine was already running by the time I climbed up on the wing. I hit the throttle, not even bothering to buckle up, and was airborne in less than a minute as I hauled the P-40 skyward.

Our SOP (standard operating procedure) was to climb to 20,000 feet, rendezvous over the field, and stay off the radio, keeping our mouths shut. By the time I had reached 12,000 feet, I had buckled myself in and was searching for the other P-40s in my flight. I began to circle the field, spiraling upward, and saw that none of the others in my flight had taken off yet.

As I was circling, I saw a flight of four aircraft off to the east, just above the haze. By the time I made my next circle, I was completely shocked at what I saw. This was no longer a flight of four aircraft; this was now four flights of twin-engine Japanese bombers! They were in their typical finger-three flight, with three in front and three in back. I counted twenty-four of them heading north and stopped counting when I saw their escort fighters suddenly appear out of the haze.

I had staggered up to 20,000 feet all alone and had a front-row seat for what was below me. I must have counted more than forty single-engine Japanese fighters flying around in loose formations, with some of the Japanese pilots performing aerobatics for the bomber crews. The Japanese planes were all over the sky, with the bombers staying down low, at 12,500 feet. The fighters, however, seemed to be all over the place, ranging from right above the bomber formation upward, to 20,000 feet. Because of the thick brown haze that hung in the air, the Japanese had not detected me as I neared the pack.

I contacted Control and reported the Japanese formation to them. They responded back and said that what I was seeing was 40 miles to the east, not the 15 miles I was reporting. I tried to tell them they were wrong—that I felt the formation was going to make a 180-degree turn and overfly the 10th Air Force headquarters and bomb it. Control assured me that wasn't going to happen because they had reliable reports from ground stations that the unknowns were farther east.

That's when the Japanese formation began a coordinated turn. When they rolled out of their turn and took up a new course, it was clear to me that I had guessed right about their intentions. I called Control and gave them the bad news and the ETA of the bomber formation over the Air Depot Group HQ. Then I called Control one last time and said, "I'm not going to let them get by for free!"

I positioned myself above the fighters and the bomber formation so I could hit the bombers just before they reached their bomb release point. I flew out in front of the bombers, off to their left, as I dove down into them. I started to fire at a long range out because I knew that the sight of my tracers would shake things up a bit. I hit the first flight and then swung around into the second flight with my finger on the trigger as I took some shots at them, too. Before I knew it, I was behind the fourth flight of bombers, looking for a target.

As soon as the shooting started, the bombers began to bounce around, moving up and down out of formation. I tacked onto the tail-end Charlie bomber in the last flight and zeroed in on his left engine. I could see flashes on the fuselage and engine area as my bullets tore into him but I couldn't stick around to watch anymore, so I dove underneath him.

I started to break and saw several Zeros heading for me. I had figured this was going to happen, so I pushed the stick full forward into the left-hand corner, pulling negative Gs as I dove away, doing outside rolls. I stayed in my dive with the throttle at war emergency power until I figured I'd shaken the Zeros.

When I looked back, I saw empty skies with nobody chasing me, so I climbed back up for another go at the bombers as they began to reform.

I don't know if the Japanese still couldn't see me in the haze, because no one made a move to cut me off. I started to make another pass on the bombers, but before I could get near them, it looked like every Zero in the sky was turning into me and wanted a piece of my P-40. I knew I couldn't get close to the bombers—it would have been like reaching into a hornet's nest—so I settled for picking off a fighter or two.

I climbed back up on top and figured I would stay out of range of the bombers, which had already dropped their bombs. I picked out one of the Zeros and tried to get a shot off at him, but he was quick and knew I was gunning for him. He made a sharp turn and disappeared as I picked out another one. This guy was a little more stupid, as he waited too long to turn. I started to fire and he turned right into my bullets. His landing gear began to drop and his engine was on fire as he went into a spiral and crashed in the jungle near Naga Hills.

I climbed back up toward the formation as they neared their lines and went for broke. I thought, "What the hell—might as well take another whack at those bombers!" Stupid jerk! I managed to get into position for another attack, but before I could get in range, I had Zeros on my right, Zeros on my left, and Zeros above me. I was outnumbered almost forty to one.

I didn't think the odds were in my favor, so I went into my escape maneuver once again. I rolled the P-40 over and all I could see was a Zero, mad as hell, coming straight up at me with his cannons and guns blazing away.

I couldn't get out of his way fast enough, but still, it sounded like a shovel full of gravel hitting my fuselage. I heard a *wham, wham, wham* followed by an explosion with a ball of fire coming out from behind the armor plate in back of my headrest. I grabbed the trim tab and turned it all the way forward to assist my escaping dive. As I pushed the P-40's nose downhill, I kept taking hits as other tracers went whizzing by just over my head. The fire in the rear area went out as the ground raced up toward me.

I tried to pull back on the stick and it wouldn't budge. I remembered the elevator trim crank and I started cranking the nose up. The trim wheel was freewheeling and the trim cables shot out as I yanked off the power and reefed the stick back with both hands. I was finally able to get my nose out of the jungle and up into the sky where it belonged, but my troubles were far from over, as I was 125 miles from my base.

It was very hard to hold the nose above the horizon even with both hands as I turned back toward friendly lines. I tried to latch my seat belt around the stick but it wasn't long enough. I kept losing altitude, and my luck turned from bad to worse as another aircraft appeared in front of me, headed in my direction. I was able to get a quarter-mile away from him and saw that it was a Zero, smoking like the devil, losing altitude faster than I was. I figured he was one of the ones I had hit earlier, and we watched one another go by in opposite directions.

I hauled the P-40 around and came screaming up his rear end with a bead on his tail. At 100 yards out with the sight dead center on his engine, I squeezed the trigger, which only brought a *kerthunk, kerthunk, kerthunk* sound of the pneumatic system recharging my empty guns! With so much forward speed, I of course went screaming by him, as I became the hunted. The Zero simply pulled over and started shooting at me. I moved out of the way as his tracers zipped over my left wing. Luckily I wasn't hit as I turned for home once and for all!

I was about 90 miles away from home and my arms were so tired from holding the stick back that I could barely keep the nose above the horizon. As my adrenaline wore off, reality set in and I knew I would never make it back to base, so I decided to bail out. I called Control and gave them the grid map location. As I looked down at the dense jungle below, I said to myself, "Man, if I can just fly another 100 yards, it will save me two days of walking."

Then it hit me—I came up with the best idea I'd had all day. I flipped *LuLu Belle* over on her back, although the jungle was still in plain view below. The P-40 ran pretty good inverted for a couple of minutes before the engine loaded up and wanted to quit. I rolled the P-40 back over, waited for the engine to clear, lost a little altitude, and flipped *LuLu Belle* back over again. I continued doing P-40 flips the rest of the way home until I reached Nagaghuli.

At about a half-mile out from the airfield and at 1,000 feet, I pointed the P-40 toward the south end of the field. I was still inverted as I pulled back on the power and flipped the gear handle down. I squeezed the pump switch, looked down, locked on the gear indicator, and rolled *LuLu Belle* back over as I hit the flap switch and cut the throttle. It wasn't my usual three-pointer, but I could have cared less; we were down in one piece.

When I finally rolled to a stop, I was so tired that I had to be pulled out of my cockpit by some of the ground crew members. On the briefing I found out that the Japanese bomb pattern had fallen short of the HQ area with little damage done to the base. I had sixteen bullet holes in *LuLu Belle*, including one that shattered my trim cable. But the P-40 was a tough old bird, and three days later we had it flying again.

NINE.

Last Man Down

Nautilus *at War*

David W. Jourdan

BY MID-1944, THE JAPANESE EMPIRE WAS IN FULL RETREAT. IN June, a massive naval fleet pounded Saipan, and in a costly battle that lasted until early July, the island was secured by US Marines. In an effort to blunt the Allied advance and force a decisive naval engagement, the Japanese fleet sortied en-masse from bases in the Philippines and elsewhere in Operation A-Go. Nine Imperial Fleet aircraft carriers and five battleships with dozens of cruisers and destroyers faced off against the American 5th Fleet, which outnumbered the Japanese in every category, most notably carrier aircraft. They met in the Philippine Sea west of Guam. In two days of pitched aerial battle, three of Japan's largest aircraft carriers were sunk along with other vessels sunk or damaged as opposed to damage to only one US battleship.

The battle was nicknamed "The Great Marianas Turkey Shoot" by American aviators who destroyed hundreds of carrier and land-based aircraft, by some estimates as many as 750 planes. What was in 1942 the greatest naval air armada ever assembled had been reduced to an impotent force that would never recover.

This was followed by the capture of the nearby island of Tinian, which became an air base for B-29s of the Twelfth Air Force, sent to bomb the homeland of Japan. At the same time, Guam was recaptured, completing the campaign in the Mariana Islands.

Meanwhile, the American Submarine Force was striking a telling blow on enemy merchant shipping. By war's end, nearly three hundred US submarines were in operation and as many as five million tons of enemy shipping had been sunk. Most of the submarines in the US fleet were of the newer *Gato* and *Balao* classes, fast and deadly.

The older *Nautilus* and *Narwhal* became the stalwarts of the Spy Squadron, with *Narwhal* conducting her first of nine Spyron patrols in November 1943. *Nautilus* would conduct her first foray into Japanese-controlled Philippines waters in June 1944, her ninth war patrol.

MINDANAO AND LEYTE

"Did you hear about Bananas?"

Nick Bruck, John Sabbe, and Foy Hester were relaxing in the chief's quarters as *Nautilus* headed southwest from Pearl Harbor, on the way to Brisbane, Australia, to begin her ninth war patrol. Nick Bruck had just heard the news that their crewmate John Peirano had been promoted to ensign.

"That would be *Mister* Bananas to you, Nick! That good-time Charlie is an officer now, believe it or not!" Sabbe chuckled with the rest of them. Peirano was a colorful character who had a reputation for carousing and telling tall tales.

"How did he get the nickname 'Bananas?'" wondered Foy.

"No one seems to know," replied Sabbe, "though it fits. Did you know he was a professional gambler before the war? At least, according to Buzz."

"Well, that explains how he always beats me at cards," mused Nick. Much of the lore surrounding Peirano had been supplied by Buzz Lee, himself a good storyteller. Peirano came aboard

Nautilus on her fourth patrol, but Buzz claimed to have served with him before the war. According to Lee, their submarine was getting underway one day without Peirano, who failed to show up in time for sailing and had been declared AWOL. As the vessel was leaving harbor, a speedboat was seen coming up astern. On board were Peirano and two women, presumably his companions during the previous night. The boat raced alongside, and the delinquent sailor managed to scramble aboard. He claimed to have paid fifty dollars (a considerable sum at the time) to hire the speedboat.

Apparently, the navy recognized Peirano's leadership abilities in spite of his flamboyant antics and, as with Porterfield, allowed him to stay on board. The freshly minted officer would join a remade wardroom led by the submarine's new commanding officer. George Sharp was the youngest commander in the navy in 1939 when as a lieutenant he captained the USS *Falcon*. The rescue ship with the new Momsen diving bell was famously used to save the lives of sailors aboard the sunken submarine USS *Squalus*. His next command was less than auspicious as he led USS *Spearfish* on patrol near Truk in June 1943. Alerted to a massive Japanese fleet of fourteen warships, including three aircraft carriers, he chose to make a conservative nighttime periscope approach. He fired torpedoes without hitting anything and was run off by an approaching destroyer without making further attacks. Admiral Lockwood was displeased by his lack of aggressiveness and relieved him. Sharp redeemed himself a few months later while commanding the rescue vessel USS *Florikan* with a daring salvage of another stricken submarine. His reward was a second chance at a submarine command.

Phil Eckert, survivor of the man overboard incident on the fourth patrol and expert diving officer, detached leaving Sharp and Executive Officer Ben Jarvis to lead a team of junior lieutenants and ensigns over the next few patrols. Porterfield and Peirano offered a significant degree of experience to the young wardroom.

Eckert took the opportunity between postings to get married, and then became executive officer on USS *Sea Robin* (SS-407). He later took command of USS *Gar* (SS-206) days before war's end. In later years, Eckert penned articles in the US Naval Academy alumni magazine *Shipmate*, including one about his experience going overboard on *Nautilus* and another detailing the fates of the 375 alumni submarine officers lost during World War II. There is no report of him requisitioning an ammunition hoist to set up and abuse at his home in Maryland.

The crew lost a half dozen veterans of the previous eight *Nautilus* war patrols along with seventeen other men, replacements bringing the crew roster to ninety-nine enlisted men and eleven officers. The ship got underway from Pearl Harbor on April 25, 1944, arriving in Brisbane on May 14, where the crew loaded assorted cargo bound for the Philippines. On May 20, they left Brisbane and cruised to Darwin via a scenic inland passage of the Great Barrier Reef and Torres Strait. Unfortunately for the engineers, continued problems with main engine cracked heads, broken head studs, cracked liners, and broken clutch shafts kept them busy in the engine room, unable to sightsee. The ship departed with only three engines operating, and thirty-six hours of labor were required to place number two main engine back in commission.

At Darwin, the crew labored to unload fourteen torpedoes and all handling gear, making room for 192,000 pounds of cargo (including some loaded in Brisbane). By May 29, all was ready for the submarine's first Spyron mission. Just before getting underway Lt. (jg) John Simmons came aboard, aiming to be put ashore on Mindanao to liaison with the guerillas. *Nautilus* headed north into the Indonesian archipelago, wending her way through narrow island passages and shallow channels, always on the lookout for enemy ships and aircraft. Charts were dubious, currents unpredictable, and weather always a challenge. Jarvis, recently promoted to lieutenant commander, served as navigator, and certainly had his hands full.

Two days into the transit, trouble struck.

"What was that?" wondered Lt. (jg) Charles Cummings, officer of the deck. An explosion had rocked the boat and was felt throughout the ship, but no enemy was in sight. *Nautilus* had been making standard speed on all four main engines, but she immediately slowed. In moments, the call came to the bridge.

"Fire in the engine room!"

Captain Sharp was on his way to the bridge while Jarvis headed aft to take charge of damage control. In moments, he reported that the fire was out and requested ventilation. It took ten minutes of forced air to clear the smoke. The long-suffering Chief Bruck made his report.

"Sir, we had a crankcase explosion on number four," he said, mopping his sweaty brow with a dirty rag. "Thank God no one was hurt, though we have a few ears ringing." He continued, "All the outboard crankcase doors blew off and the blast started a rag fire in the bilges. We put that out right away."

"So where do we stand?" inquired Jarvis.

"Will have to get in there and see, sir. Right now, I don't know what happened and how much damage there is. Fortunately, the other engines seem to be OK, but we'll have to take number two offline while we're working on four."

"Very well. Do your best." Jarvis went forward to report to the captain. *Nautilus* continued on at reduced speed while the engineers got to work. The explosion was caused by either stuck or broken piston rings in one of the sixteen cylinders, and luckily the damage was confined to that single cylinder. Bruck and his men rebuilt the unit and remarkably had the engine running again ten grueling hours later.

By the evening of June 1, *Nautilus* completed a transit of Banga Strait and entered the Celebes Sea, south of the Philippines island of Mindanao. The next morning, while cruising on the surface in glassy-calm seas, an enemy patrol craft was sighted, which immediately opened fire. All main engines cranked to full speed, but the patrol craft continued to close, firing continuously. Sharp ordered a quick dive, but kept tabs on the enemy through the periscope. The craft continued to approach, so *Nautilus* went deep and slunk away. Two days later as the boat nosed into Moro Gulf, three ships came out of a rain squall and caught *Nautilus* by surprise. Another deep dive avoided a pattern of five depth charges, and again she was able to evade.

The morning of June 5 marked the two-year anniversary of the Battle of Midway, where *Nautilus* made her first war patrol. Fourteen of the current crew were on board that day, and the men regaled their junior crew members with their exploits. There was not much time for reminiscing, however, as the periscope watch saw signals from Coastwatchers on the beach near Tukuran on Mindanao Island. With the help of Lieutenant Simmons, Sharp was able to verify the proper security code and confirm the beach was clear to approach. While lurking just offshore in Illana Bay awaiting nightfall, sonar reported propeller noises on all three sets of sonar gear with a clear turn count of 125 revolutions per minute. Could a Japanese patrol be looking for them? The tension persisted for fifteen minutes until looks through the periscope confirmed the sounds to be nothing more than a nearby playful fish.

That evening at 1910, just before sunset, *Nautilus* approached to within a mile and a half of the beach. Red Porterfield had the deck and was on the periscope.

"Christ, will you look at this!" He let out a low whistle. "There must be a thousand men on the beach!"

"That's good, we'll need the manpower," commented Sharp. "Surface the ship!"

The submarine rose from the sea and cautiously nosed close to shore. A small launch flying American colors stood out.

"Open the hatches," ordered Sharp. "Mr. Porterfield, have the men begin striking cargo topside." The first lieutenant acknowledged the captain, and the crew began manhandling the ninety-six tons of supplies to the submarine's ample deck. There was no time to lose as such a large cargo would take hours to unload. The ship hove to at times as close as eight hundred yards from the beach. Col. Robert Bowler, commanding the men ashore, came aboard with a party of ten men to assist, and around thirty bancas outriggers, and rafts of all sizes came alongside to receive cargo. Annoyingly, they brought more Filipino men who came on board and stood about the deck, more in the way than helpful.

"This won't cut it," growled Porterfield. "We'll never get this crap off the boat in those piss-ant little canoes!" He set about to have the ship's motorboats launched, and gave orders to organize the working parties. It proved to be quite a challenge, but the seasoned former chief petty officer was up to the task. Sharp later wrote: "Lack of organization or supervision of the working party from ashore was a serious matter. It was agreed that all work topside be done by the shore party, all work below decks by ship's force, but if we had waited for them to carry out that plan, we would be there yet."

Under the watchful eye and sharp tongue of Porterfield, every available ship's officer and crewman set to work, loading most of the cargo into the boats. Each boat returned with a full load of Filipinos until the deck was so covered with standing or strolling men it was almost impossible to handle the cargo. The ship's motorboats carried much of the burden, loaded to many times their rated capacity with scant inches of freeboard. Amazingly, in just three hours all cargo was on the way ashore. Sharp commented, "The spirit of the ship's company was magnificent."

Besides the assigned cargo, Sharp directed the crew to hand over any unneeded supplies from the ship's stores. *Nautilus* delivered thirty-seven cases of 20mm ammunition, 550 gallons of diesel oil, and a quantity of dry stores, including 210 pounds of white flour, all much appreciated by the ill-provisioned resistance fighters. The last trip delivered Lieutenant Simmons ashore. Boats were retrieved and stowed, and at 0247 *Nautilus* headed back out to sea, mission accomplished.

The trip back to Darwin was marked only by an encounter on the evening of June 7 with a belligerent schooner. Sharp manned battle stations and opened fire with six-inch guns, but at a range of more than six miles in growing darkness only near misses were observed. After a few salvos, Sharp broke off the attack as night fell. *Nautilus* arrived at Darwin on the morning of June 11 after a short, but successful sortie. Rear Adm. Ralph Christie, 7th Fleet commander, was pleased with the patrol and commented, "Enemy contacts were handled with sound judgment." Aggressiveness was not called for on a Spyron mission.

If the tired crew and aging submarine expected a respite for recuperation and repairs, they were profoundly misguided. Upon arrival in Darwin, the crew began immediately loading cargo for another Spyron mission. The next morning, four Filipino army enlisted men came on board bound for Negros Island north of Mindanao. At 1359, *Nautilus* was underway for her tenth war patrol, less than thirty hours after completing her ninth.

Three days later in the Banda Sea north of Timor, a two-masted schooner was sighted. Eager for action, Sharp called for battle stations and commenced firing with the main guns at five thousand yards. The sailboat crew immediately abandoned ship, but the gunners continued pumping round after round into the wreck. Finally, after twenty minutes and seventy-two shells of six-inch ammunition, Sharp called cease fire. A handful of survivors were observed, but with two lifeboats and land nearby the captain chose not to pick them up and let them fend for themselves. Regarding the prodigious expenditure of ammunition, he commented it was due to "excessive opening range, poor aiming, and my attempt to totally sink the craft."

Nautilus continued north. On June 17, she transited the narrow Sibutu Passage and entered the Sulu Sea, west of Mindanao, deep into enemy controlled waters. Aircraft sightings caused frequent dives, and radar interference was sensed all around. Heading northeast toward Negros Island, smoke was sighted over the horizon and Sharp bent on all engines making full speed. As the diesels hammered at high power, a serious knocking developed in number one. Bruck immediately shut it down, but upon stopping a violent crankcase explosion ripped through the space. As before, a fire started in the bilge and the room filled with smoke. Fifteen minutes later the fire was out, and smoke cleared, fortunately with no injuries. Sharp was forced to give up the chase as they could not close the contact at reduced three-engine speed.

Bruck and his beleaguered men set back to work on the damaged diesel. After some time, they discovered a failed bearing on one cylinder, which remained too hot to hold even after cooling for four hours. Adjacent bearings were damaged by the heat and explosion. Eventually, after four days of labor, Bruck was able to get the engine operating again by removing the entire piston and crank assembly and running the machine on fourteen cylinders. In the meanwhile, *Nautilus* limped toward her rendezvous at Negros on three diesels.

On the morning of June 20, a lookout sighted signals from Coastwatchers on Balatong Point, Negros Island. Sharp confirmed their authenticity and returned a reply, indicating they would stand offshore until evening. At 1940, the setting sun revealed a small fleet of sailboats, rowboats, and bancas heading for the submarine and Porterfield started the crew striking cargo topside. The boats came alongside and disgorged their passengers, led by Lt. Col. Salvador Abcede. As men began loading the small boats, a parade of evacuees was taken aboard, including four women, one four-year-old girl, and twelve men and boys, among them a German prisoner of war. As the men worked with Abcede's well-organized force under ideal weather conditions in still waters, *Nautilus* hove to 1,500 yards from shore. The four Filipino men embarked at Darwin went ashore. Sharp added to the assigned cargo 1,160 pounds of flour, sugar, coffee, powdered eggs, and powdered milk. By 0602, Colonel Abcede bid farewell and returned to the beach, grateful for the vital supplies and a chance to evacuate a few civilians.

Nautilus retraced her route bound for Darwin, transiting the Sibutu and Banga Passages without incident. Sharp was surprised at the lack of Japanese surface patrols and aircraft. Returning to the Banda Sea on June 25, another sail was sighted, almost in the same location as the one attacked earlier. The vessel bent on all canvas, turned tail, and tried to run, but with all four engines back on line the submarine easily outpaced the sailboat. This time Sharp closed to 2,500 yards and dispatched the vessel with only nine rounds.

The water teemed with survivors, and Sharp stood by to pick them up. The crew pulled aboard eighteen bedraggled Malaysians to add to their passenger manifest. Upon interrogation it was learned that the boat was bound for nearby Ambon under Japanese charter with more than twelve tons of pistol and rifle ammunition. The survivors also claimed that the Japanese shaved their heads and took most of their money. *Nautilus* continued south, now housing thirty-five evacuees and survivors placing extra work on the cooks and bakers. Regardless, Sharp commented that "all appeared to get a certain amount of satisfaction from feeding our half-starved passengers even to running a special menu for the children." The crew quartered the evacuees in the forward torpedo room and the Malaysian survivors in the aft torpedo room. The passengers were generally undernourished, and many suffered from malaria and tropical infections. A few of the Malaysians were treated for shrapnel wounds. Sharp concluded, "The wail of children and the stench of unwashed bodies was [*sic*] conquered by the men as are all obstacles by all good submariners."

The submarine, with her intrepid crew and grateful passengers, returned to Darwin on the afternoon of June 27. The 7th Fleet commander congratulated the officers and crew for another successful special mission, and recognized sinking of two schooners totaling 130 tons.

During the middle of 1944, MacArthur and his armies were fighting their way across New Guinea with repeated amphibious landings and attacks through dense jungles, battling desperate and determined Japanese troops as well as disease, insects, heat, hunger, and exhaustion. US, Australian, Dutch, and British soldiers fought together, assisted by air attacks from the Australian mainland. Specially modified B-25 Mitchell light bombers and A-20 Havoc attack aircraft sported extra nose-mounted heavy machine guns to give close air support to ground troops and attack Japanese shipping trying to resupply their starving men. Through these efforts, the Allies continued to hold Port Moresby in southeastern New Guinea against repeated attacks and MacArthur's forces began to make headway. Though fighting continued in islands to the east including Bougainville, Allied armies began to wear down the 350,000 Japanese defending the region and inch their way west. By July 1944, at the expense of thousands of casualties, the Allies were within five hundred miles of Mindanao and MacArthur was making plans to recapture the Philippines. The efforts of the guerrillas ashore were becoming all the more crucial to this undertaking, while Japanese efforts to curb the insurgents became all the harsher targeting guerrillas and civilians alike. Stories of gruesome reprisals abound. These measures failed to deter the freedoms fighters and only served to incite their cause as numbers increased and territory controlled by the guerrillas expanded. Supply efforts by the Spyron missions continued to be crucial to these vital forces.

The weary *Nautilus* crew began loading cargo for another patrol soon after arrival at Darwin. A scheduled departure three days hence afforded the opportunity for minor repairs, though number one main engine would continue to be run on fourteen cylinders. On June 30, Lt. Cdr. George Rowe reported aboard with a party of twenty-two men for transportation to Mindoro. Four additional army enlisted men were received aboard for transportation to Leyte and Bohol. That evening, at 1835, the ship was underway for her eleventh war patrol and third Spyron mission.

She proceeded northwest on a now familiar route into the Timor Sea. On the morning of July 1, while proceeding on the surface not yet two hundred nautical miles from Darwin, radar reported a contact.

"Conn, radar. Contact dead ahead range five miles. Believe to be an aircraft."

"Very well," replied Lt. (jg) Charles Cummings who had just come on watch as officer of the deck. "Lookouts, radar has an aircraft ahead." This close to home it was presumed to be friendly, but *Nautilus* had been attacked by friendly forces before.

In moments the lookouts spotted it. "I see a single aircraft just off the starboard bow," reported one of the sharp-eyed sailors. Through binoculars he could see details of the plane four miles in the distance and headed across the bow. "It's a twin-engine bomber."

"Probably a Beaufort," commented Cummings, referring to the British-built bomber. They watched as the plane zig-zagged away at two miles distant, then it suddenly turned and bore in at the submarine.

Cummings belatedly realized a submarine has no friends. "Dive, dive!" he yelled. Lookouts scrambled below as the young lieutenant watched a bomb tumble from the belly of the plane. The ship was just beginning to settle as the bomb hit the sea just ahead. The plane roared overhead as Cummings slammed the hatch.

"Last man down!" he rasped, breathing hard with fear and alarm in his voice. The lookout who first spotted the plane was already on the periscope. "He's coming around again!"

The aircraft reversed course and opened fire with wing-mounted guns. Luckily, his aim was no better as the rounds stitched the sea harmlessly about a hundred feet to starboard. Captain Sharp climbed into the conning tower.

"Report, Mr. Cummings!"

"Sir, we were attacked by a Beaufort bomber. A friendly." He detailed the incident. By then the submarine was safely below the waves.

"Are you sure it wasn't a Lily?" asked Sharp, which was the Allied code name for a Japanese Ki-48 light bomber, somewhat resembling the British Beaufort. The aircraft was widely used in the Philippines theater, but it would be quite a long way from home base this close to Australia.

"I don't believe so, Captain." Sharp made a point with the young officer to make no such assumptions in the future. They stayed submerged for an hour then surfaced and continued on. The next few days were uneventful, though many distant sails and other ships were seen. Nothing was deemed worthy of a chase and only once did an aircraft approach close enough to warrant another quick dive. On July 5, they completed transit of the Sibutu Passage and entered the Sulu Sea, this time continuing north along the coast of Panay to Mindoro, just one hundred miles south of enemy occupied Manila.

On July 8, *Nautilus* approached a pair of islands known as Pandan, just off the west coast of Mindoro. At 0230, three of Commander Rowe's men paddled ashore in a rubber boat to reconnoiter the landing area. The submarine, submerged, lurked just offshore for the rest of the day, dodging sailboats and patrol craft, at one point rigging for depth charges, which thankfully, never appeared. In the late afternoon security signals were seen on the beach, indicating the coast was clear for landing the remaining troops and supplies. At 2052, *Nautilus* surfaced and came as close as 250 yards to shore as cargo was unloaded into rubber boats. By 0230, Commander Rowe and his twenty-two men were ashore, along with twelve tons of supplies to sustain their clandestine mission. *Nautilus* sped away at four-engine speed, heading south to clear the area.

The crew's mission was far from complete as another rendezvous awaited them on the thirteenth. Circling the southern end of Negros Island, they entered the Mindanao Sea and spent a day patrolling the eastern end of the area, operating deep inside Japanese controlled territory in confined waters. No worthy targets were seen. The next evening, *Nautilus* transited Surigao Strait and entered Leyte Gulf, where the largest naval battle of the war would be fought in just a few months. On the morning of July 13, Sharp and his men scanned the beach off Lagoma but failed to see any signals, so they proceeded to an alternate site at San Roque the next day. These time signals were seen and that evening a flotilla of small boats led by Col. Ruperto Kangleón, a regular officer of the Filipino army. Kangleón had led an infantry regiment against the Japanese invasion but was captured and imprisoned. In December 1942, he managed to escape and returned to Leyte where he formed a guerrilla movement. By early 1944 his forces were on the offensive, keeping the Japanese on the island at bay in fortified coastal towns. Kangleón and his men would provide a bridgehead for the Allied landings on Leyte in October when MacArthur would return as promised.

Cargo was quickly moved to the waiting boats. Sounds of fighting reached them from the jungle just a few miles away. Sharp reported that the colonel's men were well organized and disciplined, and that they had but one desire: "guns and ammunition." Regardless, *Nautilus* treated the guerrillas to additional items from the ship's stores, including over a half ton of corned beef, ham and bacon, powdered eggs, and sugar. Soon after midnight on the fifteenth, the submarine headed back into Surigao Strait and west to Negros Island and the now familiar Balatong Point. On the evening of July 16, the ship made her third rendezvous of the patrol, this time reacquainting with Colonel Abcede, who turned over an unspecified "special cargo" of a box and two packages. Sharp returned the favor with two hundred pounds of food and ammunition. In just twenty minutes, *Nautilus* was on her way southwest to Sibutu Passage.

As the submarine proceeded through the Sulu Sea, many sails and a few planes were sighted. One dropped a depth bomb in their vicinity, to no effect. As the ship approached Sibutu, the crew received a welcome message.

"Did you hear the news?" Word had reached the crew, and John Sabbe was eager to share it.

"Yeah," replied Nick Bruck, dejectedly. "I heard we're almost out of coffee!"

"And we're out of flour," noted Foy Hester. "Five hundred pounds of it had to be ditched because of weevils. We gave the rest away to the guerillas. No more bread for us!"

"Oh, stop your bellyaching, that's not news. We're not going back to Darwin. We're headed to Fremantle for a refit and some R&R!"

"Really? On the level?" asked Bruck.

"Yessirree Bob!" replied Sabbe with a grin. "Forget about bread and pastries, and even coffee! Bottled sunshine awaits!"

Morale took a significant turn for the better as *Nautilus* continued south into the Makassar Strait heading for southwestern Australia. Entering the Java Sea, their progress was interrupted briefly by a rendezvous with USS *Ray* and an assignment to search for an enemy convoy spotted in the area. A day's search yielded nothing. The ship continued through the Lombok Strait east of Bali and on July 21 spent the better part of a week cruising south, short on coffee, pastries, and patience. Finally, on the morning of July 27, *Nautilus* docked at Fremantle having spent eighty-seven of the previous ninety-four days underway, covering more than twenty thousand nautical miles since the last maintenance refit.

Sharp commended Chiefs Goodman and Bruck for diligence in "maintaining an efficient main engineering plant in spite of

chronic weakness and unreliability." He also singled out Lieutenant (jg) Winner's performance as diving officer and Ensign
Porterfield's outstanding contribution to "the success and smart-
ness of the execution of all special missions." Admiral Christie
congratulated Sharp and his crew for the successful completion of
the important missions, and though they did no direct damage to
the enemy, the patrol was deemed a success. An additional measure of gratitude was offered by none other than Gen. Douglas
MacArthur, who sent letters of commendation to the entire crew,
stating:

> *The successful completion by the USS* Nautilus *of its assigned mis-*
> *sions has been a most important contribution to the strengthening of*
> *our military forces and the sustaining of our operations. I desire to*
> *commend Commander George A. Sharp, USN, and his officers and*
> *men for the splendid manner in which this task has been undertaken*
> *and executed and express to them my grateful acknowledgement of*
> *service well done.*

Captain Sharp and the officers enjoyed a fifteen-day recuperation period at Fremantle's Majestic Hotel while the crew retired
to the Ocean Beach Hotel. The respite was certainly "needed and
enjoyed by all hands."

IUISAN SHOAL AND LUZON

Nick Bruck and Joe Goodman stood dejectedly, arms crossed,
glumly regarding the massive diesel engines. They had just
returned from their two-week break, leaving the engine room in
the hands of the submarine tender mechanics who performed
a complete overhaul on all four diesels. Expecting to find them
in working order, they instead learned that all four were out of
commission. *Nautilus* was far from ready for sea. Bruck addressed
Sharp and the ship's engineer, Hal Winner, as he ticked off the
major issues.

"Well, sirs, it seems that the main engine housings are pitted and corroded. They used a kind of iron cement to patch them. We'll have serious problems with that within months. The bearings we ordered for number one came in the wrong size, so we're still on fourteen cylinders. The tender ginks ground the journal bearings too thin and so after running a battery charge they were all wiped. The rings on number two are shot. They should have replaced them, now we'll have to do it." He continued detailing the deficiencies as the captain patiently listened. Finally finished, he looked at Goodman. "Did I about cover it, Chief?"

Goodman nodded, with nothing more to say.

Winner jumped in. "Can you and your men fix all this?"

Bruck sighed. "Yes sir. We know these engines. Just keep those jerks from the tender out of our hair!"

"I'll promise you that," agreed Sharp. "Also, give me a detailed write-up of these problems. I'll put them in my next patrol report. Command needs to know what we're dealing with."

Bruck, Goodman, and the other machinists got to work. Two weeks and six hundred man hours of labor later, the main engines were hammering away on all cylinders, ready for action.

Besides the engine work, *Nautilus* received new radar equipment and an overhaul of all sea valves. The ship was fumigated, though apparently not to the captain's satisfaction. Torpedo and gunnery training helped the twenty-five new crewmen adjust to their surroundings and duties. On August 16, 1944, the crew assembled for a brief ceremony honoring Lt. Cdr. Ben Jarvis, Chief Foy Hester, Chief Joe Goodman, and Gunner's Mate Myles Banbury for "heroic and meritorious services . . . in the transporting of a Marine detachment to Japanese-occupied Apamama [Abemama] Island." The men were awarded Bronze Star medals, and forty other crewmen received letters of commendation, notably for performance during the friendly fire incident when *Nautilus* was hit by gunfire from the destroyer *Ringgold*. On August 27, the ship got underway, leaving Fremantle behind. Nine days later, vessel and crew arrived at Darwin and began loading cargo for yet another Spyron mission. Frustratingly, problems with engine clutches needed further repair, which required an extended stay in port, and more toil and sweat by the machinists. Before getting underway, a new officer came on board with the unusual name of Willard de Los Michael. Lieutenant Commander Michael would shadow Ben Jarvis to learn the art of navigating the treacherous waters around the Philippines archipelago, and was slated to eventually relieve Sharp as commanding officer. Also joining the wardroom was none other than John Sabbe, the third *Nautilus* crewman to be promoted to ensign and remain on board.

Finally, on September 17, 1944, *Nautilus* got underway for her twelfth war patrol, carrying 106 tons of cargo bound for several locations and two US Army enlisted men aiming to rendezvous with guerrilla units. Over the next week the submarine followed her former tracks, wending her way through narrow passages to enter the Sulu Sea and turn west into the Bohol Sea. This time Sharp directed the ship into the Cebu Strait, aiming for a location on the coast of the island of Cebu called Iuisan Point. Seeing proper security signals on the evening of September 25, they surfaced and saw a small boat waving an American flag, occupants "displaying length of hair to demonstrate their nationality" (that is, not Japanese). Soon a flotilla of twenty-five small boats was alongside receiving cargo. Just before 2100, forty tons of cargo was on its way to the beach and Sharp was waiting for passengers. Minutes passed, an hour passed, and no passengers appeared. One native officer explained the delays were due to "filipinitis."

Finally, out of the darkness, boats set out from shore bringing eleven evacuees and their baggage including mail and captured documents. The crew fetched them quickly, got them on board, and the ship was immediately underway, engines ahead standard speed.

The submarine swung around with full rudder, its speed increasing. Suddenly, with a grinding, screeching crunch the ship came to an abrupt stop. Unsecured baggage flew about the spaces and men staggered forward. The hull was hard aground on Iuisan Shoal, stuck on a sand and coral reef.

"Damage report!" called Hal Winner, officer of the deck. No damage was noted in any compartments, other than a few bumps, bruises, and broken coffee cups. Sharp and Porterfield were still on the bridge having just supervised the loading of passengers. Sharp took over. "Back her off, Mr. Winner." He ordered full astern, then emergency power, but the ship did not budge. "Blow forward main ballast tanks and pump all forward ballast to sea," ordered the captain, hoping to lift the bow off the bottom. As the pumps began their work, Porterfield spoke up.

"Captain, I suggest we sally ship."

"Good call, Mr. Porterfield. Make it happen!" Red set about organizing the crew and passengers to head topside and move in coordination from side to side across the large deck. This time-honored method of freeing a grounded ship involves using the weight of the crew to rock the vessel and try to break suction with the bottom. Altogether, the crew tallied nearly eight tons of weight, but the trick was to get them moving in coordination. Red did his best to set the hull in motion while the engines ran furiously, the screws churning the sea, but all efforts were futile. *Nautilus* was stuck fast.

Sharp called a halt to efforts and gathered his officers to discuss what to do. Jarvis pointed out the high tide would come at 0400. Dawn would creep in two hours later, with sunrise at 0702. Already a dozen air contacts had been logged since leaving Darwin, and as soon as they were discovered aground the Japanese air force would be on top of them. Ground troops would follow. It was critical to get off the reef before dawn.

Porterfield recommended they lighten the ship, not just forward but overall. They discussed what ballast and other weight could be offloaded. For starters, the eleven evacuees and their baggage were sent back to shore, along with the captured documents they brought on board and about forty additional tons of cargo meant for another location. Sadly, the civilians would have to wait for another opportunity to leave the island. Sharp also had all secret and confidential materials burned so none could fall into enemy hands if the ship was captured. All variable ballast was blown overboard, along with fifty-nine thousand gallons of reserve fuel amounting to two hundred tons, and all the gasoline they carried for the small boat engine. The crew jettisoned 190 rounds of six-inch ammunition amounting to ten tons. Nothing else came to mind. The tide continued to go out so that the boat was up a degree-and-a-half by the bow and listing twelve degrees to starboard. Porterfield suggested they flood the forward and middle main ballast tanks to hold the ship in place as the tide turned and flooded in, preventing her going higher up on the reef. By 0330, all excess weight was off the ship and the tide was rising quickly. It was time to go.

"Blow all main ballast tanks!" Sharp commanded. High pressure air entered the large tanks forcing hundreds of tons of seawater out. The ship began to gently roll back to vertical.

"All back two-thirds!" called Sharp. The engines responded and the screws bit. The boat shuddered but did not move. "Back full!" The diesels rumbled and the sea churned. Still no movement.

"All back emergency!" ordered Sharp. The engines roared. Bruck and Goodman crossed their fingers, hoping the old diesels would not fail them. Suddenly, the ship lurched free and began to move rapidly astern. She was off! "All stop!" yelled Sharp over the din, relieved. It was 0400 and they were clear. Moving ahead, Sharp safely passed the shoals and headed to deep water.

They were free of the reef, but not yet out of danger. So much ballast had been cast overboard they could not submerge. The oil and gasoline tanks needed to be reflooded, a process normally taking five hours, but sunrise was just three hours away. Again, Red had an idea. At his direction, the crew removed manhole covers from the tanks and rigged fire hoses to quickly fill them with seawater. By 0611, dawn was upon them, and radar reported a contact at eleven thousand yards. Sharp hoped it was the submarine USS *Mingo*, sent to render assistance, and rescue the *Nautilus* crew if necessary. At 0637, a periscope was sighted. A few minutes later, Sharp gave the order to dive. *Nautilus* started down and in short order was underwater, and sinking! Too much water ballast had been added and the submarine was now ninety thousand pounds heavy! Lieutenant Winner pumped furiously and eventually got the ship back in trim. That evening Sharp was able to contact *Mingo* and let them know that help was not needed.

Nautilus continued her mission, undeterred by the dramatic events off Cebu. She headed north to Panay Island and her second rendezvous point. On the morning of September 29, signals from the Coastwatchers were sighted and three large sailboats were observed, with much activity on the beach. Surfacing that evening, the submarine nudged near shore and began striking cargo topside. By 0144 the next morning, forty tons of supplies plus a thousand pounds of ship's dry stores were ashore, and forty-seven evacuees including twenty-two women, nine children, and sixteen men came aboard. *Nautilus* was on her way. A third rendezvous was cancelled as the supplies meant for that spot had been offloaded to lighten ship, and so much fuel had been pumped overboard they were running low. The submarine headed to Sibutu Passage and into the Celebes Sea, and from there continued east toward New Guinea. A new base was operational at Mios Woendi, with the submarine tender USS *Orion* (AS-18) serving as an impromptu submarine repair depot.

At noon on October 6, forty-seven evacuees plus one stowaway discovered shortly after departure from Panay, were transferred to a waiting vessel. Also departing were the two army enlisted men destined for the third rendezvous that was cancelled. Their names were not recorded, but the crew was sorry to see them go. Sharp reported, "They did more than their share of ship's work and during the unloading periods they worked as hard as anyone on board. They were good shipmates." At 1236, *Nautilus* moored in Woendi, completing her fourth Spyron mission. The commander of Task Force 72, Capt. John Haines, was pleased with the patrol, stating, "It was only through the coolness and good judgement of the commanding officer and the determined efforts of all hands that the *Nautilus* was saved to fight again."

In spite of all evidence to the contrary, many of the Japanese high command subscribed to the fiction that America would give up the war in the face on one major decisive defeat. Allied navy and Marine forces led by Admiral Nimitz had pushed through the Mariana Islands, breaching Japan's strategic defensive ring, and threatening the home islands. Army forces, supported by the navy and led by General MacArthur, gained ground in New Guinea. An invasion of the Philippines was imminent, and the dwindling power of the Japanese Combined Fleet prepared to meet it yet another decisive engagement code named Shō-Gō.

Though weakened by successive defeats, Japan still possessed significant land-based air power in the region, numbering some 1,500 planes operating from airfields in Luzon and the islands to the north, Formosa (now Taiwan) and Ryukyu. In a surprise move ahead of the invasion, Adm. William "Bull" Halsey led his fast carrier task force with seventeen aircraft carriers and more than a thousand aircraft on a series of raids against air bases on the northern islands from October 12–16. The Japanese counterattacked, striving to sink Halsey's carriers, but attrition had sapped Japan of her experienced pilots while well-trained American airmen flew newer aircraft. In three days of aerial combat the enemy forces were routed, losing six hundred planes, knocking the northern air forces out of the coming battles.

Thanks in large part to the successful guerrilla activity on the southern Philippine islands, MacArthur decided to bypass Mindanao and invade at the eastern beaches of Leyte, where *Nautilus* and other Spyron missions had regularly rendezvoused with guerrilla leaders. If the landing forces could quickly capture an airfield, then planes from Australia could move in and help Halsey's carrier-based aircraft to defend the beachhead. As the invasion forces landed on October 17, Japanese high command, with unfounded optimism, set operation Shō-Gō in motion. The Combined Fleet no longer had an air force, as its few remaining carriers had only a handful of planes left and few crew to fly them. However, they retained a powerful force of warships including the super battleships *Yamato* and *Musashi*, each sporting eighteen-inch naval guns, the largest ever floated, as well as five other battleships, twenty cruisers, and dozens of destroyers. With hope of air cover from land-based planes in Luzon, their mission was to approach the invasion beaches from the north through San Bernadino Straight and from the south through Surigao Strait and crush the Allied landings. To have any real chance of this they needed to neutralize Halsey's carrier force. To this end, a decoy fleet designated the Northern Force, built around the few remaining Japanese aircraft carriers, was stationed east of Luzon, about five hundred miles northeast of Leyte, hoping to lure the US fast carrier force away from the battle.

On October 23, the most powerful squadron, designated the Center Force, was heading from its base in Borneo toward Mindoro aiming to enter the Sibuyan Sea and emerge through the San Bernadino Strait, counting on the Northern Force to do its decoy job and take Halsey's carriers out of the fight. Consisting of five battleships (including *Yamato* and *Musashi*), plus ten heavy cruisers and other ships, the Center Force was detected in a narrow passage near Palawan Island by the submarines USS *Dace* and USS *Darter*. Gaining a favorable position and attacking at first light, the submarines were able to hit three of the heavy cruisers sinking two, including the commanding admiral's flagship. The formation sped on after fishing their admiral out of the sea. While following the crippled cruiser, *Darter* ran aground at Bombay Shoal and could not be refloated. Her crew was rescued by *Dace*.

NINE.

The Center Force continued to Mindoro and passed its southern point into the Sibuyan Sea. Though Halsey remained unaware of the decoy fleet, many of his ships were rearming after the Formosa raids or supporting the landings on Leyte and were not in position to counter the threat. One element of his task force was nearby and moved to block the Japanese. Three waves of land-based aircraft attacked the American ships and managed to sink the light carrier USS *Princeton*, but aircraft from the remaining carriers fell on the Japanese in the Sibuyan Sea and began scoring hits, focusing on *Musashi*. At least seventeen bombs and nineteen torpedoes struck the heavily armored battleship in a series of attacks, and she finally capsized and sank. One cruiser was also crippled, but as the Center Force retreated, it was largely intact. Halsey assumed this force was defeated, and having belatedly discovered the Northern Force with its attractive, though impotent, carriers, he gathered his ships and sent them to the north in pursuit. That evening the still powerful Center Force reversed course and headed back to the now unguarded San Bernadino Strait.

Meanwhile, the Southern Force, joined by a force of cruisers from a base in Formosa, had sailed through the Sulu Sea past Negros Island and into the Bohol Sea, following the same route taken by *Nautilus* on her eleventh and twelfth patrols. This fleet included two older battleships, four cruisers, and several destroyers. They aimed to time their arrival into Leyte Gulf with the Northern Force and make short work of the transports and landing craft there. But first they would have to negotiate the narrow thirty-five-mile-long Surigao Strait. It was a trap. Rear Adm. Jesse Olendorf of the US Seventh Fleet commanded a task force of six aging battleships (five of them sunk or damaged during the Pearl Harbor attack and subsequently refloated and repaired) that had led the preinvasion bombardment of the beachhead. Though low on ammunition (particularly of armor-piercing rounds used on ships), they formed a battle line at the head of the strait. In front of them were eight cruisers with smaller guns, and farther ahead were squadrons of fast destroyers with deadly torpedoes. At the entrance to the strait were several dozen PT boats. As the Southern Force entered the area in the predawn darkness, they swept past the little PT boats but ran into a fusillade of destroyer torpedoes from both flanks. Both Japanese battleships were hit along with several destroyers. As the crippled ships continued to press on to the head of the strait, they came under fire from the guns of USS *West Virginia* followed by the other American vessels in what was the last engagement ever to be fought between battleships. Both Japanese battleships were sunk, and the remaining vessels retired in disarray, two of them colliding in the confusion. The Southern Force was no longer a threat to the Leyte beachhead.

As the action in Surigao proceeded, the Center Force passed through the San Bernadino Strait unmolested and was bearing down on Leyte, steaming along the east cost of the island of Samar. Only fifty miles from the entrance to Leyte Gulf, *Yamato* and her eighteen-inch guns would be in range within the hour. Standing in the path were three US escort carrier units totaling sixteen small carriers with a screen of antisubmarine escort destroyers. Four battleships, eight cruisers, and eleven destroyers surprised this meager US force as it approached the beachhead. The carriers immediately launched their planes and ran for cover under a rain squall to the east, while the escort destroyers made a smoke screen to conceal their retreat. The Japanese commander, unaware that the decoy force's deception had succeeded, assumed he had encountered Halsey's fleet and prepared for air attack. He was not disappointed as the escort carriers' 450 planes fell upon the Japanese ships, unopposed by enemy fighters. These aircraft were equipped for antisubmarine operations and many had only machine guns, of little threat to the well-armored battleships and cruisers. Regardless, their attacks were relentless and certainly reinforced the impression that Halsey was afoot.

The small, unarmored destroyers steamed into the Japanese formation at flank speed, wildly maneuvering to avoid large caliber gunfire and launching torpedoes as soon as they were within range. Rather than retreating after expending their torpedoes, the little ships opened fire on the cruisers and battleships with their five-inch guns, to be joined by the single gun on each escort carrier as the Japanese continued to approach and come within range. The torpedoes did some damage, as did the five-inch fire and the air attacks. But soon the larger caliber Japanese guns began to take a toll with several destroyers and the carrier *Gambier Bay* taking fatal hits. The Japanese were in position to sweep through the opposition and take Leyte Gulf under fire. The old battleships that repelled the Southern Force were out of position and nearly out of ammunition, in any case outgunned by the larger enemy vessels. Halsey was hundreds of miles away. MacArthur's return to the Philippines hung in the balance.

At that crucial moment, the Japanese fleet reversed course and headed north in retreat. The ferocity of the near suicidal American resistance and the assumption that they were facing Halsey's carrier force discouraged the attackers. Fearing further losses, the flotilla steamed north and back into San Bernadino Strait. The liberation of the Philippines would continue.

Nautilus ended her twelfth patrol at Mios Woendi, a small atoll just off the northwest coast of New Guinea. This site was selected as a PT boat supply and repair base, and construction began in early June despite ongoing fighting in the region. In a few weeks' time, Seabees built pier and base facilities with acres of Quonset huts covering the tiny island. With more than two thousand feet of navigable beachfront adjacent to a deep water lagoon, the island would become the largest PT boat facility in the Pacific. The torpedo boats began operating from the base in late June as the camp continued to expand. A three hundred bed naval hospital, torpedo dump, dry-docking facilities, a seaplane base, and a mobile amphibious repair base for landing craft were eventually built there. Roads crisscrossed the island serving rows of tents, warehouses, stores, offices, living quarters, docks, ramps, parking areas for planes, and radio stations. The facility also served submarines and became a base for the Combined Field Intelligence Service in support of guerrillas and Coastwatchers. The submarine tender USS *Orion* was moved there, and many Spyron missions originated from that location. It was declared useable for submarines on August 7, 1944, just sixty days before *Nautilus* arrived.

The crew was disappointed to miss a visit by a USO troupe on August 11, including Bob Hope, singer Frances Langford, and dancer Patty Thomas. The Seabees built a stage in short order and the visit featured a short cruise for the entertainers on a PT boat. *Nautilus* was in Mios Woendi only four days loading for the next mission as *Orion* machinists helped with minor repairs and the ship was again fumigated, this time to Sharp's satisfaction. Some of the crew relaxed at "Club Plonk," a Quonset hut set on a barge anchored off shore that provided libations to thirsty submarine sailors. Visitors were given an official guest member card conferring mock prestige to the spartan establishment.

While *Nautilus* and her crew were enjoying a few days' respite at Woendi, submarine command was becoming increasingly worried about fellow Spyron boat USS *Seawolf* (SS-197). *Seawolf* was on her fifteenth war patrol, having departed Brisbane on September 21, assigned to deliver supplies and army personnel to the east coast of the island of Samar. In command was Lt. Cdr. Albert Bontier, who had just relieved *Nautilus* veteran Ozzie Lynch. She exchanged recognition signals with *Narwhal* along the way on October 3, but failed to report the next day when directed and was never heard from again. Eventually, she was declared lost along with eighty-three crewmen and seventeen army passengers. It was later surmised that she was sunk by the American destroyer USS *Rowell*, believing her to be an enemy submarine. The tragic loss of *Seawolf* underscored the maxim, "A submarine has no friends," and brought home the danger that *Nautilus* and other Spyron boats regularly faced.

On the afternoon of October, 10, 1944, *Nautilus* got underway for her thirteenth war patrol.

The departing crew was much the same as sailed on the previous mission but for two notable exceptions. Departing was Lt. Cdr. Ben Jarvis, who turned over executive officer and navigator duties to Lieutenant Commander Michael. Then there was the curious case of Juan Locquiao Echanes, a junior Filipino steward. The ship's official muster roll of September 30, records that Echanes "Deserted in enemy held territory," and went on to note, "Pay due $181.88. Report forwarded to BuPers."

It seems he accompanied the eleven evacuees returned ashore when the ship was aground near Iuisan Point, though no mention of his departure was found in the ship's log or patrol report. Minor cases of AWOL sailors returning late from liberty were duly noted and punishments were documented in the deck logs, so the absence of any mention in the daily log of desertion in enemy held territory, a very serious offense that in wartime could merit the death penalty, is more than puzzling.

Regardless, *Nautilus* had a Spyron mission to fulfill. With the Leyte invasion imminent and the southeastern coasts of the Philippine islands teeming with ships and aircraft, Sharp and his crew were routed along the west side of the archipelago, past Manila, through the Ryukyu Islands, and all the way around to the east coast of Luzon. Much of the eleven-day, 2,500-nautical mile transit was in view of enemy held territory, and a number of ships and aircraft were sighted. MacArthur's troops landed during this voyage and the Japanese ships of the Shō-Gō operation crossed the submarine's path just a few days later. On October 21, security signals were observed at a prearranged spot in Dibut Bay on the east coast of Luzon near Manila, but when *Nautilus* surfaced that evening no boat was seen. An hour later a series of unreadable signals were seen about a half mile from the designated spot, including a red light waving in the darkness. Sharp concluded that the shore party was ambushed, yet they bravely took the chance to warn the submarine. Sharp turned tail and sped out of Dibut Bay.

Heading farther south along the coast on October 23, *Nautilus* approached a second designated location, this one just fifty miles east of Japanese-occupied Manila. Though visibility was poor, security signals were confirmed, and that evening cargo and an unrecorded number of passengers were transferred to shore. These resistance fighters were willingly braving the most dangerous territory in the backyard of the Manila enemy garrison. MacArthur's forces would not land in Luzon to relieve them until January. Meanwhile, cargo continued to be offloaded until dawn when the submarine had to move offshore and submerge. She returned the next evening and by around midnight the job was finished. *Nautilus* bid farewell to the shore party and headed back up the coast to reconnoiter Dibut Bay.

All day they scanned the shore for signals, peering through the periscopes, seeing nothing. Finally giving up, Sharp was heading out to sea when lookouts spotted a signal. *Nautilus* reversed course and headed back into the bay. At 1910, Capt. Robert Lapham came aboard.

Lapham was a legend among the Philippines resistance. A US Army officer who was not keen to surrender when the Japanese took the islands in 1942, he helped organize a raiding party that slipped through the Japanese lines and gathered intelligence to support future operations. He so hated the prospect of surrender that he reasoned it was his duty to continue to fight the war as best he could. After the fall of Bataan, he organized a guerrilla regiment in the central plains of the northern island of Luzon, and by 1944 he commanded more than thirteen thousand men, mostly Filipino.

Among his command were several Coastwatcher units. Besides intelligence collection and sabotage, Lapham's forces were credited with helping to liberate 513 prisoners of war who were about to be executed as MacArthur's forces were approaching. Promoted to major by war's end, Lapham was awarded the Distinguished Service Cross by General MacArthur and was the third American to receive the Philippine Legion of Honor, the others being MacArthur and President Roosevelt.

One of the *Narwhal* Spyron missions delivered thirty tons of supplies to Lapham in August 1944. *Nautilus* had another twenty tons of vital cargo to offload.

To assist the unloading operation and with the beachhead secure, *Nautilus* took the unusual step of anchoring in the bay and sending a line ashore, tying the ship to a tree to stabilize its mooring. By these means the job was finished in a few hours. At 2315, the submarine weighed anchor and was underway, headed north to retrace the path around the north of Luzon and down the west coast of the archipelago. As they pulled away from the rendezvous, Japanese ships were retreating in defeat from the Battle of Leyte Gulf, as operation Shō-Gō had been thwarted.

A few days later, as the submarine was cruising south along the west coast of Luzon, Sharp received unusual orders from Task Force 72. He called his executive officer and navigator Lieutenant Commander Michael and his gunnery officer Lt. (jg) Bob Gustafson into the wardroom.

Sharp, with orders from command in hand on a clipboard, said, "Mr. Gustafson, how would you like to fire those six-inchers?" The big guns had not seen action except for training since Gustafson had come aboard as a young ensign on the tenth patrol.

"Yes sir!" he said eagerly. "The men have been itching for a chance!" Then he paused, perplexed. No targets had been sighted and with so many Allied ships now operating in the area the rules of engagement had changed requiring a vessel to be confirmed an enemy ship before attacking. "What are we shooting, sir?"

Sharp tapped the message board. "Says here the task force commander wants us to sink one of our own subs!"

"What?" blurted out the other officers in unison. "That can't be right!" said Michael.

Sharp chuckled. "It's true!" He scanned the message and paraphrased. "Seems as though USS *Darter* ran herself aground while chasing a Jap cruiser four days ago and could not get off. Fortunately, *Dace* was with her and took on the crew, but *Darter* is not worth salvaging."

"So what are we supposed to do?" asked Gustafson. "Why the guns?"

"Command is concerned that the Japs will try to salvage it. We don't want them to get a hold of one of our new *Gato*-class boats. They want us to wreck it best we can." He again looked down at the message. "Says here it's on Bombay Shoals, southwest of here."

Michael consulted his chart. "That's about three hundred miles from here." He noted a spot on the chart just west of Mindoro Island. "We're about here, and will be passing through the strait in a few hours. We need to head southwest now."

"Plot a course and make it happen." Sharp got up. "Mr. Gustafson, get your men ready for surface action. We'll be there morning after next."

"They're ready now, sir!" replied Gustafson as Michael headed up to the control room to plot a course. In a few minutes, *Nautilus* turned right and headed down the coast of Palawan toward Bombay Shoals.

When *Darter* ran aground just after midnight on October 25, the area was thick with Japanese ships and aircraft supporting (and eventually retreating) from Shō-Gō. As she tried to extricate herself with the help of *Dace*, a Japanese destroyer approached, but did not engage the helpless submarine. The enemy ship inexplicably sailed away. With the tide falling and danger lurking, it became clear that the ship could not be freed without a full salvage effort. With dawn approaching, the captain, Cdr. David McClintock, gave the order to abandon ship. Secret materials and equipment were destroyed, and scuttling charges were set inside the hull. *Dace* stood by and was able to take off the entire crew. The explosives failed to destroy the ship, so *Dace* fired several torpedoes at her erstwhile companion. The torpedoes hit the reef and exploded before reaching the submarine. *Dace* then opened up with her three-inch deck gun and managed to score twenty-one hits, but did not make much of an impression on the tough hull.

On October 27, the submarine USS *Rock* was sent to try to finish off *Darter*. Nine torpedoes (six of which spent their charges on the reef) failed to do the job. Hence the orders to *Nautilus*, with hopes that her cruiser gun battery could succeed. At 0921 on October 31, the submarine wreck was spotted off Bombay Shoals. An hour and a half later they were within range.

"Man battle stations, battle surface!" called Hal Winner, officer of the deck. *Nautilus* came to the surface and gunner's mates scrambled to ready their weapons. By 1113 all was ready. "Commence firing!" came the order. The guns erupted as the 105-pound projectiles flew to the target. After a few salvos the gunners began to score hits. As they zeroed in on the target, the men first focused on the conning tower and control room area, smashing through the hull with armor-piercing shells and setting the ship afire. Switching to high-capacity rounds, the crew worked fore and aft of the doomed ship, setting off large explosions from one end to the other. Crewmen hauled the heavy rounds up from the magazine by hand, the balky mechanical hoists having long since been removed. After forty salvoes the forward gun went quiet, the breech plug having failed, but the aft gun kept up the barrage. Dense yellow smoke poured out of *Darter*'s control room and a huge oil fire started aft. After eighty-eight rounds the captain called a cease-fire. Sharp recorded at least fifty-five hits, and commented, "It is very doubtful that any equipment on *Darter* will be useful to Japan—except as scrap."

Nautilus secured from battle stations, reversed course, and headed northwest along Palawan Island to pass through Mondoro

Strait and resumed her transit back to Mios Woendi. The route was thick with contacts, Sharp finding thirty-one vessels and fifty-six aircraft worth logging in his patrol report. Most of the sightings were Allied craft or unidentified. At one point, he commenced an approach on a vessel "hoping for a ship which would conform with the limited targets allowed us." Identifying the contact as a large power-driven sailing vessel, he let it go for reasons unexplained.

On the morning of November 9, *Nautilus* arrived at Woendi Lagoon and moored alongside the tender USS *Orion*. She only stayed long enough for the crew to refuel, load several tons of spare parts for delivery to the submarine base at Brisbane, and make a brief appearance at Club Plonk. Early afternoon the next day she set sail for eastern Australia, arriving in Brisbane without incident on November 20, ending her thirteenth patrol.

Brisbane offered a welcome opportunity for fifteen days R&R and a short refit including yet another main engine overhaul. On December 11, George Sharp detached, turning over command to his executive officer, Willard de Los Michael, who became the fourth and final wartime captain of *Nautilus*. Sharp served after the war bringing captured German submarines to the United States, and was one of the commanders in charge of atomic bomb testing in the Marshall Islands, eventually making the rank of rear admiral before retirement.

A turnover of crew saw the departure of recently promoted Lt. (jg) Floyd "Red" Porterfield who after the war commanded the submarine USS *Redfish* (SS-395), and later a destroyer. He served in the Mediterranean, including tours in Lebanon and Vietnam, and was awarded two Silver Stars, a Bronze Star, and Navy and Marine Corps medals for his service. Among the more unusual events in Porterfield's long career were opportunities to help make movies. While he was commanding officer in the spring of 1954, *Redfish* was fitted with a dummy rear fin, and played the part of Jules Verne's *Nautilus* in the Walt Disney film *20,000 Leagues*

Under the Sea. Later, in 1957, *Redfish* played the part of the fictional submarine USS *Nerka* in the 1958 motion picture *Run Silent, Run Deep*, based on the Edward Beach novel. Porterfield retired as a commander after a thirty-year naval career.

Another departure was Chief Electrician Foy Hester, like Porterfield, veteran of thirteen *Nautilus* war patrols. He first reported in 1936 and with eight years on board was one of the longest tenured men on the ship. After bidding farewell to his shipmates, Foy was transferred to the submarine repair unit in Brisbane and eventually made his way stateside. He was recommended for advancement to warrant officer and remained in the navy until he retired in 1947, having served nearly twenty-one years. While on board *Nautilus* he received a Bronze Star, the Presidential Unit Commendation, and the Philippine Presidential Unit Citation among many other awards. Foy meticulously kept his dive log for the duration of his time on board *Nautilus*, showing that from April 1942 through November 1944 the submarine made 881 dives for a total submerged time of 3,070 hours—more than 127 days under water.

An unexpected arrival was Petty Officer Juan Locquiao Echanes, "deserter" of patrol twelve. It seems that Echanes was picked up by sister submarine *Narwhal* on September 17 during her recent Spyron patrol along with refugees including six adults, fourteen children, and five Filipinos who wanted to become steward's mates in the navy. Echanes was dropped in Brisbane and awaited his own ship's return. On November 20 upon arrival in Brisbane, the *Nautilus* muster roll remarked, "Deserter returned. Reported on board for duty." The ship's deck log remained silent on the matter.

On December 15, Allied troops landed on the Philippine island of Mindoro just south of Luzon, but the southern island of Mindanao still harbored Japanese forces and the guerrillas needed supplies. *Nautilus* got underway for her fourteenth patrol and sixth Spyron mission on January 3, 1945, after loading ninety-five tons of cargo. Just days later on January 9, landings on Luzon, the island of Manila, began the culminating drive to recapture the Philippines. The ship made Darwin on January 13, refueled, and after minor repairs headed north the next day.

Nautilus followed similar routes to earlier patrols and made her way into the Celebes Sea and the west coast of Mindanao without incident, though many aircraft were sighted. Entering Moro Gulf on January 20, Captain Michael sighted security signals at a spot off Linao Bay, and that evening saw a motor whaleboat standing offshore with "Old Glory" hoisted. The submarine surfaced, and though the danger of Japanese attack was waning, Michael took no chances. He had the crew make ready four 20-mm machine guns and trained out both six-inch guns with five rounds for each on hand. He commented, "Should be able to return the average surprise with dividends."

Before midnight, all forty-five tons of cargo was ashore and a single evacuee was taken on, a soldier who was sick and malnourished, having subsisted on rice and fish for the last three years.

Departing the area, *Nautilus* continued around the south of Mindanao, sighting wave after wave of American aircraft, mainly flights of B-24 Liberator heavy bombers. Over the course of the patrol thirty-one air contacts were logged, in groups of as many as sixteen planes. From time to time recognition flares were fired if an aircraft seemed threatening, and on a few occasions a quick dive was in order. By this time, sea and air spaces were well under control by Allied forces, so ships and aircraft were to engage targets only after verifying they were enemy. Still caution was in order, as submarines have no friends.

On January 23, the ship made the east coast of the island and sighted signals at Baculin Bay. That evening, a banca flying the American flag came alongside and the crew began transferring cargo. As few boats were available from shore, Michael had the ship's rubber boats broken out and shortly after midnight all remaining supplies were ashore. The progress of Allied forces in the theater was such that the thousand pounds of dry stores provided by the submarine included such nonmilitary items as books, magazines, and office supplies.

Nautilus proceeded south returning to Darwin late morning on January 30, completing her fourteenth and final war patrol. The task group commander congratulated Captain Michael, officers, and crew upon the "expeditious completion of another hazardous assignment." Adm. James Fife, Seventh Fleet Commander of Submarines had the following to say:

> *It is noted that this fourteenth patrol of the* Nautilus *terminates the active patrol duty of this gallant ship, during which several hazardous special missions were successfully completed in the SOW-ESPAC area. Her departure from this force is met with regret and pride in a job well done.*

Seven men made all fourteen *Nautilus* war patrols: Ens. John Sabbe, Chiefs Myles Banbury, Nick Bruck, Peter Freitas, and Joe Goodman, and First Class Mates Colin Campbell and Robert Hyde.

Supported mainly by *Nautilus* and *Narwhal*, but with other submarines as well, Spyron missions delivered 1,325 tons of supplies, sent ashore 331 military personnel, and evacuated 472 people, most of them civilians, many women and children. A 1948 assessment of Spyron said, "The practical importance of this efficient supply service by cargo submarine can scarcely be overestimated. It became the life-line of the guerrilla resistance movement."

The Spyron program was ended after *Nautilus* completed her special mission at Baculin Bay with Allied forces on the ground and the battle for the Philippines well in hand, though it would be weeks before Manila was captured, and pockets of resistance continued through the end of the war. The Philippines campaign cost the US Army nearly fourteen thousand lives lost against more than three hundred thousand Japanese. It is estimated that some nine hundred thousand civilians perished over the course of the invasion, occupation, and retaking of the islands.

Most of his shipmates have since departed on "eternal patrol," but their legacy lives in every submariner who serves today. May their service and sacrifices never be forgotten.

TEN.

Operation Ginny

Vincent dePaul Lupiano

THE STORY OF OPERATION GINNY STARTS AT OLD HARBOR, Bastia, the capital of Corsica, an island in the Mediterranean Sea west of the Italian Peninsula and immediately north of the Italian island of Sardinia. Italian and Free French forces started to push the Germans off the island after the Italian armistice in September 1943, making Corsica the first French Department to be freed.

On the afternoon of February 27, 1944, there were telltale signs of a brutal battle in Bastia: The citadel's walls were pocked with bullet holes, and the streets showed signs of shell damage. The sound of sporadic gunfire started to diminish. The Germans and the French resistance forces pursuing them were still here and there but in a dwindling capacity.

In the northeastern corner of Nouveau Port, cordoned off from the rest of the waterfront, two American patrol boats, *PT 214* and *PT 210*, were preparing to put out to sea and initiate a secret, historic mission.

Navigation was left entirely to these boats' radar and compasses. Four hours and fifty minutes after departure, they arrived three hundred yards off the pinpoint. The terms "pinpoint" and "target" are often confused. A pinpoint in this context means the point onshore nearest the target; the target is self-explanatory. In the US Air Force, the pinpoint is the target—the point at which to drop bombs.

The boats were seventy-eight feet long and powered by three modified marine derivations of the 1,500-hp Packard V-12 aircraft engine, water-cooled, making 4,500 hp each. They were built by Higgins Industries and utilized an innovative V-shaped Quadraconic hull design subsequently used in later years in yachts, sailboats, and racing boats. The hull, two double diagonal mahogany planking layers, incorporated a glue-impregnated cloth layer between inner and outer planks held together by thousands of copper rivets and shiny bronze screws—one of many artisanal works of World War II equipment that can be admired today in various museums.

Overall, a light and robust hull was constructed from three-thousand-year-old white cedar logs recovered from the Mountain Lake sphagnum bog in New Jersey. On January 20, 1943, they were commissioned at the Municipal Yacht Basin at Lake Pontchartrain, New Orleans. They were part of Motor Torpedo Boat Squadron Fifteen, referred to as MTBRon 15 or, as the sailors called it, Ron 15.

They were tough old gals, the first two PT boats to arrive in the Mediterranean at the end of April 1944. They fought against the Axis forces across the Western Mediterranean, North Africa, Sicily, and the southern Italian coast.

In the US Navy inventory of warships, these were the fastest boats afloat and could attain 40 knots.

The boats bristled with gunnery: two large-bore Swedish-manufactured Bofors 40mm cannons with a firing rate of 120 rounds/minute, a range of 10,750 yards, and an aircraft ceiling of 23,500 feet; it took four men to aim, fire, and load. Ammo loaded from the top in four-round clips. Each round weighed 4.75 pounds, and the projectile it fired weighed almost 2 pounds. Two twin M2 .50 caliber machine guns were mounted on turrets on the port and starboard sides. The twin-fifties were an icon of the boat's image. Crews preferred to mix armor-piercing, incendiary, and tracer ammunition firing at a rate of 730 rounds per minute.

Their maximum range was 7,300 yards, and their effective range was about 2,000 yards. Mounted on the forecastle were two Oerlikon 20mm cannons. A sixty-round drum magazine mounted on the top of the gun housed the ammunition—a high-explosive tracer or incendiary round weighing approximately one-half pound.

The maximum range was 4,800 yards, with a ceiling of 10,000 feet and an effective range of 1,000 yards. A gunner and a loader were needed to operate the weapon, one to cock it and fire it, and another to clear the jams that occurred. To qualify as a gunner, this team had to achieve a rate of fire between 250 and 300 yards per minute. The best crews practiced with their eyes closed to be able to perform the same tasks instinctively. Each boat had four Mark XVII torpedoes on the starboard and port sides weighing 2,600 pounds and containing 466-pound Torpex-filled warheads; Torpex was a secondary explosive, with 50 percent more knockout power than TNT. The torpedoes were known to crew members as "fish" and the torpedomen who operated them as "lovely ladies."

Each vessel had a crew of fifteen to twenty sailors.

The cabin interior and exterior components were constructed of two layers of cross-hatched mahogany wood with a layer of canvas treated with anti-rot paint brushed between the planking. The cabin interior and exterior were plywood and mahogany, elegant enough to appear in *Architectural Digest* magazine.

Weight was kept to a minimum to allow for more incredible speed and maneuverability. The future president of the United States John F. Kennedy, who would be forever associated with the sinking of his PT boat—he would be blown out of the water on his *PT 109* by a Japanese cruiser—said the PT boats were "small, fast, versatile, strongly armed vessels." They could make

TEN.

a maximum sustained speed of 39.7 knots and a top speed of 44.1 knots with a heavy ordnance load.

Maneuverability was satisfactory, with a turning circle of 368 yards. The structural strength was also adequate, and it had a moderate tendency to "pound" in the sea. By war's end, the US Navy PT boat would have more "firepower-per-ton" than any other vessel in the fleet. All the boats were painted Navy gray above and red below the waterline for camouflage. A few added a personal touch: a shark's eyes and a toothy grin on the bow, painted red, white, and blue.

The only similar boat was the German *Schnellboote* ("fast boats"), also known as *S-Boot* or *E-Boot*. They were formidable: 115 feet in length, a beam of 17 feet, a top speed of 50 knots, and 7,500 hp. The US Navy PT boat would outfire the German boat in a gunfight, but the speed differential went to the *Schnellboot*. So the idea for the PT boat was to shoot and run and leave the German boat wallowing.

Tonight, *PT 204* would have a considerable shark jaw painted around the nose on the flank—red lips and sharp white teeth; it also had shark's eyes, which gave it a menacing, pulverizing appearance. Because of this, it was nicknamed "Shark's Head." The nickname for *PT 203* was "Aggie Maru," the Corsican dialect version of Agatha Mary.

On February 27, 1944, as the sun diminished behind the mountains on Corsica, Lt. (jg) Eugene S. A. Clifford, the senior officer in charge, began prepping for the mission; he checked each boat for anything that might be incorrect. Often, mishaps happened when loose wiring caused the navigation lights or searchlights to switch on accidentally, revealing their location to the enemy.

Tonight's mission was super stealthy: The boats would have to carry fifteen American commandos—an Organizational Group (OG) from the Office of Strategic Services, or OSS—through the darkness and travel 120 miles to the Ligurian coast and the

256

province of La Spezia, where the Germans had a massive force of Wehrmacht troops. The OGs would disembark the PT boats, paddle to shore in bright yellow rubber boats, and blow up railroad tunnels crucial to the Germans.

The PT boats would loiter off the coast and pick up the OGs once they completed their mission. On the way to La Spezia and back, they would have to cross shipping lanes the Germans and their *Schnellboote* patrolled regularly but not with any predictability. Thus, they had to be watchful.

As Clifford finished his inspections, two Army trucks pulled up at the dock with the fifteen commandos inside. At that moment, a light rain began; it would get heavier, and stay with them all night throughout the mission.

There were nineteen OGs—fifteen enlisted men and four officers for this mission. Clifford knew most of them from prior tasks: They were known as the "Italian Operational Groups (OGs)," thus the name "Ginny." They were first- or second-generation Italian Americans from a unit formally known as Unit A, First Contingent, Operational Group, 2677th Headquarters Company Experimental (Provisional), attached to Allied Forces Headquarters. All had volunteered to join the Operational Group Command of the OSS, received basic Army training and commando training in the United States, and shipped over here. Their purposes were to sabotage operations, stir guerrilla warfare in enemy territory, and go deep behind front lines.

As soon as the OGs boarded the PT boats, 1st Lt. Albert R. Materazzi, the mission commander, instructed the enlistees to haul their weapons and equipment into the forward cabin of each boat. He gathered them in the chart house, which was the boat's nerve center. All maneuvers were directed from here by the captain or whoever was in charge of the boat at any given time. The radar display, radio communications gear, and nautical maps were in the chart house.

TEN.

The OGs knew what the mission was—they had rehearsed for the last time the day before at L'Ile-Rousse, topographically like the La Spezia coast—but the officers took them through it one more time. Standing by with Materazzi and Clifford were Lieutenant (Junior Grade) Wittibort, skipper of *PT 203*; an observer, Capt. Donald B. Wentzel; and the two officers who would lead the mission: 1st Lt. and engineer Vincent J. Russo, an explosives expert from Montclair, New Jersey, and 1st Lt. Paul J. Traficante, overall commander of Operation Ginny, who would remain on one of the PT boats.

Most vital for this mission were the highly informative aerial photos taken a couple of days prior. They showed the railroad tunnel entrances—the targets—on the La Spezia–Genoa line, five hundred yards southeast of Stazione di Framura (Framura Station), the Germans' main supply line to run vital equipment and weaponry to the fighting at Cassino and Anzio. The photographs also highlighted about one thousand feet of railroad tracks between the tunnel entrances; Stazione di Framura was situated almost equidistant between the two vaulted tunnel entrances.

The mission's plan called for the PT boats to depart Bastia, land the fifteen men in their rubber boats on the craggy coastline, then loiter until the OGs completed the mission and returned to the waiting PT boats. Then they would head back to Corsica— that was the plan.

It did not work out that way because of serious errors and miscalculations. Not least was navigational and disorientation among the OGs paddling ashore.

Once ashore, Lieutenant Traficante and his security party were to neutralize the railroad's signal house near one of the tunnels and then examine and evaluate both tunnel entrances and come up with a plan to blow them—and do this at a preset time. While he and one other man did this, the other members of the security party kept a lookout.

Vincent Russo and his men would go to the targets, prepare them for detonation, and then leave for the PT boats. He would not do this until he was sure the PT boats were waiting for them. Materazzi would remain with the boats, maintaining communications and updates via radio. One of the men would adjust the timers on the explosives to the time it would take for his party to leave the tunnels and get back to the boats.

The explosive to be used was C4 (cyclonite, or cyclotrimethylene trinitramine), which makes up around 91 percent of C4 by mass: potent, deadly, and powerful. The plan was to cause the tunnel entrances to implode onto the tracks, which would require months of reconstruction and put the trains out of business. Once the boats left their loitering stations, the timers—according to plan—would kick off the charges at the tunnels, giving the party ample time to escape the area without engaging the Germans. Again, that was the plan. It never got that far.

Now, at the dock at Bastia, all aboard the boats took to their stations and listened to the powerful engines cough to life. They slowly moved away from the docks, their windshield wipers slashing across the rain-spattered windscreens.

"The first thing that dies in any battle is the plan of attack." So said, accurately, Carl von Clausewitz—formally, Carl Philipp Gottfried (Gottlieb) von Clausewitz—a military theorist of absolute respect, a thousand times admired. He stressed "morality" in war, or, in today's terminology, "psychology." More than anything, von Clausewitz was a realist when pondering the cannonade and splattering of body parts on the rustic hills and grassy valleys of warfare. Had he been aboard one of the PT boats right now, von Clausewitz would have allowed a faint roll of his patrician's eyes: "I am not surprised," he might have uttered.

The boats were no more than a hundred yards from the dock when Eugene Clifford announced they had to return to the dock—his radar unit was on the fritz. Hopefully it could be repaired quickly. When they got to the dock, the maintenance sailors went to work. Ten minutes later, Clifford was told that his radar unit would need a few hours to repair; they suggested he swap out *PT 203* with *PT 214*. "Shark Head" was going nowhere that night. It took about thirty minutes to transfer all the men, equipment, and weapons from *PT 203* to *PT 214*. Frustration and anxiety started to mount—and they had a strict schedule facing them when they reached the disembarkation point on the Ligurian coast.

At this point, perhaps they should have thought about delaying the mission. After all, nothing said the tunnels had to be blown that night. But they didn't delay, and that might have contributed to their failure that night. They persevered, obviously thinking they could make up the lost time. Not so.

Departure from Bastia had been scheduled for 1800 hours. It was now 1845, so they were behind schedule by forty-five minutes.

With the Packards' exhaust notes burbling, the boats forged a stable speed of 30 knots, spewing rooster tails of frothy white spray and an arrogant nose-high attitude marking their path through the chilly rain.

Leaving the Ligurian Sea, they sped into the Gulf of Genoa, the Italian Riviera—that crescent-shaped region of historic Mediterranean coastline arcing between the South of France and Tuscany—now 153 miles off their bows. The eastern half, the Riviera di Levante, is defined by rugged cliffs, turquoise coves, colorful fishing villages, and a lovely broach of cities and towns with centuries-old names: La Spezia, Portofino, Camogli, San Remo. A few miles northwest, situated in the crux of the region, Genoa, the birthplace of Christopher Columbus. The Apennine Mountains cut midsection, a range of three parallel mountains extending 750 miles along the length of Italy. In the northwest, they meld with the Ligurian Alps at Altare. They conclude at Reggio di

Calabria in the southwest, the coastal city at the peninsula's tip that cups the northern portion of the horseshoe-shaped area. At almost any other time in history, the area would be unmistakably fetching and romantic. Tonight, it could be lethal.

Fifteen miles northwest of La Spezia, the two tunnels sat on opposite ends of the small railroad station named Stazione di Framura (Framura railway station) and Bonassola, a small fishing village. Occasionally, writers and historians mark the forces' landing point as La Spezia and other as Bonassola because they are close. The tunnels were on the railroad line—the only one—that *Generalfeldmarschall* (General Field Marshal) Albert Kesselring liked to use to transport supplies to his embattled troops in the north, specifically the Cassino area of northern Italy.

OSS intelligence agents had obtained construction documents of the tunnels. They spent time interviewing engineers from the maintenance section of the Italian railways about the tunnels near Framura. If the tunnels were imploded onto the tracks, all rail transportation—all the Wehrmacht's vital supplies—would cease rolling for many months, starving an irreplaceable supply chain and shutting down the entire German offensive in Italy.

At about 2230 hours, another obstacle arose.

The PT boats' radar screens picked up hits that could have been enemy vessels—specifically, the fast-moving, lethal German *Schnellboote*. The PT boats were about four miles from the coastline and could make out lights. From here, the boats went into "silent mode": Each muffler had butterfly flap valves fitted in the main exhaust that ran the usually loud exhaust down through the muffler and under the water line. Usually, this was only done at low speeds.

The OGs came out of their reverie and began gathering their equipment and blowing up the two rubber boats. Lieutenant Clifford set a course for Stazione di Framura. His calculations were only made through the cockpit instruments and the onboard maps. This form of navigation was probably responsible for his missing the pinpoint. Clifford was up against a moonless night, near-zero visibility, and light rain.

At this point, the only distinguishable objects onshore were two mountains to the north. Since that might have "appeared" to be the pinpoint area, Clifford headed the boats in their direction.

At 2230 hours, Vincent Russo, standing with Clifford in the cockpit, told Clifford he believed they were heading in the wrong direction. Clifford ordered a course change again, heading them south—until they came to Scoglia Ciamia and stopped.

Russo and his men started to disembark. When all the men and equipment were aboard the rubber boats, Russo gave Materazzi his best salute, unhooked the lines, and pushed off the PT boat. The OGs started paddling to the shore; the serious part of the mission had begun.

No one among them was calm; there were a lot of butterflies. They all knew that several mistakes, miscalculations, and errors had already been made—most important, they were now ninety minutes off schedule. The combination of the errors, the darkness, and the rain just added to their trepidation. All knew that for a mission to go well, it had to run like clockwork; tonight was running like a clock, only this one was broken. They could not get the ninety minutes back. They could not stop the rain. They could not guarantee the pinpoint. The only thing to do was move forward and pray things would somehow fall into place. But at this point, they knew they were against stiff odds.

Aboard the PT boats, the gunners were on high alert for enemy vessels.

At 0145, Materazzi's radio came alive with Russo's voice saying they had found the fissure that would lead them up the cliff. Russo said he would personally inspect the area and report back. Meanwhile, the clock kept ticking. Russo climbed the fissure to the top of the cliff, nearly falling several times because the rain made the rocks slick as ice. As soon as Russo reached the top of the cliff, he heard a train northwest of where he was standing. He took a deep breath, knowing he was in trouble. Again, he realized they were in the wrong spot.

Aboard *PT 214*, Materazzi and Eugene Clifford started to make calculations; they told Russo to stand by while they tried to figure things out.

According to their mission timetable, they should have been leaving the coastline with the OGs at 0330—this would provide cover from the overcast skies and the rain. They told Russo that they could only loiter until 0400 at the latest, then they had to leave for Bastia. If they waited any longer, it would be daylight, the weather could worsen, they could be exposed to German patrols, and would generally be way off the timetable and in serious jeopardy of losing control of the whole mission. It could evolve into a deadly situation.

Materazzi concluded that it would take Russo and his men until 0530 to reach the tunnels—and then they would need thirty minutes to set the time fuses and attach the C4 to the tunnel openings. When Materazzi rolled this over in his mind, he ordered Russo and his men to return to the PT boats. By 0315, the OGs were aboard the PT boats and heading for Bastia, where they arrived at 0730.

They would try again March 22.

The plan was considered generally sound enough to be used for the second attempt to blow up the tunnels.

Despite their unsuccessful attempt, the Ginny OGs were determined to get the job done and now had more knowledge and experience regarding the overall mission. Things would be better the second time out, they felt. They practiced getting in and out of the PT boats and into the rubber boats until they could do it with their eyes closed; they went through inflating the boats and anything else related to the sea trip that had to be done with precision. They checked their weapons so many times they thought they would wear them thin. They thought they had a better shot at blowing the tunnels than they did the first time. The experience had been a good teacher.

Even more than before, they had the spirit they needed to succeed. On March 22 they would put the time to good use.

OSS agents in Naples "obtained" the tunnels' construction documents, and interviewed engineers from the construction crews. They then went to pilots of the Eighth Air Force and obtained photographs, studied them over and over, and asked the pilots to go up and shoot another batch for them. All this information was new and helped them better understand the topography around the tunnels.

Vincent Russo, the mission's engineer, studied all the latest information. He concluded that instead of using 375 pounds of C4, 650 pounds would be better—half for one tunnel, the other half for the second tunnel. He and the rest of the OGs rehearsed this at L'Ile-Rousse, a location on the island of Corsica opposite Bastia, similar to La Spezia. At night on March 20, two days before the raid date, they made a dry run.

The PT boats would arrive at the disembarkation point, a cove below Capeneggio three hundred yards southwest of the pinpoint. Once there at 2300 hours, March 22, the shore party would transfer from the two PT boats to the three rubber dinghies. They would follow a ravine, or fissure, that extended 150 meters to the open section of the railroad track and the tunnel openings on either side of Stazione Framura and neutralize the signal house, or linesman's shed. There, at 0300 hours on March 23, they would commence work.

Lieutenant Traficante would lead the security party, head toward the signal house, and neutralize it. Included in his party were Technical Specialists Grade 5 (T/5s) Joseph Noia, Rosario F. Squatrito, and Storo Calcara. They would do an immediate reconnaissance of the targets and then pass along the signal to proceed to Lieutenant Russo.

Upon receiving the signal, Russo and his party would set the charges. With him were Sgt. Alfred L. De Flumeri, Sgt. Dominick C. Mauro, and T/5s Liberty J. Tremonte, Joseph J. Leone, Thomas N. Savino, and Joseph A. Libardi. However, if Russo determined that the explosives could not be set on time, he would signal Materazzi, telling him they would be back on the boats by 0300. Some of the party would remain onshore, hide during the day, and then, at 2300 hours the next night, with only two men at the tunnels, finish setting the C4. Only after contact with the PT boats with a red "R" signal would they initiate the C4 charges—weather permitting. All this depended on the PT boats' ability to return the following night and loiter until the OGs came aboard.

At 1755 hours on March 22, 1944, the PT boats departed Bastia, arriving at Stazione Framura at 2245 hours; they had come within three hundred yards of the shore. Ten minutes later, the OGs had inflated the rubber boats, had them in the water, loaded the C4, shoved off from the PT boats, and headed for shore. So far, no glitches. But the night was young.

At 2315 hours the shore party sent a garbled message to Materazzi; there was no response. Ten minutes later, Russo got on the radio and said he was at the shoreline looking for a spot to land the rubber boats. Materazzi replied, "OK." Ten minutes later, Russo was on the radio again to Materazzi, saying he thought he had found the target. Materazzi did not know what this meant. Thirty minutes later, Russo radioed Traficante, saying, "We see you. Wait for us." That was the last communication from the Ginny fifteen.

Almost at that moment, several *Schnellboote* were running at the PT boats at high speed. As a diversionary tactic, one of the PT boats broke off, taking enemy fire from the lead *Schnellboot*. By now, Materazzi's PT boat had drifted two miles from its loitering spot and waited five hundred yards offshore. But Materazzi had been spotted from the shore: A green flare shot up and outlined his PT boat. Then, from the sea came a red flare, a response to the green light, clearly showing the outline of Materazzi's PT boat. Materazzi thought he saw machine-gun fire coming at them from the shore, but the bullets were splashing too far off their bow to be effective.

Materazzi quickly determined this was not a good spot for the PT boats. He ordered both to head west for five miles. Once there, they would join up, turn around, head back to where they had been, and try to reestablish a connection with the shore party.

At 0200 hours the rendezvous was successful, but more *Schnellboote* appeared simultaneously. The PT boats effectively initiated evasive maneuvers, and one hour later the *Schnellboote* were gone.

But misfortune struck again.

One of the PT boats had a serious problem, actually, two problems: Both the main and auxiliary steering mechanisms were not functioning, and both boats had to wait while the malfunctions were repaired. It was now 0415, too late for the boats to return to the pinpoint, retrieve the OGs, and get out of there before sunrise.

Materazzi held a meeting with the other boat's skipper. They concluded it would be best to go back to Bastia and return the next night, as per the contingency plan, and off they went back to their home base in Bastia.

The PT boats returned to the pinpoint on March 23, but before they reached it, their radar indicated several large enemy craft at sea. They were blocked from making shore and the pinpoint. From where they were, they saw blinking lights coming from the shore—a possible enemy trap to lure them. With no way they could loiter, they headed back to Bastia. A photo reconnaissance mission flown the next morning revealed no damage to the tunnels and no sign of the OGs. The Ginny OGs had not succeeded in blowing the tunnels. But where were they?

A final attempt was made on the night of March 25, but again there was no sign of the OGs. That was the end of the attempts to bring them home. Initially, the OSS listed them as missing in action; later, as captured by the enemy.

From here, events become debatable, often confusing, and conflicting. There is of course no rendering on the part of the OGs as to what they endured—no record of their communications or the decisions they had to make. Once they left the shoreline and proceeded up the cliff, the last communication Lt. Materazzi heard was, "We are here. Come to us."

So, WHAT HAPPENED TO THE GINNY OGS AFTER THEY LANDED?

After the OGs left the PT boats on March 24, they paddled to the shore to discover sheer cliffs rising formidably, straight from the sea. They moved up the coast to seek a more suitable place. The rough seas complicated their rowing and the direction they were heading. Several OGs fell into the water and had to swim to shore, and they lost fifteen cases of C4 explosives.

THE MISSION WAS DETERIORATING WITH ALARMING SPEED. WHAT TO DO?

Once ashore, they discovered they were in the wrong spot. Traficante tried to reconnect with Materazzi—no luck. The walkie-talkies had been ruined. Russo decided that demolishing the tunnels was out of the question, at least tonight. As dawn approached, the OGs pulled the rubber boats up about fifty feet from the beach and set out to camouflage them. The entire party of OGs then went about four hundred yards uphill until they found an abandoned barn, where they decided to hide for the day.

Partial communications from the OGs and reports from local Italians and Germans provide a lessthan-clear picture of their arrival at the pinpoint and ascent up the fissure.

Once ashore, the OGs had attempted to camouflage the dinghies with leaves, tree limbs, and brush; the attempt was inept. Yes, the dinghies could not be seen from the cliff above, but they could be seen from the sea, and a fisherman reported them. Further, the rubber boats were bright orange. (Why would the powers that be have permitted that color for the boats?) This set off an immediate German and partisan search.

More than anything else, bungling the camouflaging of the rubber boats was probably the OGs, biggest mistake and would, sadly, lead to their capture.

The only helpful information at this time regarding the OGs came from the enemy's intercepted telex reports and communiqués monitored by the BBC in London. Using the sparse details from enemy telex communiqués, this is what occurred immediately after the OGs landed.

While the records of *Brigade Almers* could not be found, the war diary (*Kriegstagebuch*) of LXXV Army Corps showed that the Ginny OGs were captured midmorning on March 24. The enemy's GSO (intelligence office) entry stated:

> Mar. 44: 500 meters west of Bonassola (22 kilometers northwest of La Spezia), an American sabotage team consisting of two officers and thirteen NCOs and other ranks, landed and were slaughtered (*abgeschlachtet*) by troops of Fortress Brigade for Special Use stationed there.

The GSO's report was only partially correct—the OGs had not been *slaughtered*—and the hour and day were not recorded. Instead, the OGs had been captured but were still alive.

Information gathered by OSS Captains Lanier and Manzini during an interview of an eyewitness recorded on May 5 provided essentials in reconstructing the movement of the Ginny OGs on March 23 and their capture the next day.

The witness was a sixteen-year-old herdsman, Franco Lagaxo, who lived with his mother near Carpeneggio—a locality on Monte Pastorelli four hundred meters northwest of Bonassola and southeast of the Framura station. Young Lagaxo's deposition was taken at the Carpeneggio town hall. He spoke clearly and simply, without elaboration or artifice. He did not have a vested interest in the matter, which could have motivated him to lie. He did not face any criminal charges so was not trying to make a deal for himself. Nor could he profit from falsifying or embellishing his account. Lagaxo's rendering is essential for understanding what happened to the OGs during the last thirty-four hours of their lives. Here is a verbatim translation:

> On March 23, 1944, around 0900 hours, I was in the vicinity of my house when I noted two armed men in military uniform who were asking about us. They asked my mother and I, too, went into the house. The two soldiers identified themselves as American, and [upon entering] the house placed themselves near the fire [,] as they were wet. They immediately told me to say nothing and [asked] if I could bring them to the "little house" of the railroad. I told them "Yes," and after about 5 minutes we left. Following the path of the woods, I accompanied them to the locality of Paggio, which is about 800 meters from my house, and in about 10 minutes, we arrived [at] the place.
>
> They immediately told me that it was not what they were seeking, [*sic*] and leaving me free, they charged me with buying them fish, eggs, and wine and said they would return to get them at my house. The soldiers remained [at] the place, and I returned home and, given some money, I went into town where I bought fifteen eggs and a liter of wine. Bringing the purchase home, I remained there to wait, and about noon, they returned, three of them, the two of the morning and another. They entered the house and ate with us some "polenta" and after having taken the eggs and the wine they left again agreeing that about 15 hours I would go to get them, near a little stable which is about 200 meters from my house to accompany them to [another] "little house."
>
> At 15 hours, I went to the place, and together with all three, I conducted them above the second "little house," [which required about an hour's walk to reach it]. Upon arrival, they

said, "This is the place where we were supposed to land." After about 15 minutes, they told me I could leave, and they remained on the spot. They were speaking with each other in American, and I could not understand anything. I returned home, leaving them alone. In the evening towards dusk I noted the same two were seated about 50 meters from my house. On the morrow [March 24] at about 0800 hours, while I was going fishing, I saw in the distance the Americans who were climbing from the sea towards the house.

Arriving at the rocks, I noted some fisherman gathering material, and I noted that with them was the Fascist Bertone. Instead of fishing, I returned home, and I found the two Americans by the door . . . waiting for mother. I asked them if they had left the material on the rocks, informing them that Fascists were taking it in the boat. They answered "Yes" and said they were leaving because they were causing too much bother, and my mother arriving at that time gave them some bread and jam. Out of curiosity, I then went to the mule trail that leads to the town, and I saw a group of Germans and Fascists who were coming up. On my own initiative, I ran to the little stable to warn the Americans, and for the first time, I saw that they were a numerous group. I turned back, taking another path, and I met the Fascists Bertone and Ferri who asked me if I had seen anyone. I answered "no" and despite their insistence I stayed on the negative. The Fascists proceed and in the vicinity of my house the groups of German and other Fascists dispersed. I, from the vicinity of the house, watched to see what would happen, and after several minutes I saw that the two Fascists Bianchi and Bertone were about 15 meters above a small grove where were hiding the two Americans I knew.

Bertone then yelled to them, "What are you doing here, ugly pigs." The two answered, "We are Italians." Bertone added, "you are traitors." In that moment, Bianchi threw a hand grenade and then asked where the other [sic] were. Having received a reply that there was no one else, Bertone said, "Do you want to bet that if I blow the whistle, the others will come out?" He emitted a whistle and almost immediately [yelled] in

Italian, "Here they are!" I, however, from my position, did not see them.

In the meantime, I head shooting with machine gun [*sic*] and rifles but only for a short while. After a little time, I saw coming towards my house the group of Americans with their hands raised surrounded by Fascists and two Germans. The others continued to search the vicinity and towards 1100 hours they returned, taking away with them the Americans imprisoned in the storehouse. While they were leaving, the Fascists Bertone and Bertine were saying that they had made a good catch, adding that they had taken the English and that we never saw anything. In the evening, the Germans came for the guard, and they asked me if I had seen someone else and if it were true that I was feeding them. I denied everything, and on the following day, I was interrogated by Commissioner of the Commune [*sic*] Guglielmini to whom I always denied having seem them.

(Signed) Lagaxo Franco. Bonassola, May 5 1945.

While the above statement offers a general idea of how the OGs were captured, it does not offer an explanation as to why they gave up so easily—a bothersome question that has been debated for many, many years and an action for which the OGs have long been criticized. Only speculation can approach an answer. Russo knew the area was covered with Germans and Fascists and that it would be difficult to elude them. He also knew that if they did manage to get back to the rubber boats, where would they go? The PT boats were not loitering, not waiting for them. And since their radios had been ruined, there was no way of communicating with friendly forces.

Russo knew he was in a difficult, if not impossible, position and probably figured that the odds were against them—they were. The idea of a clean escape without bloodshed looked ridiculous because they were outgunned in a foreign land and without any form of backup. But countless Americans—not present at that moment, of course—would have liked to have seen the fifteen Italian Americans at least try to fight their way out of an ugly confrontation and have them shed their blood to the last man, the last bullet. That's what Americans did, after all, and nothing less would suffice. Of course none of these critics were on-site the moment the Germans appeared with their machine pistols and hand grenades. Further resistance would only have produced bloodshed and loss of lives; Russo knew this for sure. It was one thing to go down with the ship, another to die without a sense of achievement. Besides, Russo knew the rules of engagement, the treatment of POWs—he had learned it in basic training—and he wrongly assumed that if captured the OGs would be treated as POWs. After all, they were in regulation US Army uniforms. They would raise their arms, drop their weapons, and surrender.

And up to this point, the OGs had done nothing destructive, had not shot any Germans. Their only offense, a mild one, was that they had landed on enemy territory, and not disguised but in US Army uniforms. However, the grand old American tradition of "never give up the ship" prevailed for numerous years, causing many to criticize Russo's (to them) impotent response to imminent capture. For many, it was not the American way. You stood up and fought back, even if it meant dying. Of course, in the end, no matter the issue of surrender, Vincent Russo and the OGs died for their country.

Franco Lagaxo gave us a picture of what the OGs did after the sun came up on March 23. He saw two uniformed men, armed, walk toward him. They said they were Americans, were in US Army uniforms, and said they wished to speak with him and his mother inside their house. Inside, they stood around the fire; they were still wet after having fallen in the water. They told Lagaxo and his mother that they were looking for a little house (the signal house) near the railroad tracks. Lagaxo said he would take them there.

The group took a path in the woods, and ten minutes later arrived at the little house. Vincent Russo told Lagaxo that this was not the place they sought; this was the southern exit of the tunnel at Bonassola. They wanted the northern entrance, at Framura. After taking some money from Russo, Lagaxo went to town to buy eggs, cheese, and wine, then went home and waited for the OGs; they came back at noon and ate some polenta. Before they left, they told Lagaxo to meet them at 1500 hours at the stable near the house.

They all met at the agreed time and walked for an hour until they arrived at a spot where they could see Stazione Framura below. "This is the place where we were supposed to land," one of the Americans said. They sent Lagaxo away and remained there, evaluating the situation.

The next morning two of the OGs were descending the cliff, going down the fissure to the cove, apparently going back to either finish camouflaging the boats or, perhaps, retrieve some items—the remainder of the explosives—they had left behind in their haste. What Lagaxo saw when he got closer was some fishermen gathering items under the direction of Vito Bertone, a local Fascist. The evening before, Gaetano Oneto, a villager, had noticed the bright orange rubber boats poorly camouflaged among the rocks. (Couldn't they have picked a different color? No wonder the boats were spotted.) Oneto went in for a better look.

A box in one of the boats had a stencil painted on one side that read "EXPLOSIVE." Lagaxo returned home, and two Americans were standing by the front door; he asked if they had left anything in the boats. They said they had, and Lagaxo told them the Fascists had taken one boat and whatever was inside.

At that moment, the OGs realized they had been discovered; they had to rethink the mission and would eventually have to leave the area. There probably was little hope that they could continue the mission and destroy the tunnels. The OGs returned to the stable.

TEN.

The poor camouflaging had been their undoing.

His curiosity piqued, Lagaxo took a mule path back to where the boats were. Before he got there, he spotted a group of Fascists and German soldiers coming toward him. He ran back home and saw several German soldiers and Fascists who had just arrived. They set out searching the area. Two Fascists, Gibatta Bianchi and Bertone, walked to a grove where Lagaxo knew two Americans were hiding.

Bertone spotted them and yelled, "What are you doing here, you ugly pigs?"

"We are Italians," an American replied.

"You are traitors," Bertone said, asking where the other Americans were.

Bertone assumed that because there were three boats, there had to be more than two Americans. A brief exchange of gunfire ensued, and hand grenades were thrown. Vincent Russo was slightly wounded in the face with shrapnel.

At 1030, the Americans surrendered and were disarmed.

Lagaxo saw the Americans coming toward his house with their hands raised; they were immediately surrounded by the Germans and Fascists and locked in the storehouse. The search for more Americans continued until they were satisfied they had caught the whole group.

At 1100 hours, satisfied they had caught all the Americans, the Germans and their Fascist collaborators marched the prisoners to Fascist headquarters in Bonassola, where the prefect, *Commissario* Guglielmini, was the first to interrogate them.

Il Commissario Guglielmini, the prefect of Bonassola, filed an official report concerning what he saw and what happened after the OGs were captured:

The patrol [involved in the capture] was composed of the following Fascists: Gio Batta Bianchi, Political Secy; Vittorio Bertone, Fascist; Giovanni Ferri, Fascist; Vincenzo Bertini,

Station Master, and Luigi Perrone (who later joined of his own volition), Fascists. (The patrol) having learned [about the discovery of the rubber boats] went to the aid of his comrades who had united with a patrol of seven German soldiers located in the [zone on the mountain] indicated by Bertone as the spot where the enemy soldier would probably be found.

They initiated an accurate inspection of the zone, roughly from Scalo to Carpenettoia. The Fascist Bertone Vittorio and Ferri Giovanni detached themselves from the principal group and at about 1015 hours, they discovered two soldiers of enemy nationality who had evidently been placed as sentinels. They caught them by surprise and captured them without the soldier having time to place themselves on guard or alert their companions. But Bertone immediately interrogated one of the two soldiers, seeking to learn if there were others nearby. The interrogated soldiers, who spoke Italian, answered in the negative, stating that the two of them were alone.

But Bertone was not convinced inasmuch as he justly surmised that numerous persons and not merely two soldiers must have landed in three rubber boats. He took from his pocket a whistle which he had found in one of the rubber boats and showing it to the captured soldier, said, "Do you want to see how, if I blow this whistle the others will come out?"

Bertone then blew the whistle. At the sound, several enemy soldiers who had been hiding in a little vale about a hundred meters [distant] from the place where the first two were captured, jumped to their feet firing their weapons. Fortunately, the [principal] group of Fascists and a German FF.AA. [sic] were only a short distance away in a favorable position. So, making use of hand grenades and small arms, they were able promptly to intervene and surround the enemy who, seeing themselves outnumbered, surrendered time was approximately 1030 hours. During this brief fight the North American Engineer (Lieutenant Russo) was slightly wounded. After being disarmed the enemy soldiers were temporarily located in a stable that was close at hand and were guarded by two Fascists and two Germans while the remainder of the patrol continued to search the entire zone to make sure that there were no other enemy soldiers hiding out.

After an accurate search the patrol was convinced that there were no other enemy soldiers in the vicinity. The patrol recovered some arms and ammunition found at the place of capture and the enemy soldiers were conducted to Bonassola, where they arrived at about 1200 and were locked in the Fascist headquarters while awaiting orders from qualified higher headquarters. About this time, I [the prefect] came back from Framura, and having been told of the capture I went to Fascist headquarters to proceed with an interrogation of the captured soldiers, who numbered 15, including two officers.

The captured soldiers, who were dressed [in khaki-colored uniforms], turned out to be of North American nationality, the majority of them being of Italian. Some of them spoke Italian. From the interrogation of the two officers, I was able to ascertain that following orders received by them from high headquarter in Naples they had left Corsica on a [sic] PT boat and that when they neared the Italian coast, they had been transferred to three rubber boats, also that they landed about 0200 hours on March 22 [sic] at the point where the boats were found.

Their mission was to blow up the portion of the railroad from Bonassola to Framura. Having landed, they went up the mountain and took lodging in a stable which they found empty and abandoned. They claimed that they saw Bertone when he passed in front of the stable in which they were hidden and that had they wanted to, they could have captured him. I got the impression that they had no desire to complete the mission which they had been sent and were content to have been captured. When I asked Lt. Vincent Russo if he, the son of an Italian, did not feel ashamed to carry arms against his fatherland, he lowered his head, became red, and did not answer, but gave me the impression that my words struck home.

At Fascist headquarters the enemy soldiers were searched by the Germans who found various documents, 30,000 lira, and some French notes on the prisoners, all of which were consigned to the German headquarters. German headquarters directed that the prisoners be sent to Chiaverri [*sic*]. The work of Political secretary Bianchi and of the other Fascists above mentioned was beyond any eulogy. Their intuitive and courage [deserve] vivid recognition and I hereby inform the head of the province of their spirit of sacrifice and their devotion to duty. I attach a list of the captured North American soldiers.

(Signed) The prefect, *Il Commissario* Guglielmini.

According to this report, the OGs were captured by twelve of the enemy: five Italian Fascists and seven German soldiers. In another report, only one German officer and two men made the capture. Lack of clarity here does nothing to evoke an accurate picture of what actually happened.

The Fascist captors had learned much before the Germans arrived, obtaining this information from Lieutenants Traficante and Russo.

After the war ended, statements were obtained from the Fascists. As would be expected, eyewitness reports differ significantly and are often confusing.

Fascist Vittorio Bertone's statement is brief and an example of the confusion surrounding the incident. Some said he was one of the leaders involved in the capture; he was not. While his statement is short, it nonetheless provides some fascinating details not found elsewhere:

I, the undersigned Bertone, Vittorio, residing at Bonassola, hereby declare the following: One day in March 1944, while employed by the Todt Organization, I was sent by the secretary of the Fascio, Bianchi, Giobatta, to see about retrieving a box which had been reported to him the previous evening by Oneto Gaetano. Oneto accompanied me, and when we arrived at [the cove] we found not only the case, but some rubber rafts. We saw three men fishing from a boat, and with their help we brought the rafts into [shore]. Soon after, a German soldier came down from his OP nearby to see what our activity was all about; when he saw the rafts, he asked us where we got them. Oneto told him that it had been the spot where we found the box, and the German reported the incident to his First Sergeant (who was located in [Bonassola]. The First Sergeant sent eleven men and another Sgt. to investigate, and I went along with them. [Alongside of] the mule path, we found two soldiers in American uniforms—they surrendered without resistance. A Sgt. and a German soldier remained with the two Americans while the other men continued in a search for more. They found thirteen others—also in American uniform. /s/ Bertone, Vittorio.

Fascist Vincenzo di Pietro Bertini's statement also gives us many details not found in the others':

In reference to the incident about which the Prefect of Bonassola wrote regarding the capture of fifteen American soldiers, Bertini swears as follows: On March 24, 1944, at about 0900 hours, I heard rumors that some Americans had landed. It was said that a certain Oneto Gaetano, mason, had found a box on which was written ["munition," "explosives,"] in a strange language. Coming to Bonassola he informed the secretary of the Fascist party, Bianchi, G. B., of his discovery.

Bianchi then sent Bertone and Oneto to cover the case of explosive but it was no longer there. Instead of finding the box, they found rubber boats hidden among the rocks. These boats were brought to Bonosola [*sic*] later. Bianchi alerted the German garrison and six Germans along with Bianchi, Ferri, and Berton Vittorio set out. The distance from [Bonassola] to the point where the boats were located was about 800 air line meters. I was located in the general vicinity.

I met two Germans of this patrol, who invited me to go with them. However, I lagged behind, and when I arrived, the Americans [had already surrendered and were captives]. They held their hands on their heads. Going back to Fascist headquarters, I remained about a hundred meters behind Perrone

Luigi. At Fascist headquarters the prisoners said they were hungry. I was present and talked with almost all the prisoners because they talked Italian. I asked who the officer was, and they showed me an insignia which he had under his collar. I went to the Commissioner to get something for them to eat but he shouted that he would give them nothing. In the meantime, he continued to interrogate the officers. I procured water and aspirin for one of the prisoners. Upon my insistence, they were finally given bread. This was about 1300 hours. Then I went to eat at home. When I returned for the second time to give the prisoners bread, I heard the Commissioner, Guglielmone, say to Lt. Vincent Russo, "Aren't you the son of Italians, ashamed to fight against your brothers?" The Lt. did not answer.

The Commissioner asked how long they had been there. He (Russo?) answered: two days. "We disembarked from a PT boat about two miles off the coast about 2300 hours, and we landed on shore about midnight." The Commissioner asked why they had remained there for two days and what they had done. I heard the Lt. answer, "We have not yet located the actual place for our mission." Some people said that the Americans were to have blown the tunnel from Framura to [Bonassola]. After this I was through but returned about 1530 hours to give Lt. Russo some bread. At that time, a German truck with about ten men arrived.

The Germans cleared the place where the prisoners were and went in. The Fascist Commissioner and the Secretary remained. About 1700 hours the American prisoners were put on the truck and taken toward La Spezia. After the departure of the prisoners, I did not speak of the incident with anyone, and I heard no further information about them. Commissioner Guglielmone made a report against me to the Prefect and the Federal Secretary because I did not want to assume responsibility as Fascist Political Secretary. (signed) Bertini, Vincenzo, Genoa, 1 May 1945.

TEN.

The OSS, still hanging on to a sliver of hope that the OGs were alive and hiding out somewhere, believed for the briefest of moments that they could have been on their way or, perhaps, had already arrived at the pre-designated safe house in Babio, in accordance with their contingency plan.

Then news arrived in Bastia that reduced this hope to almost zero.

On March 27, the Wehrmacht transmitted an ominous communiqué at 1500 hours (GMT time) via Berlin that was monitored by the BBC; it was broadcast in German and then English:

> The Supreme Command of the Armed Forces announces: On the East Coast of the Gulf of Genoa, a party of US Commandos consisting of two officers and thirteen men, which landed northwest of Spezia, was wiped out.

Attached was a duplicate version that aired from Rome on March 28 at 2300 hours, a couple of days after the OGs had been murdered by firing squad. The communiqué deliberately used the term *ausgelöscht* ("wiped out") when what they meant was "executed," which had occurred on the morning of March 26. And by that time the OGs were, indeed, all dead and buried and in a common grave.

The OSS had good reason to doubt this report, perhaps believing it was disinformation by the Germans. At the time, OSS had no way to validate the report, mainly the worth or meaning of "wiped out." They felt helpless.

The disposition of the OGs after they landed was becoming more apparent: They had come ashore around midnight (22/23 March) at a cove in their orange rubber boats below Carpeneggio, La Spezia province. (Bonassola, Carpeneggio, and La Spezia are interchangeable as the pinpoints where the OGs land because the towns are so close to one another; they are all in La Spezia province.) As soon as they arrived, they hastily attempted to camouflage the orange dinghies before they ascended a fissure at the 150-meter mountain—this camouflaging was done hastily and ineffectively. A fisherman could see the dinghies from his fishing boat and he reported what he saw.

Meanwhile, the OSS pressed on, desperate to find their brother commandos and determine whether the "wiped out" report was accurate or they had misinterpreted the German version of the communiqué.

Another eyewitness to the events after the Ginny OGs arrived at Carpeneggio, Angelonia Viviani, who lived on the mountaintop near Carpeneggio, added some rich details:

> On the morning of March 24, 1944, at about 0915 hours, I saw that from my stable . . . some smoke arising, and I neared it to see what was happening. At about 15 meters from [my] stable, I heard myself called by a soldier whom I later learned to be an American officer . . . called me closer.
>
> When I was near him, he inquired of me if many armed Germans or Fascists were at the "Salto dell Lepre" battery. To this . . . I responded that there were 3 or 4 Germans . . . but some 15 Fascists, after which they courteously asked me if I could furnish them with some food. I agreed, [saying] that I would bring him [*sic*] the said food at 1600 hours of the same day. After this, the officer returned into my stable where, I presume, they warmed themselves and dried their clothes because from what I had seen they were very wet, and I went back to getting some greens. About 15 minutes later, I heard an explosion of a hand grenade. I learned later that said hand grenade was thrown by Bianchi against two American soldiers who were acting as sentinels about 100 meters from the stable. Eight of the two were wounded and were therefore captured and taken to the site near the stable. Shortly thereafter, the Germans descended, and I saw an American officer fire a burst against a German who was nearing the stable.
>
> Those remaining in the stable gave themselves up, [were] made to come out, [and] were taken to the site where [the

Fascists] Bertini, Ferri, Perrone, Bianchi, and Bertone, were very elated and Perone also stated the following, "I am going to see those 'cowardly' Americans to spit on their faces."

Interrogated at the spot by a German, who accused me of having brought something to eat to the Americans; the same stated that I [would be punished]. After this interrogation, I returned home, where I arrived at about 1000 hours. Other than this I have nothing to add.

Sources

"Omaha Beach: Following General Cota" from *D-Day General: How Dutch Cota Saved Omaha Beach on June 6, 1944.* Noel F. Mehlo Jr. Lanham, MD: Stackpole Books, 2021.

"Taking Mount Suribachi" from *Closing In: Marines in the Seizure of Iwo Jima.* Joseph H. Alexander. Marines in World War II Commemorative Series. Washington, DC: US Marine Corps Historical Center, 1994.

"Doolittle Hits Tokyo" from *The Greatest Air Aces Stories Ever Told.* Colonel Robert Barr Smith and Laurence J. Yadon. Essex, CT: Lyons Press, 2017.

"Treacherous Passage," from *Eight Survived: The Harrowing Story of the USS Flier.* Douglas A. Campbell. Essex, CT: Lyons Press, 2010.

"Sugar Loaf" from *The Battle of Okinawa.* George Feifer. Essex, CT: Globe Pequot, 1992.

"Crash Boat" from *Crash Boat: Rescue and Peril in the Pacific during World War II.* George Jepson and Earl McCandless. Essex, CT: Lyons Press, 2023.

"Hell Is Green: A War Rescue" from *Hell Is So Green: Search and Rescue over the Hump in World War II.* William Diebold. Essex, CT: Globe Pequot, 2012.

"Gunslingers: The Pilots Remember" from *Gunslingers: Allied Fighter Boys of WWII.* James P. Busha. Essex, CT: Lyons Press, 2022.

"Last Man Down: Nautilus at War" from *Last Man Down: USS Nautilus and the Undersea War in the Pacific.* David W. Jourdan. Essex, CT: Lyons Press, 2022.

"Operation Ginny" from *Operation Ginny: The Most Significant Commando Raid of WWII.* Vincent dePaul Lupiano. Essex, CT: Lyons Press, 2023.